Berlitz®

Finnish
PHRASE BOOK
& DICTIONARY

Easy to use features
- Handy thematic colour coding
- Quick Reference Section—opposite page
- Tipping Guide—inside back cover
- Quick reply panels throughout

How best to use this phrase book

● We suggest that you start with the **Guide to pronunciation** (pp. 6-9), then go on to **Some basic expressions** (pp. 10-15). This gives you not only a minimum vocabulary, but also helps you get used to pronouncing the language. The phonetic transcription throughout the book enables you to pronounce every word correctly.

● Consult the **Contents** pages (3-5) for the section you need. In each chapter you'll find travel facts, hints and useful information. Simple phrases are followed by a list of words applicable to the situation.

● Separate, detailed contents lists are included at the beginning of the extensive **Eating out** and **Shopping guide** sections (Menus, p. 39, Shops and services, p. 97).

● If you want to find out how to say something in Finnish, your fastest look-up is via the **Dictionary** section (pp. 164-189). This not only gives you the word, but is also cross-referenced to its use in a phrase on a specific page.

● If you wish to learn more about constructing sentences, check the **Basic grammar** (pp. 159-163).

● Note the **colour margins** are indexed in Finnish and English to help both listener and speaker. And, in addition, there is also an index in Finnish for the use of your listener.

● Throughout the book, this symbol ☛ suggests phrases your listener can use to answer you. If you still can't understand, hand this phrase book to the Finnish-speaker to encourage pointing to an appropriate answer. The English translation for you is just alongside the Finnish.

Revised edition–4th printing–July 2000   Printed in Spain

Contents

Travelling around 65

Sightseeing 80

Relaxing 86

Making friends 92

Shopping guide 97

Acknowledgements
We are particularly grateful to Mr Ilkka Lavonius for his help in the preparation of this book, and to Dr T J A Bennet and Mrs Rayne Bensky who devised the phonetic transcription.

Guide to pronunciation

This chapter is intended to make you familiar with the phonetic transcription we have devised and to help you get used to the sounds of Finnish.

An outline of the spelling and sounds of Finnish

The writing system in Finnish is systematic: each letter corresponds to one and the same phoneme (basic sound) and each phoneme corresponds to one and the same letter. The number of phonemes is smaller than in most European languages. Letters like **b, c, f, q, w** and **z** are only found in words recently borrowed from foreign languages.

You'll find the pronunciation of the Finnish letters and sounds explained below, as well as the symbols we're using for them in the transcriptions. The imitated pronunciation should be read as if it were English except for any special rules set out below. Of course, the sounds of any two languages are never exactly the same; but if you follow carefully the indications supplied here, you'll have no difficulty in reading our transcriptions in such a way as to make yourself understood.

Letters written in bold type should be stressed.

Consonants

Letter	Approximate pronunciation	Symbol	Example	
k, m, n **p, t, v**	as in English			
d	as in rea**d**y, but sometimes very weak	d	**taide**	**tah**iday
g	in words of Finnish origin, only found after **n**; **ng** is pronounced as in si**ng**er	ng	**sangen**	**sahn**gayn
h	as in **h**ot, whatever its position in the word	h	**lahti**	**lahh**ti
j	like **y** in **y**ou	y	**ja**	yah

l	as in let	l	**talo**	**tah**loa
r	always rolled	r	**raha**	**rah**hah
s	always as in set (never as in present)	s/ss*	**sillä** **kiitos**	**sill**æ **kee**toass

*To make doubly sure that the Finnish s receives its correct pronunciation as s in English set, and not as a z sound in present, we often use ss in our phonetic transcriptions. Similarly, we sometimes employ a double consonant after i to ensure this is pronounced like i in pin, and not like i in kite. In these cases you can quickly check with the Finnish spelling whether you should pronounce a single or a double consonant.

Vowels

a	like a in car; short or long	ah aa	**matala** **iltaa**	**mah**tahlah **il**taa
e	like a in late; but a pure vowel, not a dipthong; short or long	ay $\overline{ay}$	**kolme** **teevati**	**koal**may **tāy**vati
i	like i in pin (short) or ee in see (long); ir + consonant like i in pin (short)	i ee eer	**takki** **siitä** **kirkko**	**tah**kki **see**tæ **keer**koa
o	a sound between aw in law and oa in coat; short or long	oa $\overline{oa}$	**olla** **kookas**	**oa**llah **kōa**kahss
u	like oo in pool; short or long	oo $\overline{oo}$	**hupsu** **uuni**	**hoop**soo **ōo**ni
y	like u in French sur or ü in German über; say ee as in see, and round your lips while still trying to pronounce ee; it can be short or long	ew $\overline{ew}$	**yksi** **syy**	**ewk**si s$\overline{ew}$

ä	like **a** in h**a**t; short or long	æ	**äkkiä**	**aekki**æ
		ǣ	**hyvää**	**hewv**ǣ
ö	like **ur** in f**ur**, but without any **r** sound, and with the lips rounded; short or long	ur ūr	**tyttö** **likööri**	**tewtt**ur **likk**ūr**ri**

N.B. The letters **b, c, f, q, s, sh, w, x, z, ž** and **å** are only found in words from foreign languages, and they are pronounced as in the language of origin.

Diphthongs

In Finnish, diphthongs occur only in the first syllable of a word, except those ending in **-i**, where they can occur anywhere. They should be pronounced as a combination of the two vowel sounds represented by the spelling. The list below shows you how the Finnish diphthongs are written in our imitated pronunciation.

The first vowel is pronounced louder in the following diphthongs:

ai = ahⁱ   **iu** = i^{oo}   **äi** = æⁱ
au = ah^{oo}   **oi** = oaⁱ   **äy** = æ^{ew}
ei = ayⁱ   **ou** = oa^{oo}   **öi** = urⁱ
eu = ay^{oo}   **ui** = ooⁱ   **öy** = ur^{ew}
ey = ay^{ew}   **yi** = ewⁱ

The second vowel is louder in:

ie = ⁱay   **uo** = ^{oo}oa   **yö** = ^{ew}ur

Double letters

Remember that in Finnish *every* letter is pronounced, therefore a letter written double is pronounced long. Thus, the **kk** in ku**kk**a should be pronounced like the two **k** sounds in the words thi**ck c**oat. Similarly the **aa** in k**aa**tua should be pronouced long (like **a** in English c**a**r). These distinctions are important, not least because ku**k**a has a different meaning to ku**kk**a and k**a**tua a different meaning to k**aa**tua.

Compound words

Finnish uses a great number of compound words. We have indicated the separate parts as in the examples below:

rauta|tie means 'railway', the compound being made up of *rauta* (iron) and *tie* (road); similarly: *maito|suklaa* (milk chocolate), *yli|opisto* (university).

This splitting of compound words has been done to help you with pronunciation. It will also provide you with an aid to stress, one of the distinctive features of Finnish.

Stress

A strong stress always falls on the first syllable of a word. In compound words, the first syllable of each part of the word receives a stress.

Pronunciation of the Finnish alphabet

A	aa	K	kōā	U	ōō
B	bāy	L	æl	V	vāy
C	sāy	M	æm	W	**kak**sois-vāy
D	dāy	N	æn	X	æks
E	āy	O	ōā	Y	ēw
F	æf	P	pāy	Z	tsayt
G	gāy	Q	kōō	Å	**ruot**salainen ōā
H	hōā	R	ær	Ä	ǣ
I	ee	S	æs	Ö	ūr
J	yee	T	tāy		

Some basic expressions

Yes.	Kyllä/Joo.	kewllæ/yōo
No.	Ei.	ay^i
Please.	Olkaa hyvä.	oalkaa hewvæ
Thank you.	Kiitos.	keetoass
Thank you very much.	Kiitos paljon.	keetoass pahlyoan
That's all right/You're welcome.	Ei kestä.	ay^i kaystæ

Greetings *Tervehdyksiä*

Good morning.	(Hyvää) huomenta.	(hewvǣ) h°oamayntah
Good afternoon.	(Hyvää) päivää.	(hewvǣ) pæ^{i}vǣ
Good evening.	(Hyvää) iltaa.	(hewvǣ) iltaa
Good night.	Hyvää yötä.	hewvǣ °°urtæ
Goodbye/Bye-bye.	Näkemiin/Hei hei.	nækaymeen/hay^i hay^i
See you later.	Näkemiin/Hei sitten.	nækaymeen/ hay^i sittayn
Hello/Hi!	Hei/Terve!	hay^i/tayrvay
This is Mr/Mrs/Miss...	Tässä on herra/rouva/neiti...	tæssæ oan hayrrah/roa°°vah/nay^{i}ti
How do you do? (Pleased to meet you.)	Hyvää päivää. (Hauska tutustua.)	hewvǣ pæ^{i}vǣ (hah°°skah tootoost°°a)
How are you?	Mitä kuuluu?	mittæ kōolōo
Very well, thanks. And you?	Kiitos, hyvää. Entä teille/sinulle?*	keetoass hewvǣ ayntæ tay^{i}llay/sinnoollay
How's life?	Miten menee?	mittayn maynāy

* Many of the expressions in this book vary depending on whether they are used formally or informally. These are shown with the formal expression first followed by the informal.

Fine, thanks.	**Kiitos, hyvin.**	keetoass hewvin
I beg your pardon?	**Anteeksi?**	ahntäyksi
Excuse me. (May I get past?)	**Anteeksi. (Pääsenkö ohi?)**	ahntäyksi (pääsaynkur oahhi)
Sorry!	**Anteeksi!**	ahntäyksi

Questions *Kysymyksiä*

Where?	**Missä?**	missæ
How?	**Kuinka?**	koo¹nkah
When?	**Milloin?**	milloa¹n
What?	**Mitä?**	mittæ
Why?	**Miksi?**	miksi
Who?	**Kuka?**	kookah
Which? (of these/of two)	**Mikä?/Kumpi?**	mikkæ/koompi
Where is...?	**Missä on...?**	missæ oan
Where are...?	**Missä ovat...?**	missæ oavaht
Where can I find/get...?	**Mistä löydän...?**	mistæ lurᵉʷdæn
How far?	**Kuinka kaukana?**	koo¹nkah kah°°kanah
How long (time)?	**Kuinka kauan?**	koo¹nkah kah°°ahn
How much/How many?	**Kuinka paljon/Kuinka monta?**	koo¹nkah pahlyoan/koo¹nkah moantah
How much does this cost?	**Paljonko tämä maksaa?**	pahlyoankoa tæmæ mahksaa
When does... open/close?	**Milloin... aukeaa/suljetaan?**	milloa¹n... ah°°kayaa/soolyaytaan
What do you call this/that in Finnish?	**Mitä tämä/tuo on suomeksi?**	mittæ tæmæ/t°°oa oan s°°oamayksi
What does this/that mean?	**Mitä tämä/tuo tarkoittaa?**	mittæ tæmæ/t°°oa tahrkoa¹ttaa

Do you speak...? *Puhutteko...?*

Do you speak English?	**Puhutteko englantia?**	poohoottaykoa aynglahntiah
Does anyone here speak English?	**Puhuuko kukaan täällä englantia?**	poohōōkoa kookaan tællæ aynglahntiah
I don't speak (much) Finnish.	**En puhu (paljon) suomea.**	ayn poohoo (pahlyoan) s°°oamayah

Could you speak more slowly?	**Voisitteko puhua hitaammin?**	voaⁱsittaykoa **poo**hooah **hit**taammin
Could you repeat that?	**Voisitteko toistaa sen?**	voaⁱsittaykoa **toa**ⁱstaa sayn
Could you spell it?	**Voisitteko tavata sen?**	voaⁱsittaykoa **tah**vahtah sayn
How do you pronounce this?	**Kuinka äännätte tämän?**	kooⁱnkah **ǣn**nættay sayn
Could you write it down, please?	**Voisitteko kirjoittaa sen?**	voaⁱsittaykoa **keer**yoaⁱttaa sayn
Can you translate this for me?	**Voitteko kääntää tämän minulle?**	voaⁱttaykoa **kǣn**tǣ tæmæn **min**noolay
Can you translate this for us?	**Voitteko kääntää tämän meille?**	voaⁱttaykoa **kǣn**tǣ tæmæn mayⁱllay
Could you point to the... in the book, please?	**Voisitteko osoittaa... kirjassa.**	voaⁱsittaykoa **oa**soaⁱttaa... **keer**yahssah
word	**sanaa**	**sah**naa
phrase	**sanontaa**	**sah**noantaa
sentence	**lausetta**	**lah**^{oo}sayttah
Just a moment.	**Hetkinen.**	**hayt**kinayn
I'll see if I can find it in this book.	**Katson, voinko löytää sen tästä kirjasta.**	**kaht**soan voaⁱnkoa lur^{ew}tǣ sayn tæstæ **keer**yastah
I understand.	**Ymmärrän.**	**ewm**mærræn
I don't understand.	**En ymmärrä.**	ayn **ewm**mærræ
Do you understand?	**Ymmärrättekö?**	**ewm**mærrættaykur

Can/May...? *Voiko/Saako...?*

Can I have...?	**Saanko...?**	**saahn**koa
Can we have...?	**Saammeko...?**	**saahm**maykoa
Can you show me...?	**Voitteko näyttää minulle...?**	voaⁱttaykoa næ^{ew}ttǣ **min**noolay
I can't.	**En voi.**	ayⁱn voaⁱ
Can you tell me...?	**Voitteko sanoa minulle...?**	voaⁱttaykoa **sah**noah **min**noollay

Can you help me?	**Voitteko auttaa minua?**	voa'ttaykoa ah°°ttaa minnooah
Can I help you?	**Voinko auttaa teitä?**	voa'ankoa ah°°ttaa tay'tæ
Can you direct me to...?	**Voitteko opastaa minut...-n luo?**	voa'ttaykoa oapahstaa minnoot...-n l°°oa

Do you want...? *Haluatteko...?*

I'd like...	**Haluaisin...**	hahlooah'sin
We'd like...	**Haluaisimme...**	hahlooah'simmay
What do you want?	**Mitä teille saisi olla?**	mittæ tay'llay sah'si oallah
Could you give me...?	**Antaisitteko minulle...?**	ahntah'sittaykoa minnoollay
Could you bring me...?	**Toisitteko minulle...?**	toa'sittaykoa minnoollay
Could you show me...?	**Näyttäisittekö minulle...?**	næ°°ttæ'sittaykur minnoollay
I'm looking for...	**Haen...**	hahayn
I'm searching for...	**Etsin...**	aytsin
I'm hungry.	**Olen nälkäinen.**	oalayn nælkæ'nayn
I'm thirsty.	**Olen janoinen.**	oalayn jahnoa'nayn
I'm tired.	**Olen väsynyt.**	oalayn væsewnewt
I'm lost.	**Olen eksynyt.**	oalayn ayksewnewt
It's important.	**Se on tärkeä.**	say oan tærkayæ
It's urgent.	**Sillä on kiire.**	sillæ oan keeray

It is/There is... *Se on/On...*

It is...	**Se on...**	say oan
Is it...?	**Onko se...?**	oankoa say
It isn't...	**Se ei ole...**	say ay oalay
Here it is.	**Tässä se on.**	tæssæ say oan
Here they are.	**Tässä ne ovat.**	tæssæ nay oavaht
There it is.	**Tuolla se on.**	too°°llah say oan

14

There they are.	**Tuolla ne ovat.**	too°°llah nay oavaht
There is/There are ...	**On ...**	oan
Is there/Are there ...?	**Onko ...?**	oankoa
There isn't/aren't ...	**Ei ole ...**	ay[i] oalay
There isn't/aren't any.	**Ei ole yhtään.**	ay[i] oalay ewhtæ̅n

It's ... *Se on ...*

beautiful/ugly	**kaunis/ruma**	kah°°nis/roomah
better/worse	**parempi/huonompi**	pahraympi/h°°oanoampi
big/small	**suuri/pieni**	soori/p[i]ayni
cheap/expensive	**halpa/kallis**	hahlpah/kahlliss
early/late	**aikainen/myöhäi-nen**	ah[i]ka[i]nayn/m[ew]urhæ[i]nayn
easy/difficult	**helppo/vaikea**	haylppoa/vah[i]kayah
free (vacant)/occupied	**vapaa/varattu**	vahpaa/vahrahttoo
full/empty	**täysi/tyhjä**	tæ[ew]si/tewhyæ
good/bad	**hyvä/huono**	hewvæ/h°°oanoa
heavy/light	**raskas/kevyt**	rahskahs/kayvewt
here/there	**täällä/tuolla**	tæ̅llæ/t°°oallah
hot/cold	**kuuma/kylmä**	koomah/kewlmæ
near/far	**lähellä/kaukana**	læhayllæ/kah°°kahnah
next/last	**seuraava/viimeinen**	say°°raavah/veemay[i]nayn
old/new	**vanha/uusi**	vahnhah/ōōssi
old/young	**vanha/nuori**	vahnhah/n°°oari
open/shut	**avoin/suljettu**	ahvoa[i]n/soolyayttoo
quick/slow	**nopea/hidas**	noapayah/hiddahss
right/wrong	**oikea/väärä**	oa[i]kaya/væ̅ræ

Quantities *Määriä*

a little/a lot	**vähän/paljon**	væhæn/pahlyoan
few/a few	**harvat/muutamat**	hahrvaht/mootahmaht
much	**paljon**	pahlyoan
many	**monta**	moantah
more(than)/less(than)	**enemmän (kuin)/vähemmän (kuin)**	aynaymmæn (koo[i]n)/væhaymmæn (koo[i]n)
enough/too	**tarpeeksi/liiaksi**	tahrpāyksi/leeahksi
some/(not) any	**hieman/ei yhtään**	hi[ew]mahn/ay[i] ewhtæ̅n

A few more useful words *Muutama hyödyllinen sana lisää*

above	**-n yllä/yli**	-n **ewl**læ/**ewl**i
after (time)	**-n jälkeen**	-n **jæl**kāyn
and	**ja**	yah
at	**-n kohdalla**	-n **koah**dahllah
before (time)	**ennen -a**	**ayn**nayn -a
behind	**-n takana/taakse**	-n **tah**kahnah/**taak**say
below	**-n alla/alle**	-n **ahl**lah/**ahl**lay
between	**-n välissä/välillä**	-n **væ**lissæ/**væ**lillæ
but	**mutta**	**moot**tah
down	**alas/alhaalla**	**ah**lahs/**ahl**haallah
downstairs	**alakerrassa**	**ah**lahkayrrassah
during	**aikana**	**ahⁱ**kahnah
for	**-n suuntaan/-n sijaan**	-n **soon**taan/-n **si**yyaan
from	**-n suunnasta**	-n **soon**nahstah
in	**-n sisässä/-llä**	-n **si**ssæssæ/-llæ
inside	**sisään/sisälle**	si**ssā**en/si**ssæl**lay
near	**lähellä/lähelle**	**læ**hayllæ/**læ**hayllay
never	**ei koskaan**	ayⁱ **koas**kaan
next to	**vieressä**	**vⁱay**rayssæ
none	**ei yhtään**	ayⁱ **ewh**tāen
not	**ei**	ayⁱ
nothing	**ei mitään**	ayⁱ **mit**tāen
now	**nyt**	newt
on	**-n päällä/päälle**	-n **pāel**læ/**pāel**lay
only	**vain**	vahⁱn
or	**tai**	tahⁱ
outside	**ulkona/ulos**	**ool**koanah/**oo**loas
perhaps	**ehkä**	**ayh**kæ
since	**alkaen**	**ahl**kahayn
soon	**pian**	pⁱahn
then	**sitten**	**sit**tayn
through	**läpi**	**læ**pi
to	**-n kohdalle**	-n **koah**dayllay
too (also)	**myös**	mᵉʷurss
towards	**-a kohti**	-a **koah**ti
under	**alla/alle**	**ahl**lah/**ahl**lay
until	**asti**	**ahs**ti
up	**ylös/ylhäällä**	**ewl**urss/**ewl**hāellæ
upstairs	**yläkerrassa**	**ewl**ækayrrahssah
very	**tosi**	**toa**si
with	**-n kanssa**	-n **kahn**ssah
without	**ilman**	**il**mahn
yet	**vielä**	**vⁱay**læ

Arrival

Passport control *Passin|tarkastus*

Here's my passport.	**Tässä on passini.**	tæssæ oan **pahs**sini
I'll be staying...	**Viivyn...**	**vee**vewn
a few days	**muutamia päiviä**	mōōtahmiah pæ'viæ
a week	**viikon**	**vee**koan
2 weeks	**kaksi viikkoa**	kahksi **veek**koah
a month	**kuukauden**	kookah°°dayn
I don't know yet.	**En tiedä vielä.**	ayn t'aydæ v'aylæ
I'm here on holiday.	**Olen täällä lomalla.**	oalayn tǣllæ **loam**ahllah
I'm here on business.	**Olen täällä liike-|asioissa.**	oalayn tǣllæ **lee**kayahsioa'ssah
I'm just passing through.	**Olen vain läpi-|kulku|matkalla.**	oalayn vah'n **læpi**koolkoomahtkahllah

If things become difficult:

| I'm sorry, I don't understand. | **Anteeksi, en ymmärrä.** | ahnt**ā**yksi ayn **ewm**mærræ |
| Does anyone here speak English? | **Puhuuko kukaan täällä englantia?** | poo**hōō**koa **koo**kaan tǣllæ **ayng**lahnt'ah |

TULLI
CUSTOMS

After collecting your baggage at the airport (*lentokenttä—***layn**toa**kaynt**æ) you have a choice: use the green exit if you have nothing to declare. Or leave via the red exit if you have items to declare (in excess of those allowed).

tullattavia tavaroita
goods to declare

ei tullattavaa
nothing to declare

The chart below shows what you can bring in duty-free:*

	Cigarettes	Cigars	Tobacco	Spirits	Wine
European residents	200	or	250 g. of other tobacco products	1 l. and 1 l.	
Non-European residents	400	or	500 g. of other tobacco products	1 l. and 1 l.	

I have nothing to declare.	**Minulla ei ole mitään tullattavaa.**	minnoollah ay¹ oalay mittæn toollahttahvaa
I have...	**Minulla on...**	minnoollah oan
a carton of cigarettes	**kartonki savukkeita**	kartoanki sahvookkay¹tah
a bottle of whisky	**pullo viskiä**	poolloa viskiæ
It's for my personal use.	**Se on henkilö|kohtaiseen käyttööni.**	say oan haynkillurkoahtah¹ssāyn kæᵉʷttūrni
It's a gift.	**Se on lahja.**	say oan lahhyah
Your passport, please.	**Passinne, olkaa hyvä.**	pahssinnay oalkaa hewvæ

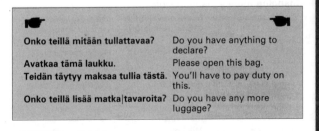

Onko teillä mitään tullattavaa?	Do you have anything to declare?
Avatkaa tämä laukku.	Please open this bag.
Teidän täytyy maksaa tullia tästä.	You'll have to pay duty on this.
Onko teillä lisää matka|tavaroita?	Do you have any more luggage?

---

* All allowances are subject to change without notice

Baggage—Porter *Kantaja*

In the absence of porters, you'll find plenty of luggage trolleys at the airport. You might find porters at the railway stations, but they are becoming scarce.

Porter!	Kantaja!	kahntahyah
Please take (this/my)...	Olkaa hyvä ja ottakaa (tämä/minun)...	oalkaa hewvæ ya oattahkaa (tæmæ/minnoon)...
luggage	matka|tavarani	mahtkahtahvahrani
suitcase	matka|laukku|ni	mahtkahlah°°kkooni
(travelling) bag	(matka)laukku|ni	(mahtkah)lah°°kkooni
That one is mine.	Tuo on minun.	t°°oa oan minnoon
Take this luggage...	Ottakaa tämä laukku...	oattahkaa tæmæ lah°°kkoo
to the bus	bussille	boossillay
to the luggage lockers	säilytys|lokeroille	sæilewtewsloakayroaillay
to the taxi	taksille	tahksillay
How much is that?	Paljonko tämä maksaa?	pahlyoankoa tæmæ mahksaa
There's one piece missing.	Yksi laukku puuttuu.	ewksi lah°°kkoo poott°°o
Where are the luggage trolleys (carts)?	Missä on työntö|kärryjä?	missæ oan t°°urnturkærrewyæ

Changing money *Rahan\|vaihto*

Where's the currency exchange (office)?	Missä on valuutan vaihto (toimisto)?	missæ oan vahlootahn vahitoa (toaimistoa)
Can you change these traveller's cheques (checks)?	Voitteko vaihtaa nämä matka|sekit?	voaittaykoa vahihtaa næmæ mahtkahsaykit
I want to change some dollars/pounds.	Haluaisin vaihtaa dollareita/puntia.	hahlooahisin vahihtaa doallahrayitah/poontiah
Can you change this into Finnish marks?	Voitteko vaihtaa tämän Suomen markoiksi?	voaittaykoa vahihtaa tæmæn s°°oamayn mahrkoaiksi
What's the exchange rate?	Mikä on vaihto|kurssi?	mikkæ oan vahihtoakoorssi

BANK-CURRENCY, see page 129

Where is...? *Missä on...?*

Where is the...?	**Missä on...?**	missæ oan
booking office	**lippu|myymälä**	lippoomēw̄mælæ
duty (tax)-free shop	**vero|vapaa myy-mälä**	vayroavahpaa mēw̄mælæ
newsstand	**lehti|myymälä**	layhtimēw̄mælæ
restaurant	**ravintola**	rahvintoalah
How do I get to...?	**Miten pääsen...-n/-lle?**	mittayn pǣsayn...-n/-llay
Is there a bus into town?	**Meneekö kaupun-kiin bussia?**	maynāȳkur kah°°poonkeen boossiah
Where can I get a taxi?	**Mistä voin saada taksin?**	mistæ voaᶦn saadah tahksin
Where can I hire (rent) a car?	**Mistä voin vuok-rata auton?**	mistæ voaᶦn v°°oakrahtah ah°°toan

Hotel reservation *Hotellin varaus*

Do you have a hotel guide (directory)?	**Onko teillä hotelli|opasta?**	oankoa tayᶦllæ hoatayllioapahstah
Could you reserve a room for me?	**Voisitteko varata minulle huoneen.**	voaᶦsittaykoa vahrahtah minnoollay h°°oanāȳn
in the centre	**keskustassa**	kayskoostahstah
near the railway station	**lähellä rauta|tie|asemaa**	læhayllæ rah°°tahtᶦayahsaymaa
a single room	**yhden hengen huone**	ewhdayn hayngayn h°°oanay
a double room	**kahden hengen huone**	kahhdayn hayngayn h°°oanay
not too expensive	**ei liian kallis**	ayᶦ leeahn kahlliss
Where is the hotel/guesthouse?	**Missä on hotelli/matkustaja|koti?**	missæ oan hoataylli/mahtkoostahjahkoati
Do you have a street map?	**Onko teillä kau-pungin karttaa?**	oankoa tayᶦllæ kah°°poongin kahrttaa

HOTEL/ACCOMMODATION, see page 22

Car hire (rental) *Auton vuokraus*

All the major international agencies are represented in Finland.
To hire a car you must show a valid driving licence from your
country of residence. The minimum age varies from 19 to 23
and one year's driving experience is required. Most companies
require a cash deposit but this is often waived for holders of
major credit cards.

I'd like to hire (rent) a car.	**Haluaisin vuokrata auton.**	hahlooah'sin v°°oakrahtah ah°°toan
small	**pieni**	p'ayni
medium-sized	**keski|kokoinen**	kayskikoakoanayn
large	**suuri**	soori
automatic	**automaatti| vaihteella**	ah°°toamaattivah'htæyllah
I'd like it for a day/a week.	**Haluaisin sen päi-väksi/viikoksi.**	hahl°°ah'sin sayn pæ'væksi/ veekoaksi
Are there any week-end arrangements?	**Onko vii-kon|lopuksi eri tarjouksia?**	oankoa veekoanloapooksi ayri tahryoa°°ksiah
Do you have any special rates?	**Onko teillä mitään erikois|hintoja?**	oankoa tay'llæ mittæn ayrikkoa'shintoayah
What's the charge per day/week?	**Mikä on päivä|maksu/ viikko|maksu?**	mikkæ oan pæ'væmahksoo/ veekkoamahksoo
Is mileage included?	**Kuinka suuri kilo|metri|määrä sisältyy hintaan?**	koo'nkah soori killoamaytrimææræ sissæltew hintaan
What's the charge per kilometre?	**Mikä on kilo|metri|maksu?**	mikkæ oan killoamaytrimahksoo
I'd like to leave the car in...	**Haluaisin jättää auton ...-n/-lle**	hahlooah'sin yættæ ah°°toan ...-n/-llay
I'd like full insurance.	**Haluaisin täy-den|vakuutuksen.**	hahlooah'sin tæ°ᵉʷdaynvahkootooksayn
How much is the deposit?	**Kuinka suuri on ennakko|maksu?**	koo'nkah soori oan aynnahkkoahmahksoo
I have a credit card.	**Minulla on luotto|kortti.**	minnoollah oan l°°oattoakoartti
Here's my driving licence.	**Tässä on ajo|kortti|ni.**	tæssæ oan ahyoakoarttini

CAR, see page 75

Taxi *Taksi*

Taxis are easy to spot as they all have a yellow *Taxi* or *Taksi* sign. If this sign is lit the cab is available. All taxis have meters and a surcharge is added at weekends and at night. Drivers don't expect a tip but a few extra coins for good service is customary.

Where can I get a taxi?	**Mistä voin saada taksin?**	mistæ voa'n saadah tahksin
Where is the taxi rank (stand)?	**Missä on taksi|asema?**	missæ oan tahksiahsaymah
Could you get me a taxi?	**Voitteko hankkia minulle taksin?**	voa'ttaykoa hahnkkiah minnoollay tahksin
What's the fare to...?	**... – Mitä maksaa ajaa sinne?**	mittæ mahksaa ahyaa sinnay
How far is it to...?	**Kuinka kaukana on...?**	koo'nkah kah°°kahnah oan
Take me to...	**Viekää minut...**	v'aykæ minnoot
this address	**tähän osoitteeseen**	tæhæn oasoa'ttæyssäyn
the airport	**lento|kentälle**	layntoakayntællay
the town centre	**kaupungin keskustaan**	kah°°poongin kayskoostaan
the... Hotel	**hotelli...-n/-lle**	hoataylli...-n/-llay
the railway station	**rauta|tie|asemalle**	rah°°taht'ayahsaymahllay
Turn... at the next corner.	**Kääntykää... seuraavassa kulmassa.**	kæntewkæ... say°°raahvassah koolmahssah
left/right	**vasemmalle/ oikealle**	vahsaymmallay/ oa'kayahllay
Go straight ahead.	**Ajakaa suoraan eteen|päin.**	ahjahkaa s°°oaraan aytäynpæin
Please stop here.	**Pysähtykää tässä.**	pewssæhtewkæ tæssæ
I'm in a hurry.	**Minulla on kiire.**	minnoollah oan keeray
Could you drive more slowly?	**Voisitteko ajaa hitaammin?**	voa'sittaykoa ahyaa hittaammin
Could you help me carry my luggage?	**Voisitteko auttaa kantamisessa?**	voa'sittaykoa ah°°ttaa kahntahmissayssah
Could you wait for me?	**Voitteko odottaa?**	voa'ttaykoa oadoattaa
I'll be back in 10 minutes.	**Tulen takaisin kymmenessä minuutissa.**	toolayn tahkah'sin kewmmaynayssæ minnoottissah

TIPPING, see inside back-cover

Hotel—Other accommodation

Finnish hotels maintain high standards. During the last few years many modern, tastefully furnished hotels and motels have been built. In a typical hotel (*hotelli*) you're likely to find not only a *sauna* but a swimming pool as well. Finnish Tourist Board offices in Finland and abroad supply the brochure *Hotels*, which details all the facilities provided.

motelli
(**moat**aylli)

Accommodation for motorists, all modern and of a very good standard.

kongressi|hotelli
(**koang**rayssihoa**tay**lli)

These are modern, big hotels with a special emphasis on congress facilities and other services.

kesä|hotelli
(**kays**æhoa**tay**lli)

These are usually student living quarters which open as hotels in the summer months (June-August); thus the name 'summer hotels'. Comfortable accommodation in modern buildings at attractive rates.

hospiz, hospitsi
(**hoas**pitsi)

Small hotels operated by the YMCA or YWCA.

matkustaja|koti
(**maht**koostahjah**koat**i)

Small, modest hotels providing basic accommodation at affordable prices.

retkeily|maja
(**rayt**kay'lewmah**jah**)

Youth hostels open during the summer months only. Despite the name they welcome visitors of any age (it is worth checking with individual hostels if children are allowed). Most require membership of a national youth hostel organisation, however non-members are admitted upon payment of a small surcharge. Foreigners can buy a visitor's card from any youth hostel in Finland.

loma|kylä
(**loam**ahkewlæ)

Finland has more than 200 holiday villages consisting of self-contained bungalows in rustic settings. Some are open all year round and are excellent for winter holiday stays.

mökki
(**murk**ki)

Cabins found on well-equipped camping sites.

maatalo|majoitus
(maatahloamah
yoa'tooss)

A number of farmhouses take in guests, who have their meals with the family on a full-board, half-board or bed-and-breakfast basis and can participate in the work of the farm if they wish.

täysi|hoitola
(tæ"ssihoa'toalah)

These boarding houses may offer specialized holidays such as sports, health cures etc.

kesä|mökki
(kaysæmurkki)

Summer cottages are available for rent through the local tourist office.

Can you recommend a hotel/guesthouse?	**Voitteko suositella hotellia/matkus-taja|kotia?**	voa'ttaykoa s°°oasittayllah hoataylliah/ mahtkoostahjah|koatiah
Are there any flats (apartments) vacant?	**Onko yhtään huoneistoa vapaana?**	oankoa ewht°n h°°oanay'stoaah vahpaanah

Checking in—Reception Ilmoittautuminen—Vastaanotto

My name is...	**Nimeni on...**	nimayni oan
I have a reservation.	**Minulla on varaus.**	minnoollah oan vahra°°s
We've reserved 2 rooms.	**Olemme varanneet kaksi huonetta.**	oalaymmay vahrahnnayt kahksi h°°oanayttah
Here's the confir-mation.	**Tässä on vahvistus.**	tæssæ oan vahhvistooss
Do you have any vacancies?	**Onko teillä vapaita huoneita?**	oankoa tay'llæ vahpah'tah h°°oanay'tah
I'd like a...	**Haluaisin...**	hahlooah'sin
single room	**yhden hengen huoneen**	ewhdayn hayngayn h°°oanāyn
double room	**kahden hengen huoneen**	kahhdayn hayngayn h°°oanāyn
We'd like a room...	**Haluaisimme huo-neen,...**	hahlooah'simmay h°°oanāyn
with twin beds	**jossa on kaksi vuodetta**	yaossah oan kahksi v°°oadayttah
with a double bed	**jossa on kaksois|vuode**	yaossah oan kahksoa'sv°°oaday
with a bath	**jossa on kylpy|huone**	yaossah oan kewlpewh°°oanay
with a shower	**jossa on suihku**	yaossah oan soo'hkoo

CHECKING OUT, see page 31

with a balcony	jossa on parveke	yoassah oan **pahr**vaykay
with a view	josta on näkö|ala	yoastaah oan næ**kurahlah**
at the front	joka on julki|sivun puolella	yoakah oan **yool**kisivoon p°°oalayllah
at the back	joka on taka|osassa	yokah oan **tahk**ahoassahssah
It must be quiet.	Sen täytyy olla hiljainen.	sayn tæ°°tew oallah **hil**yah'nayn
Is there...?	Onko...	oankoa
air conditioning	ilmastointia	**il**mahstoa'ntiah
a conference room	neuvottelu|huonetta	**nay°°**voattaylooh°°oa nayttah
a laundry service	pyykki|palvelua	**pew**kkipahlvaylooah
a private toilet	oma wc	oamah **vay**sā̄y
a radio/television in the room	huoneessa radio/ televisio	h°°oa**nayss**ah rahdioa/ taylayvissioa
a sauna	saunaa	**sah°°**naa
a swimming pool	uima-allasta	oo'mah**al**lahstah
hot water	kuuma vesi	**kōō**mah vayssi
room service	huone|palvelua	h°°oa**nay**pahlvaylooah
running water	juokseva vesi	y°°oaksayvah **vay**ssi
Could you put an extra bed/a cot in the room?	Voitteko tuoda huoneeseen lisä-sängyn/lapsen sängyn?	voa'**ttay**koa t°°oadah h°°oa**nay**sā̄yn lissæ**sæng**gewn/**lahp**sayn **sæng**gewn

How much? *Paljonko?*

What's the price...?	Mitä hinta on...	**mitt**æ **hin**tah oan
per day	päivältä	**pæ'**vælltæ
per week	viikolta	**vee**koaltah
for bed and breakfast	aamiaisen kanssa	aamiah'sayn **kahns**sah
excluding meals	ilman aterioita	**il**mahn ahtayrioa'tah
for full board (A.P.)	täysi|hoidosta	tæ°°**sih**oa'doastah
for half board (M.A.P.)	puoli|hoidosta	p°°oa**lih**oa'doastah
Does that include...?	Sisältyykö siihen...?	sissæl**tew**kur **see**hayn
breakfast	aamiainen	aamiah'nayn
service	palvelu|palkkio	pahlvayloo**pahlkk**ioa
value-added tax (sales tax)	liike|vaihto|vero	leekayvah'**htoa**vayroa
Is there any reduction for children?	Onko lapsille alennusta?	oankoa **lahp**sillay ahlaynnoostah

NUMBERS, see page 147

Do you charge for the baby?	**Veloitatteko pikku|lapsesta?**	**vayloa'tahttaykoa pikkoolahpsaystah**
That's too expensive.	**Se on liian kallista.**	say oan **leeahn kahl**listah
Do you have anything cheaper?	**Onko teillä mitään halvempaa?**	**oan**koa tay'llæ mit**tæn hahl**vaympaa

How long? *Kuinka kauan?*

We'll be staying...	**Viivymme...**	**vee**vewmmay
overnight only	**vain yhden yön**	vah'n **ewh**dayn ᵉʷurn
a few days	**muutamia päiviä**	**moo**tahmiah pæ'viæ
a week (at least)	**(vähintään) viikon**	(væhin**tæn**) **vee**koan
I don't know yet.	**En tiedä vielä.**	ayn t'aydæ v'aylæ

Decision *Päätös*

May I see the room?	**Saanko nähdä huoneen?**	**saan**koa næhdæ hᵒᵒoan**ayn**
That's fine. I'll take it.	**Tämä on hyvä. Otan sen.**	**tæ**mæ oan **hew**væ **oa**tahn sayn
No. I don't like it.	**Ei. En pidä siitä.**	ay' ayn **pi**dæ **see**ttæ
It's too...	**Se on liian...**	say oan **lee**ahn
cold/hot	**kylmä/kuuma**	**kewl**mæ/**koo**mah
dark/small	**pimeä/pieni**	**pimm**ᵉʸæ/p'ayni
noisy	**meluisa**	mayloo'sah
I asked for a room with a bath.	**Pyysin huonetta, jossa on kylpy|huone.**	**pew**sin hᵒᵒnayttah **yoas**sah oan **kewl**pewhᵒᵒoanay
Do you have anything...?	**Onko teillä mitään...?**	**oan**koa tay'llæ mit**tæn**
better	**parempaa**	**pah**raympaa
bigger	**suurempaa**	**soo**raympaa
cheaper	**halvempaa**	**hahl**vaympaa
quieter	**rauhallisempaa**	**rah**ᵒᵒhahllissaympaa
Do you have a room with a better view?	**Onko teillä huonetta, josta on parempi näkö|ala?**	**oan**koa tay'llæ hᵒᵒoanayttah **yaos**tah oan **pah**raympi **næ**kurahlah

Registration *Kirjoittautuminen*

Upon arrival at a hotel or guesthouse you'll be asked to fill in a registration form (*matkustaja|kortti*—**maht**koostahyah-**koart**ti).

Suku|nimi/Etu|nimi	Name/First name
Koti|kaupunki/Katu/Numero	Home town/Street/Number
Kansallisuus/Ammatti	Nationality/Occupation
Syntymä|aika/|-paikka	Date/Place of birth
Tulossa/Menossa	Coming from.../Going to...
Passin numero	Passport number
Paikka/Päivä	Place/Date
Alle|kirjoitus	Signature

What does this mean?	**Mitä tämä tarkoit-taa?**	mittæ tæmæ tahrkoa'ttaa

Saanko nähdä passinne.	May I see your passport?
Voisitteko täyttää tämän matkustaja|kortin.	Would you mind filling in this registration form?
Allekirjoittakaa tähän.	Please sign here.
Kuinka kauan viivytte?	How long will you be staying?

What's my room number?	**Mikä on huonee|ni numero?**	mikkæ oan h°°oanayni noomayroa
Will you have our luggage sent up?	**Toimitatteko matka|tavaramme ylös?**	toa'mittahttaykoa mahtkahtahvahrahmmay ewlurss
Where can I park my car?	**Minne voin pysä-köidä auto|ni?**	minnay voa'n pewsækur'dæ ah°°toani
Does the hotel have a garage?	**Onko hotellilla auto|tallia?**	oankoa hoatayllillah ah°°toatahliah
I'd like to leave this in the hotel safe.	**Haluaisin jättää tämän hotellin talle|lokeroon.**	hahlooah'sin jættæ tæmæn hoatayllin tahllayloakayroan

TELLING THE TIME, see page 153

Hotel staff *Hotellin henkilökunta*

hall porter	**portieeri**	**poarti°yri**
maid	**siivooja**	**seevoayah**
manager	**johtaja**	**yohtahyah**
porter	**kantaja**	**kahntahyah**
receptionist	**vastaan|otto**	**vahstaanoattoa**
switchboard operator	**keskus**	**kayskooss**
waiter	**tarjoilija**	**tahryoa¹liyah**
waitress	**tarjoilija**	**tahryoa¹liyah**

General requirements *Yleisiä tarpeita*

The key to room..., please.	**Avain huoneeseen numero..., kiitos.**	**ahvah¹n h°°oanāyssāyn noomayroa... keetoass**
Could you wake me at... please?	**Voisitteko herättää minut kello...?**	**voa¹sittaykoa hayrættā̄ minnoot kaylloa**
When is breakfast/ lunch/dinner served?	**Mihin aikaan tarjoillaan aamiainen/ lounas/päivällinen?**	**mihin ah¹kaan tahryoa¹llaan aamiah¹nayn/ loa°°nahs/ pæ¹vællinayn**
May we have breakfast in our room, please?	**Voisimmeko saada aamiaisen huoneeseen?**	**voa¹simmaykoa saadah aamiah¹ayn h°°oanāyssāyn**
Is there a bath on this floor?	**Onko tässä kerroksessa kylpy|huonetta?**	**oankoa tæssæ kayrroaksayssa kewlpewh°°oanayttah**
What's the voltage?	**Mikä on jännite?**	**mikkæ oan yænnittay**
Where's the shaver socket (outlet)?	**Missä on parran|ajo|koneen pisto|rasia?**	**missæ oan pahrrahnahyoakoanāyn pistoarahsiah**
Can you find me a...?	**Voitteko hankkia minulle...?**	**voa¹ttaykoa hahnkkiah minnoollay**
babysitter	**lapsen|vahdin**	**lahpsaynvahhdin**
secretary	**sihteerin**	**sihhtāyrin**
typewriter	**kirjoidiskone**	**keeryoa¹diskoanay**
May I have a/an/ some...?	**Voisinko saada...**	**voa¹sinkoa saadah**
ashtray	**tuhka|kupin**	**toohkahkoopin**
bath towel	**kylpy|pyyhkeen**	**kewlpewpēwhkāyn**
(extra) blanket	**(lisä-) peiton**	**(leesæ-) pay¹toan**
envelopes	**kirje|kuoria**	**keeryayk°°oariah**
(more) hangers	**(lisää) vaate|ripustimia**	**(leesæ) vaatayrippoostimmiah**

BREAKFAST, see page 40

hot-water bottle	kuuma|vesi|pullon	koomahvayssipoolloan
ice/ice cubes	jäitä/jää|kuutioita	yæ'tæ/yækootioa'tah
needle and thread	neulan ja lankaa	nay°°lahn ya lahnkaa
(extra) pillow	(lisä-) tyynyn	(leesæ-) tēwnewn
reading lamp	luku|lampun	lookoolahmpoon
soap	saippuaa	sah'ppooaa
writing paper	kirjoitus|paperia	keeryoa'toospahpayriah
Where's the...?	Missä on...?	missæ oan
bathroom	kylpy|huone	kewlpewh°°oanay
dining-room	ruoka|sali	r°°oakahsahli
emergency exit	hätä|ulos|käynti	hætæooloaskæ°°nti
hairdresser's	kampaaja	kahmpaayah
lift (elevator)	hissi	hissi
Where are the toilets?	Missä ovat WC:t?	missæ oavaht vāysāyt

Telephone—Post (Mail) *Puhelin—Posti*

Can you get me Kuusamo 123-45-67?	Saanko Kuusamo 123-45-67.	saankoa koosahmoa 123-45-67
Do you have any stamps?	Onko teillä posti|merkkejä?	oankoa tay'llæ poastimayrkkayyæ
Would you post this for me, please?	Voisitteko postittaa tämän?	voa'sittaykoa poastittaa tæmæn
Are there any letters for me?	Onko minulle kirjeitä?	oankoa minnoollay keeryay'ttæ
Are there any messages for me?	Onko minulle viestejä?	oankoa minnoollay v'aystayyæ
How much is my telephone bill?	Kuinka suuri on puhelin|laskuni?	kooinkah soori oan poohaylinlahskooni

Difficulties *Vaikeuksia*

The... doesn't work.	... ei toimi.	ay' toa'mi
air conditioning	ilmastointi	ilmahstoa'nti
bidet	bidet	bidday
fan	tuuletin	tōolaytin
heating	lämmitys	læmmittewss
light	valo	vahloa
radio	radio	rahdioa
television	televisio	taylayvissioa
The tap (faucet) is dripping.	Vesi|hana tippuu.	vayssihahnah tippoo
There's no hot water.	Ei tule kuumaa vettä.	ay toolay kōomaa vayttæ

POST OFFICE AND TELEPHONE, see page 132

The washbasin is blocked.	Pesu|allas on tukossa.	payssooahllahs oan tookoassah
The window is jammed.	Ikkuna on juuttunut kiinni.	ikkoonah oan joottoonoot keenni
The curtains are stuck.	Verho on juuttunut kiinni.	vayrhoa oan joottoonoot keenni
The bulb is burned out.	Lamppu on palanut.	lahmppoo oan pahlahnoot
My bed hasn't been made up.	Vuodettani ei ole sijattu.	v°°oadayttahni ayⁱ oalay siyyahttoo
The... is broken.	... on rikki.	oan rikki
blind	kaihdin	kahⁱhdin
lamp	lamppu	lahmppoo
plug (electricity)	pistoke	pistoakay
plug (water)	tulppa	toolppah
shutter	ikkuna|luukku	ikkoonahlookkoo
switch	katkaisija	kahtkahⁱsiyah
Can you get it repaired?	Voitteko korjata sen?	voaⁱttaykoa koaryahtah sayn

Laundry—Dry cleaner's *Pesula*

I'd like these clothes...	Haluaisin nämä vaatteet...	hahlooahⁱsin næmæ vaattayt
cleaned	puhdistukseen	poohdistooksäyn
dry-cleaned	kuiva|pesuun	kooⁱvahpaysoon
ironed	silitykseen	sillittewksäyn
pressed	prässäykseen	præssæ^{ew}ksäyn
washed	pesuun	paysoon
When will they be ready?	Milloin ne ovat valmiit?	milloaⁱn nay oavaht vahlmeet
I need them...	Tarvitsen ne...	tahrvitsayn nay
today	tänään	tænään
tonight	tänä iltana	tænæ iltahnah
tomorrow	huomenna	h°°oamaynnah
before Friday	ennen perjantaita	aynnayn payryahntahⁱtah
Can you... this?	Voitteko... tämän?	voaⁱttaykoa... tæmæn
mend	korjata	koaryahtah
patch	paikata	pahⁱkahtah
stitch	ommella	oammayllah
Can you sew on this button?	Voitteko ommella tämän napin kiinni?	voaⁱttaykoa oammayllah tæmæn nahpin keenni
Can you get this stain out?	Voitteko poistaa tämän tahran?	voaⁱttaykoa poaⁱstaa tæmæn tahhrahn

Is my laundry ready?	**Onko pyykkini valmis?**	oankoa pēwkkini vahlmiss
This isn't mine.	**Tämä ei ole minun.**	tæmæ ay¹ oalay minnoon
There's something missing.	**Jotain puuttuu.**	yatah¹n pōottōo
There's a hole in this.	**Tässä on reikä.**	tæssæ oan ray¹kæ

Hairdresser—Barber *Kampaaja—Parturi*

Is there a hairdresser/ beauty salon in the hotel?	**Onko hotellissa kampaajaa/kauneushoitolaa?**	oankoa hoatayllissah kahmpaajaa/ kah°°nayooshoa¹toalaa
Can I make an appointment for Thursday?	**Voinko varata ajan torstaiksi?**	voa¹nkoa vahrahtah ahyahn toarstah¹ksi
I'd like a cut and blow dry.	**Haluaisin leikkauksen ja föönauksen.**	hahlooah¹sin lay¹kkah°°ksayn yah fūrnah°°ksayn
I'd like a haircut, please.	**Saisinko tukanleikkuun?**	sah¹sinkoa tookahnlay¹kkōōn
blow-dry	**föönaus**	furnah°°ss
colour rinse	**väri|huuhtelu**	værihōōhtayloo
dye	**värjäys**	væryæ⁰ʷss
face pack	**kasvo|naamio**	kahsvoanaammioa
hair gel	**hius|geeli**	hi°°sghāyli
highlights	**raidat**	rah¹daht
manicure	**käsien hoito/mani-kyyri**	kæs¹ayn hoa¹toa/ mahnikkēwri
perm(anent)	**permanentti**	payrmahnayntti
setting lotion	**kampaus|neste**	kahmpah°°snaystay
shampoo and set	**pesu ja kampaus**	paysoo yah kahmpah°°ss
with a fringe (bangs)	**otsa|tukka**	oatsahtookkah
I'd like a shampoo for... hair.	**Haluaisin shampoon... hiuksille.**	hahlooah¹sin shahmpōan...h¹ooksille
normal/dry/greasy (oily)	**normaaleille/kuiville/rasvaisille**	noarmaalay¹llay/koo¹villay/ rahsvah¹sillay
Do you have a colour chart?	**Onko teillä väri|karttaa?**	oankoa tay¹llæ værikahrttaa
Don't cut it too short.	**Älkää leikatko liian lyhyeksi.**	ælkǣ lay¹kahtkoa leeahn lewh⁰ʷayksi
A little more off the...	**Vähän lyhyem-mäksi...**	væhæn lewh⁰ʷaymmæksi
back	**takaa**	tahkaa
neck	**niskasta**	niskahstah

DAYS OF THE WEEK, see page 151

sides	sivuilta	sivvoo'ltah
top	päältä	pæltæ
I don't want any hairspray.	En halua mitään hius|lakkaa.	ayn hahl°°ah mittæn hi°°uslahkkaa
I'd like a shave.	Haluaisin parran|ajon.	hahlooah'sin pahrrahnahyoan
Would you trim my..., please?	Voisitteko siistiä....	voa'sittaykoa seestiæ
beard	parta|ni	pahrtahni
moustache	viiksiä|ni	veeksiæni
sideboards (sideburns)	pulisonki|ni	poolissoankinni

Checking out *Lähtö*

May I have my bill, please?	Saisinko lasku?	sah'sinkoa lahskoo
I'm leaving early in the morning.	Lähden aikaisin aamulla.	læhdayn ah'kah'sin aamoollah
Please have my bill ready.	Kirjoittaisitteko laskuni valmiiksi.	keeryoa'ttah'sittaykoa lahskooni vahlmeeksi
We'll be checking out around noon.	Lähdemme puolen|päivän aikoihin.	læhdaymmay p°°oalaynpæivæn ah'koa'hin
I must leave at once.	Minun täytyy lähteä heti.	minnoon tæ°wtew læhtayæ hayti
Is everything included?	Sisältyykö siihen kaikki?	sissæltewkur seehhayn kah'kki
Can I pay by credit card?	Voinko maksaa luotto|kortilla?	voa'nkoa mahksaa l°°oattoakoartilla
I think there's a mistake in the bill.	Tässä laskussa taitaa olla virhe.	tæssæ lahskoossah tah'taa oallah virhay
Can you get us a taxi?	Voitteko hankkia meille taksin?	voa'ttaykoa hahnkkiah may'llay tahksin
Could you have our luggage brought down?	Voisitteko toimittaa matka|tavara|mme alas?	voa'sittaykoa toa'mittaa mahtkahtahvahrahmmay ahlahs
Here's the forwarding address.	Tässä on seuraava osoittee|ni.	tæssæ oan say°°raavah oasoa'ttæyni
You have my home address.	Teillä on koti|osoittee|ni.	tay'llæ oan koatioasoa'ttæyni
It's been a very enjoyable stay.	Olen viihtynyt erinomaisesti.	oalayn veehtewnewt ayrinoamah'saysti

TIPPING, see inside back-cover

Camping *Leirintä*

There are more than 350 camp sites, 200 of which belong to the Finnish Travel Association (*Suomen Matkailuliitto*). Sites are graded by stars from one to three, the best offering riding, water-skiing, rowing and fishing. The Finnish camping season starts around the end of May in the south and lasts into September. An international or Finnish camping card is required - obtainable at the sites. It is forbidden to light fires in the countryside so bring a camping stove if you intend to cook.

Is there a camp site near here?	**Onko lähellä leirintä|aluetta?**	oankoa læhayllæ lay'rintæahlooayttah
Can we camp here?	**Voimmeko leiriytyä tässä?**	voa'mmaykoa lay'riewtewæ tæssæ
Do you have room for a tent/caravan (trailer)?	**Onko teillä tilaa teltalle/asunto|vaunulle**	oankoa tay'llæ tillaa tayltahllay/ ahsoontoavah°°noollay
What's the charge...?	**Mitä on maksu...?**	mittæ oan mahksoo
per day	**päivältä**	pæ'væltæ
per person	**hengeltä**	hayngayltæ
for a car	**autosta**	ah°°toastah
for a tent	**teltasta**	tayltahstah
for a caravan (trailer)	**asuntovaunusta**	ahsoontoavah°°noostah
Is tourist tax included?	**Sisältyykö matkailija|vero hintaan?**	sissæltewkur mahtkah'liyahvayroa hintaan
Is there/Are there (a)...?	**Onko...?**	oankoa
drinking water	**juoma|vettä**	y°°oamahvayttæ
electricity	**sähköä**	sæhkuræ
playground	**leikki|kenttää**	lay'kkikaynttǣ
restaurant	**ravintolaa**	rahvintoalaa
shopping facilities	**myymälää**	mēwmælǣ
swimming pool	**uima|allasta**	oo'mahahllahstah
Where are the showers/toilets?	**Missä ovat suihkut/vessat?**	missæ oavaht soo'hkoot/ vayssaht
Where can I get butane gas?	**Mistä voin saada butaania/ neste|kaasua?**	mistæ voa'n saadah bootaaniah/ naystaykaassooah
Is there a youth hostel near here?	**Onko lähellä retkeily|majaa?**	oankoa læhayllæ raytkay'lewmahyaa

CAMPING EQUIPMENT, see page 106

Eating out

Eating places in Finland range from the basic to the very smart; the list below will help you decide where to choose. However, remember that restaurants are not allowed to serve alcoholic drinks before 11 a.m.

Baari
(baari)

A 'snack-bar', unlicensed as a rule, although some serve beer, so don't head for one of these if what you want is a stiff drink! Actually the ones which do not offer any alcoholic beverages at all generally have a more pleasant atmosphere. You will see the sign *Baari* everywhere in Finland. The menu usually consists of snacks, simple meals, pastries and ice cream. They will be happy to serve just a cup of coffee or tea; there is no obligation to order a full meal. However, some of these may close quite early in the evening.

Grilli
(grilli)

A small informal restaurant, sometimes licensed to serve beer and wine. More popular for luncheons than for dinner.

Kahvio, Kahvila
(kahhvioa kahhvillah)

Kahvila is a cafe or a snack-bar usually specializing in pastries and cakes. Light meals may also be available. *Kahvio* is just a self-service cafeteria, for example in a department store or a service station.

Krouvi
(kroa^{oo}vi)

A small restaurant offering a hearty menu and usually licensed to serve beer and wine. Very similar in style to the restaurants called *Grilli*.

Pub
(poob)

An imitation of an English pub, although sometimes only in name. Many pubs in Finland serve meals and have waitress service as in a restaurant.

Ravintola
(rahvintoalah)

The general name for a restaurant. This can cover anything from a small intimate eating place to a grand establishment with live music and a dance floor. A *ravintola* may be either licensed or unlicensed.

Yö|kerho
(^{ew}urkayrhoa)

A night-club, always licensed, mostly to be found in big hotels. Open until 2 - 3 a.m.

Eating habits *Ruoka|tavat*

The Finns are coffee drinkers and most of them start their day with a cup of black coffee. A healthy breakfast may then consist of oat porridge or muesli and some black rye bread. In Finland tea is served extremely weak and never with milk.

Most workplaces have subsidized canteens where the employees may have a two or three course lunch which is often their main meal of the day. Nowadays in many families a full dinner is cooked at home only at weekends as the parents have their main meal at work and the children are given theirs at school or at a creche.

In general Finnish food is hearty and homely. Pork, beef and chicken casseroles are common, while lamb and veal are less popular. Cold milk is the typical drink at meal times, wine only being served on special occasions or when entertaining.

Meal times *Ateria-ajat*

In Finland, lunch and dinner are eaten earlier than in most other European countries. Lunch (*lounas*—**loa**°°nahss) at 11 a.m. is not unusual and when at home most families eat dinner (*päivällinen*—**pæ**ᶦvællinnayn) around 5 p.m. However, restaurants continue serving evening meals until late and it is possible to have dinner in a restaurant quite late in the evening, for example after a visit to the theatre or cinema.

Finnish cuisine *Suomalainen keittiö*

Finnish cuisine is a mixture of Scandinavian, European and Russian cooking. The staple diet consists of various potato and meat dishes. Milk is the traditional drink with meals and there are many Finnish dishes in which milk is a prominent ingredient. Pickled and smoked fish is a speciality and there are numerous types of these. Finnish bread is delicious and there is an endless variety. Very dark, sour rye bread is very popular in Finland.

Wild mushrooms and fresh wild berries are widely used. Try *sienisalaatti* (**s**'**aynisah**laatti), a salad of wild mushrooms in sour cream. A bright red jam, *puolukkahillo* (**poa**lookka**hill**oa), made of uncooked lingonberries which grow wild in the Finnish forests, is a regular accompaniment to meat dishes.

Savoury pasties are another Finnish delicacy. Try *kaalipiirakka* (**kaali**pee**rah**kah) made with cabbage and minced meat, or *karjalanpiirakka* (**kahr**yahlahn**peer**ahkkah) which is a traditional Carelian delicacy often served with chopped cooked egg mixed with a knob of butter. Smoked reindeer meat, which resembles venison but is slightly stronger, is a speciality from Lapland.

Mitä saisi olla?	What would you like?
Suosittelen tätä.	I recommend this.
Mitä haluaisitte juoda?	What would you like to drink?
Meillä ei ole...	We don't have...
Ottaisitteko...?	Would you like...?

Hungry? *Nälkäinen?*

I'm hungry/I'm thirsty.	**Olen nälkäinen/ Olen janoinen.**	oalayn nælkæinayn/oalayn yahnoa'nayn
Can you recommend a good restaurant?	**Voitteko suositella hyvää ravintolaa?**	voa'sittaykoa s°°sittayllah hewvæ rahvintoalaa
Are there any inexpensive restaurants around here?	**Onko täällä|päin edullista ravinto- laa?**	oankoa tællæpæin aydoollistah rahvintoalaa

If you want to be sure of getting a table in a well-known restaurant, it may be better to book in advance.

I'd like to reserve a table for 4.	**Varaisin pöydän neljälle.**	vahrahisin p°ewdæn nayljællay
We'll come at 8.	**Tulemme kello 8.**	toolaymmay kaylloa kahhdayksahn

Could we have a table...?	Voimmeko saada...?	voa'mmaykoa saadah
in the corner	nurkka|pöydän	noorkkahp"ewdæn
by the window	ikkuna|pöydän	ikkoonahp"ewdæn
outside	pöydän ulkoa	p"ewdæn oolkoaah
on the terrace	pöydän terassilta	p"ewdæn tayrahssiltah
in a non-smoking area	pöydän savuttomalta alueelta	p"ewdæn sahvoottoamahltah ahlooaÿltah

Asking and ordering *Kysyminen ja tilaaminen*

Waiter/Waitress!	Tarjoilija!	tahryoa'liyah
I'd like something to eat/drink.	Haluaisin jotain syötävää/juotavaa	hahlooah'sin yoatahin sew'"tævæ/y''oatavaa
May I have the menu, please?	Saisinko ruoka|listan.	sah'sinkoa r°°oakahlistahn
Do you have a set menu/local dishes?	Onko teillä vakio|listaa/paikallisia erikoisuuksia?	oankoa tay'llæ vahkioalistaa/ pah'kahllissiah ayrikoa'sōōksiah
What do you recommend?	Mitä suosittelisitte?	mittæ s°°oasittaylissittay
Do you have anything ready quickly?	Onko teillä jotakin nopeasti valmista?	oankoa taillæ yoatahkin noapayahsti vahlmisstah
I'm in a hurry.	Minulla on kiire.	minnoollah oan keeray
I'd like...	Saisinko...	sah'sinkoa
Could we have a/an..., please?	Voisimmeko saada...?	voa'simmaykoa saadah
ashtray	tuhka|kupin	toohhkahkoopin
cup	kupin	koopin
fork	haarukan	haarookahn
glass	lasin	lahsin
knife	veitsen	vay'tsayn
napkin (serviette)	lautas|liinan	lah°°tahsleenahn
plate	lautasen	lah°°tahsayn
spoon	lusikan	loossikkahn
May I have some...?	Voisinko saada...?	voa'sinkoa saadah
bread	leipää	lay'pǣ
butter	voita	voa'tah
lemon	sitruunaa	sitrōōnaa
oil	öljyä	urlyewæ

pepper	pippuria	**pip**pooriah
salt	suolaa	s°°oalaa
seasoning	mausteita	mah°°stay'tah
sugar	sokeria	soakayriah
vinegar	viini|etikkaa	veeniayttikkaa

Special diet *Erikois\|ruoka\|valio*

Some useful expressions for those with special requirements:

I'm on a diet.	Olen dieetillä.	oalayn d'aytillæ
I'm a vegetarian.	Olen kasvis|syöjä	oalayn kahsvissew'''yæ
I don't drink alcohol.	En juo alkoholia.	ayn y°°oa ahlkoahoaliah
I don't eat meat.	En syö lihaa.	ayn sew'' lihaa
I mustn't eat food containing...	En voi syödä ruo-kaa, jossa on...	ayn voa' sew'''dæ r°°oakaa yoassah oan
flour/fat	jauhoa/rasvaa	yah°°hoaah/rahsvaa
salt/sugar	suolaa/sokeria	s°°oalaa/soakayriah
Do you have... for diabetics?	Onko teillä... dia-beetikoille?	oankoa tay'llæ...diahbātikkoa'llay
cakes	kakkuja	kahkkooyah
fruit juice	hedelmä|mehua	haydaylmæmayhooah
a special menu	erikois|ruoka|listaa	ayrikkoa'sr°°oakahlistah
Do you have any vegetarian dishes?	Onko teillä kasvis|syöjän annoksia?	oankoa tay'llæ kahsvissew'''yæn ahnnoaksiah
Could I have... instead of dessert?	Voisinko saada...-a jälki|ruoan asemasta?	voa'sinkoa saadah...-a yælkirr°°aahn asaymahstah
Can I have an artificial sweetener?	Voinko saada makeutus|ainetta?	voa'nkoa saadah mahkayootoosah'nayttah

And...

I'd like some more.	Saisinko vähän lisää.	sah'sinkoa væhæn lissǣ
Can I have more..., please?	Saisinko lisää...-a, kiitos.	sah'sinkoa lissǣ...-a keetoass
Just a small portion.	Vain pieni annos.	vah'n p'ayni ahnnoass
Nothing more, thanks.	Kiitos, riittää.	keetoass riittǣ
Where are the toilets?	Missä ovat WC:t?	missæ oavaht vāȳsāyt

What's on the menu? *Mitä on (ruoka)|listalla?*

During the summer many restaurants offer a tourist menu. Known as the *Finland Menu*, it features a selection of typical dishes. There are three price categories which vary according to the establishment.

Under the headings below you'll find alphabetical lists of dishes that might be offered on a Finnish menu with their English equivalents. You can simply show the book to the waiter. If you want some fruit for example, let *him* point to what's available on the appropriate list. Use pages 36 and 37 for ordering in general.

Reading the menu *Ruoka|listan luku*

Talon erikoisuudet	Specialities of the house
Paikkakunnan erikoisuuksia	Local specialities
Päivän tarjous/annos	Dish of the day
... tapaan	... style
Kotitekoista	Home-made
Valintanne mukaan	Of your choice
Vuodenajan erikoisuudet	In season

alku|paloja	ahlkoopahloayah	appetizers
hampurilaisia	hahmpoorillah'sia	burgers
hedelmiä	haydaylmiæ	fruit
juomat	y°°amaht	beverages
jälkiruokia	yælkirr°°oakiah	desserts
jäätelöä	yǣtayl^{ur}æ	ice cream
kalaa	kahlaa	fish
kanaa	kahnaa	chicken
keittoja	kay'ttoayah	soups
lintua	lint°°ah	poultry
muna|ruokia	moonahr°°oakiah	egg dishes
olut	oaloot	beer
pasta	pahstah	pasta
riistaa	reestaa	game
salaatteja	sahlaattayyah	salads
vihanneksia	vihahnnayksiah	vegetables
viinit	veenit	wine
väli|palaa	vælipahlaa	snacks
väli|ruokia	vælirr°°oakiah	entrees
äyriäisiä	æ^{ew}riæissiæ	seafood

Breakfast *Aamiainen*

A Finnish breakfast is a hearty meal usually consisting of coffee or tea with bread, butter and cheese, cold meats and sometimes eggs or perhaps porridge. Most hotels can also provide an English or American breakfast.

I'd like breakfast, please.	**Saisinko aamiaisen.**	sah'sinkoa aamiah'ssayn
I'll have a/an/some...	**Ottaisin...**	oattah'sin.
bacon and eggs	**pekonia ja munia**	paykoaniah yah **moo**niah
boiled egg	**keitetyn munan**	kay'taytewn **moo**nahn
soft/hard	**kovaksi/pehmeäksi**	koavahksi/**payhm**ayæksi
cereal	**hiutaleita**	hi°°tahlay'tah
eggs	**munia**	**moo**niah
fried eggs	**paistettuja munia**	pah'stayttooyah **moo**niah
scrambled eggs	**muna|kokkelia**	moonahkoak**kay**liah
poached eggs	**hyydytettyjä munia**	hēwdewtayttewyæ **moo**niah
fruit juice	**hedelmä|mehua**	haydaylmæ**may**hoo
grapefruit	**greippi|mehua**	grayppi**may**hoo
orange	**appelsiini|mehua**	appaylseeni**may**hoo
ham and eggs	**kinkkua ja munia**	kinkkooah yah **moo**niah
jam	**hilloa**	**hill**oah
marmalade	**marmelaadia**	mahr**may**laadiah
toast	**paahto|leipää**	paahhtoalay'pǣ
yoghurt	**jogurttia**	yoa**goor**ttiah
May I have some...?	**Voinko saada vähän...**	voa'nkoa saadah væhæn
bread	**leipää**	lay'pǣ
butter	**voita**	voa'tah
(hot) chocolate	**kaakaota**	**kaa**kahoatah
coffee	**kahvia**	**kahh**viah
decaffeinated	**kafeiinitonta**	**kah**fayeenitoantah
black/with milk	**mustana/maidon kanssa**	**moos**tahnah/**mah**'doan **kanss**ah
honey	**hunajaa**	**hoo**nahjaa
milk	**maitoa**	**mah**'toa
cold/hot	**kylmää/kuumaa**	kewlmǣ/**koo**maa
pepper	**pippuria**	**pip**pooriah
rolls	**sämpylöitä**	sæampewlur'tæ

salt	suolaa	s°°oalaa
tea	teetä	tāytæ
with milk	maidon kanssa	mah'doan kahnssah
with lemon	sitruunan kanssa	sitrōonahn kahnssah
(hot) water	(kuumaa) vettä	kōomaa vayttæ

Seisova pöytä

Finland also has its own variation of the Swedish *smörgåsbord* known as *seisova pöytä*. This is a sumptuous do-it-yourself stand-up cold buffet. Also common in Finland is *voi|leipä|pöytä* which literally means 'bread and butter table'.

This buffet can consist of 50 or more different dishes! You can choose it either as a first course or as a fixed-price complete meal, in which case the only limit on the number of trips you make to the serving table is your own capacity.

The meal is often divided into three phases. The first plateful consists of fish, the second of cold meats and the third of hot foods such as meatballs and casseroles. In addition there are salads, cheese, fruit, several types of bread, milk or buttermilk and beer, all included in the price.

Starters (Appetizers) *Alkuruokia*

Pickled or smoked fish, smoked fish roe, smoked reindeer meat and wild mushrooms are the starters which give a regional flavour to a Finnish meal.

I'd like an appetizer.	Ottaisin jotain alku|ruokaa.	oattah'sin yoatah'n ahlkoor°°oakaa
What would you recommend?	Mitä suositteli-sitte?	mittæ s°°oasittaylissittay
anjovista	ahnyoavisstah	anchovies
katka|rapua	kahtkahrahpooah	shrimp
kaviaaria	kahv'aariah	caviar
keittoja	kay'ttoayah	soup
kinkkua	kinkkooah	ham
leikkeleitä	lay'kkaylaytæ	cold meats

lohta	**loah**tah	salmon
makkaraa	**mahk**kahraa	sausage
mätiä	**mæ**tiæ	roe
parsaa	**pahr**saa	asparagus
poron︱kieltä	**poa**roank'ayltæ	reindeer tongue
poron︱lihaa	**poa**roanlihaa	reindeer meat
rapuja	**rah**pooyah	crayfish
salaattia	**sah**laattiah	salad
sardiineja	**sahr**deenayyæ	sardines
silakoita	**sil**lahkoa'tah	Baltic herring
savu︱silakoita	**sah**voosillahkoa'tah	smoked Baltic herring
silliä	**sil**liæ	salted herring

Soups and stews *Keittoja ja muhennoksia*

A steaming hot bowl of soup is a perfect dish in winter, particularly after skiing or skating, as it warms up the whole body. Thick pea soup with cubed fatty pork *hernekeitto* (**hayr**nay**kay'**ttoa) is traditionally served on Shrove Tuesday. *Kesäkeitto* (**kay**ssae**kay'**ttoa) - 'summer soup' is another Finnish speciality which is most often served in summertime, as its name indicates. This soup is made of fresh summer vegetables stewed in milk, the main ingredient being cauliflower.

I'd like some soup.	**Haluaisin (jotain) keittoa.**	hahlooah'sin (yoatah'n) **kay'**ttoah
artisokka︱keitto	**ahr**tisoakkah**kay'**ttoa	artichoke soup
(herkku︱)sieni︱keitto	(**hayr**kkoo) s'**ay**nikay'ttoa	mushroom soup
herne︱keitto	**hayr**naykay'ttoa	pea soup
härän︱häntä︱liemi	**hæ**rænhæntæl'aymi	oxtail soup
juusto︱keitto	**yōōs**toakay'ttoa	cheese soup
kaali︱keitto	**kaa**likay'ttoa	cabbage soup
kala︱keitto	**kah**lahkay'ttoa	fish soup
kana︱keitto	**kah**nahkay'ttoa	chicken soup
kukka︱kaali︱keitto	**kook**kahkaalikay'ttoa	cauliflower soup
liha︱keitto	**lih**hahkay'ttoa	meat stew
mustikka︱keitto	**mus**tikkahkay'ttoa	whortleberry soup
parsa︱keitto	**pahr**sahkay'ttoa	asparagus soup
pinaatti︱keitto	**pin**naattikay'ttoa	spinach soup
raparperi︱keitto	**rah**pahrpayrikay'ttoa	rhubarb soup
tomaatti︱keitto	**toa**maattikay'ttoa	tomato soup
vihanes︱keitto	**vih**ahnnaykay'ttoa	vegetable soup

Salads *Salaatteja*

hapan|kaali|salaatti	**hah**pahnkaalisahlaatti	sauerkraut salad
kaali-puolukka| salaatti	kaalip°°oalookkah **sah**laatti	cabbage and lingonberry salad
rosolli	**roa**soalli	beetroot salad with salt herring
savu|silakka|salaatti	**sah**voosilahkkah **sah**laatti	salad with smoked Baltic herring

Egg dishes *Muna\|ruokia*

I'd like an omelet.	**Haluaisin munak- kaan.**	**hah**looah'sin **moo**nahkkaan
hyydytetty muna	h$\overline{\text{ew}}$dewtayttew **moo**nah	poached egg
keitetty muna	kay'tayttew **moo**nah	boiled egg
kovaksi	**koa**vahksi	hard
pehmeäksi	**payh**mayæksi	soft
munakas	**moo**nahkahs	omelet
hillo|munakas	**hill**ooa**moo**nahkahs	cheese omelet
juusto-munakas	y$\overline{\text{oo}}$stoa**moo**nahkahs	ham omelet
kinkku|munakas	**kink**koo**moo**nahkahs	bacon omelet
pekoni|munakas	**pay**koani**moo**nahkas	jam omelet
peruna|munakas	**pay**roonah**moo-** nahkahs	potato omelet
sieni|munakas	s'aynimoonahkahs	mushroom omelet
muna|kokkeli	**moo**nahk**oa**kkayli	scrambled eggs
paistettu muna	pah'stayttoo **moo**nah	fried egg

Fish and seafood *Kalaa ja äyriäisiä*

With all its lakes, and the Baltic, you'd think Finland would be a land of fish fanciers. Surprisingly, the average Finn eats little fish except for Baltic herring. Restaurants, though, nearly always offer interesting dishes like smoked whitefish or salmon. An excellent lake fish is *muikku*, mainly eaten in the province of Savo.

| I'd like some fish. | **Haluaisin (jotain) kalaa.** | **ha**looah'sin (**yo**atah'n) **kah**laa |
| What kind of seafood do you have? | **Mitä äyriäisiä teillä on?** | **mit**tæ æ°ʷriæ'ssiæ **tay**'llæ oan |

ahven	**ahh**vayn	perch
anjovis	**ahn**yoavis	anchovies
ankerias	**ahn**kayriahss	eel
hauki	**ha**°°ki	pike
hummeri	**hoom**mayri	lobster
kampela	**kahm**paylah	flounder
katka|rapu	**kaht**kahrahpoo	shrimp
kaviaari	**kah**viaari	caviar
kilo|haili	**kil**loahah'li	sprats
kirjo|lohi	**kir**yoaloahi	rainbow trout
kolja	**koal**yah	haddock
kuha	**koo**hah	pike perch
lahna	**lahh**nah	bream
lohi	**lo**ahi	salmon
made	**mahd**ay	burbot
makrilli	**mahk**rilli	mackerel
meri|antura	**may**riahntoorah	sole
muikku	**moo**'kkoo	vendace
muste|kala	**moos**taykahlah	cuttlefish
mäti	**mæt**i	roe
nahkiainen	**nahh**kiah'nayn	lamprey
osterit	**oas**tayri	oysters
pikku|silli	**pik**koosilli	whitebait
puna|kampela	**poo**nah**kahm**paylah	plaice
rapu	**rah**poo	crayfish
sampi	**sahm**pi	sturgeon
sardiinit	**sahr**deenit	sardines
siika	**see**kah	whitefish
silakka	**sil**lahkkah	Baltic herring
silli	**sil**li	herring
sini|simpukat	**sin**nisimpookaht	mussels
särki	**sær**ki	roach
taimen	**tah**'mayn	trout
tonni|kala	**toan**nikahlah	tuna
turska	**toors**kah	cod

baked	**uunissa paistettu**	**ōō**nissah **pah'**stayttoo
fried	**paistettu**	**pah'**stayttoo
grilled	**grillattu**	**grill**ahttoo
marinated	**marinoitu**	**mahr**inoa**'**too
poached	**keitetty**	**kay'**tayttew
sautéed	**ruskistettu/käristetty**	**roos**kistayttoo/
		kæristayttew
smoked	**savustettu**	**sah**voostayttoo
steamed	**höyryssä keitetty**	**hur**ᵉʷrewssæ **kay'**tayttew

Fish dishes *Kala*|*ruokia*

Janssonin kiusaus
(**yahnss**soanin
kiᵒᵒsah**ᵒᵒ**ss)
'Jansson's temptation'; sliced potatoes, onions and anchovies in cream sauce, baked in the oven

kala|**kukko**
(**kah**lah**kook**koa)
'fish loaf'; sort of loaf of dark bread with *muikku* (sometimes perch) and pork inside and baked in the oven; speciality of the province of Savo

kulibjaka
(**koo**libyahkah)
a savoury pie filled with salmon, rice, hard-boiled eggs and dill, served in slices with melted butter

lasi|**mestarin silli**
(**lahsi**maystahrin **silli**)
'glass master's herring'; pickled herring with spices, vinegar, carrot and onion

lipeä|**kala**
(**lippa**yækahlah)
a Christmas speciality; codfish soaked in lye solution, boiled and served with a white sauce

lohi|**laatiko**
(**loah**ilaatikkoa)
a potato and salmon casserole, baked in the oven

mateen|**mäti** ,
muikun|**mäti**
(**mah**tāȳnmæti
moo'koonmæti)
roe from burbot or whitefish, seasoned with onion; often accompanies *bliny* (small pancakes)

silaaka|**laatikko**
(**sill**ahkkahlaatikkoa)
casserole made of alternating layers of potato slices, onion and Baltic herring, with an egg and milk sauce, baked in the oven

suutarin|**lohi**
(**sōō**tahrinloahi)
'cobbler's salmon'; marinated Baltic herring in vinegar with onion and peppers

venäläinen silli
(**vay**nælæ**'**nayn **silli**)
'Russian herring'; herring fillets with mayonnaise, mustard, vinegar, beetroot, gherkins and onion

Meat *Liha|ruokia*

You'll find most of the familiar meat dishes in Finland, with pork predominating. You'll also meet some exciting novelties: roast elk or reindeer from Lapland, or even bear (mostly imported from Russia).

What kind of meat do you have?	**Mitä liha|ruokia teilä on?**	**mittæ lihahr°°oakiah tay'llæ oan**
beef	**naudan|lihaa**	**nah°°dahnlihaa**
lamb	**lammasta**	**lahm**mahstah
pork	**porsaan|lihaa**	**poar**saanlihaa
veal	**vasikan|lihaa**	**vah**sikkahnlihaa
filee	**filay**	fillet
hirven|liha	**hir**vaynlihah	elk
härän|häntä	**hæræn**hæntæ	oxtail
jauheliha|pihvi	**yah°°hay**lihah**pihvi**	beefburger
kani	**kah**ni	rabbit
karhun|paisti	**kahr**hoon**pah'sti**	bear steak
kieli	**k'ay**li	tongue
kinkku	**kink**koo	gammon
kyljys/kotletti	**kewl**yews/**koat**laytti	chop/cutlet
lammasta	**lahm**mahstah	mutton
(lampaan) jalka	(**lahm**paan) **yah**lkah	leg (of lamb)
leike	**lay'**kay	escalope
liha|pyörykät	**lihah**pew°°rewkæt	meatballs
makkara	**mahk**kahrah	sausage
maksa	**mahk**sah	liver
munuaiset	**moonooah'**sayt	kidneys
nakit	**nah**kit	frankfurters
paisti	**pah'**sti	sirloin
pekoni	**pay**koani	bacon
pihvi	**pih**vi	steak
poron|liha	**poar**oanlihah	reindeer meat
(savustettu) kinkku	(**sah**voostayttoo) **kink**koo	(smoked) ham

baked	**uunissa paistettu**	o͞onissah **pah**ˈstayttoo
barbecued	**pariloitu**	pahriloaˈtoo
boiled	**keitetty**	**kay**ˈtayttew
braised	**haudutettu**	hah͞o͞odootayttoo
fried	**paistettu**	**pah**ˈstayttoo
grilled	**grillattu**	grillahttoo
roast	**paahdettu**	paahdayttoo
sautéed	**ruskistettu/käristetty**	roo͞o͞oskistayttoo/
		kæristayttew
stewed	**muhennokseksi**	moohaynnoaksayksi
	keitetty	**kay**ˈtayttew
very rare	**vain vähän paistettu**	vah**ˈ**n **væh**æn **pah**ˈstayttoo
underdone (rare)	**puoli|kypsä**	p͞o͞oali**kewps**æ
medium	**keski-kypsä**	**kay**ski-**kewps**æ
well-done	**hyvin/kypsäksi**	**hewv**in/**kewps**æksi
	paistettu	**pah**ˈstayttoo

Meat specialities *Liha|erikoisuuksia*

joulu|kinkku
(yoa͞o͞olookinkkoo)

Christmas ham; whole ham served as the traditional Finnish Christmas dish with various stews, e.g. *lanttulaatikko*, rutabaga casserole or *porkkanalaatikko*, carrot casserole, peas, plums, etc.

kaali|kääryleet
(kaalikæ͞ærewlayt)

cabbage rolls; cabbage leaves stuffed with minced meat and rice

kaali|piirakka
(kaalipeerahkkah)

pie made with cabbage and minced meat

karjalan|paisti
(kahryahlahnpahˈsti)

'Carelian stew'; beef, pork and sometimes mutton with allspice

lammas|kaali
(lahmmahskaali)

stew or soup made with mutton and cabbage

Lindströmin pihvi
(lindsrurmin **pihv**i)

beefburger made with beetroot, served with fried onions and a piquant cream sauce

maksa|laatikko (**mahk**sahlaatikkoa)	baked liver purée made with rice and raisins
meri|mies|pihvi (**mayrim**'ayspihvi)	'seaman's beef'; casserole of alternate layers of potato slices and meat patties (or minced meat), baked in the oven
pala|paisti (pahlahpah'sti)	beef ragout
pipar|juuri|liha (pippahy<u>oo</u>rilihah)	boiled beef with horseradish sauce
poron|käristys (poaronkæristewss)	sautéed reindeer stew, a Lapp speciality
veri|ohukaiset (vayrioahookah'sayt)	thin pancakes made with blood, eaten with lingonberry jam
wienin|leike (veeninlay'kay)	veal cutlet, breaded and fried (wiener schnitzel)

Game and Poultry *Riistaa ja lintua*

Finland is noted for its game birds but you may consider the prices high.

ankka	ahnkkah	duck
fasaani	fahsaahni	pheasant
hanhi	hahnhi	goose
hirvi	hirvi	venison
jänis	yænia	hare
kalkkuna	kahlkkoonah	turkey
kana	kahnah	chicken
rinta/koipi/siipi	rintah/koa'pi/seepi	breast/leg/wing
grillattu kana	grillahttoo kahnah	barbecued chicken
pelto|pyy	payltoap<u>ew</u>	partridge
teeri	t<u>ay</u>ri	grouse
villi|sika	villisikah	wild boar

Vegetables *Vihanneksia*

artisokka	ahrtisoakkah	artichokes
avokado	ahvoakahdoa	avocado
endive	ayndivay	endive (chicory)
espanjan|pippuri	ayspahnyahnpippoori	chili
herneet	hayrnāyt	peas
kaali	kaali	cabbage
kastanja	kahstahnyah	chestnuts
kesäkurpitsa	kaysækoorpitsah	courgette (zucchini)
kukka|kaali	kookkahkaali	cauliflower
kurkku	koorkkoo	cucumber
kurpitsa	koorpitsah	pumpkin (squash)
lanttu	lahnttoo	swede (rutabaga)
lehti|salaatti	layhtisahlaatti	lettuce
linssit	linssit	lentils
maissi	mah'ssi	(sweet) corn
muna|koiso	moonahkoa'soa	aubergine (eggplant)
nauriit	nah°°reet	turnips
parsa	pahrsah	asparagus (tips)
parsa|kaali	pahrsakaali	broccoli
pavut	pahvoot	beans
perunat	payroonaht	potatoes
pinaatti	pinnaatti	spinach
pippuri	pippoori	(sweet) peppers
vihreä/punainen	vihrayæ/ poonah'nayn	green/red
porkkanat	poarkkahnaht	carrots
puna|juuri	poonahyōōri	beetroot
purjo(|sipuli)	(pooryoa(sippooli)	leeks
retiisit	rayteesit	radishes
ruusu|kaali	rōōsookaali	Brussels sprouts
(saksan|)kumina	(sahksahn)koominah	fennel
seka|vihanneket	saykahvihahnaykayt	mixed vegetables
selleri	sayllayri	celery
sieni	s'ayni	mushrooms
sipulit	sippoolit	onions
tomaatit	toamaatit	tomatoes

lanttu|laatikko
(**lahntt**oolaatikkoa)
swede casserole; a Christmas speciality - mashed swede baked in the oven, served with Christmas ham

porkkana|laatikko
(**poark**kahnah**laatikkoa**)
carrot casserole; mashed carrots and rice baked in the oven

peruna|laatikko
(**pay**roonah**laatikk**oa)
potato bake

makaroni|laatikko
(**mah**kahroani**laatikkoa**)
macaroni bake with milk and egg sauce

pinaatti|ohukaiset
(**pinnaattioa**hookah'**sayt**)
spinach pancakes

porkkana|ohukaiset
(**poark**kahnah**oa** hookah'**sayt**)
carrot pancakes

kesä|keitto
(**kay**ssae**kayt**toa)
cauliflower and milk soup

Sauces *Kastikkeita*

etika	**ay**tikkah	vinegar
herkku|sieni|kastike	**hayr**kkoos'**ayni**-**kah**stikkay	mushroom sauce
juusto|kastike	y**oo**stoa**kah**stikkay	cheese sauce
kastike	**kah**stikkay	sauce
liemi	**l'ay**mi	broth
majoneesi	**mah**yoan**āy**ssi	mayonnaise
ranskalainen **saalatti|kastike**	**rahns**kahlah'**nayn** **sah**laatti**kah**stikkay	French dressing
ruskea kastike	**roos**kayah **kah**stikkay	brown sauce
sian|liha|kastike	**sia**hnlihah**kah**stikkay	gravy prepared wth sliced pork
tomaatti|kastike	**toa**maatti**kah**stikkay	tomato sauce
valko|kastike	**vahl**koa**kah**stikkay	white sauce
öljy|kastike	**url**yew**kah**stikkay	oil sauce

Herbs and spices *Yrttejä ja mausteita*

anis	**ah**nis	aniseed
basilika	**bah**silikah	basil
inkivääri	**inki**vǣri	ginger
kaneli	**kah**nayli	cinnamon
kumina	**koo**minah	caraway
laakerin lehti	**laah**kayrinlayhti	bay leaf
meirami	**may**'rahmi	marjoram
minttu	**minnt**too	mint
muskotti	**moos**koatti	nutmeg
oregano	**o**araygahnoa	oregano
paprika	**pap**rikah	paprika
persilja	**payr**silyah	parsley
pipar|juuri	**pi**pahry<u>oo</u>ri	horseradish
pippuri	**pip**poori	pepper
rakuuna	**rah**k<u>oo</u>nah	tarragon
ros|mariini	**ross**mahreeni	rosemary
ruoho|laukka	r^{oo}**oa**hoalah^{oo}kkah	chives
salvia	**sahl**viah	sage
sinappi	**si**nahppi	mustard
suola	s^{oo}**oa**lah	salt
tilli	**tilli**	dill
tinjami	**tin**yahmi	thyme
valko|sipuli	**vahl**koasipooli	garlic
yrtti|sekoitus	**ewrtti**saykoa'toos	mixed herbs

To follow ... *Jatko ...*

Cheese *Juustoa*

Most Finns eat cheese at breakfast, cut in thin slices, or with the main course, not as a dessert. However, the custom of eating cheese after a meal is spreading. The fine cheeses of Finland are comparable to French or Swiss cheese, which they often resemble. Try some:

Aura (**ah**^{oo}rah)	blue veined, strong cheese of the Roquefort type
Hovi (**hoa**vi)	mild, soft cheese, similar to petit-suisse
Emmental (**aym**mmayntahl)	Finnish emmental (*tahko|juusto*) reminiscent of the Swiss cheese, in mild and strong varieties

Ravintolat

Edam (aydahm)	the most common cheese in Finland, not unlike Dutch Edam
Juhla (yoohlah)	hard cheese with a strong flavour, along the lines of Cheddar
Kappeli (kahppayli)	soft, creamy cheese with a strong flavour
Kartano (kahrtahnoa)	cheese resembling Gouda, though milder
Kesti (kaysti)	strong carraway-flavoured cheese
Kreivi (kray'vi)	strong cheese of the Tilsit type
Luostari (l°°oastahri)	soft cheese with a delicate flavour, in the syle of Port-Salut
Turunmaa (tooroonmaa)	mild, creamy cheese

Fruit and nuts *Hedelmiä ja pähkinöitä*

| Do you have any fresh fruit? | **Onko teillä tuoreita hedelmiä?** | oankoa tay'llæ t°°oarayitah haydaylmiæ |
| I'd like a (fresh) fruit cocktail. | **Haluaisin (tuore|) hedelmä|cocktailin.** | hahlooah'sin (t°°oaray) haydaylmækoaktah'lin |

ananas	ahnahnahss	pineapple
appelsiini	ahppaylseeni	orange
aprikoosi	ahprikkōāssi	apricots
banaani	bahnaani	banana
greippi	gray'ppi	grapefruit
hassel-pähkinät	hahssaylpæhkinæt	hazelnuts
karviais|marjat	kahrviah'smahryaht	gooseberries
kastanjat	kahstahnyaht	chestnuts
kirsikat	keersikkaht	cherries
kookos|pähkinä	kōākoaspæhkinæ	coconut
kuivatut hedelmät	koo'vahttoot haydaylmæt	dried fruit
kuivatut luumut	koo'vahttoot lōōmoot	prunes
limetti	limaytti	lime
luumut	lōōmoot	plums
maa|pähkinät	maahpæhkinnæt	peanuts
mandariini	mahndahreeni	tangerine
mansikat	mahnsikkaht	strawberries

mantelit	**mahn**taylit	almonds
meloni	**may**loani	melon
musta viini|marjat	**moos**tah **veeni**mahryaht	blackcurrants
nektariini	**nayk**tahreeni	nectarine
omena	**oa**maynah	apple
persikka	**payr**sikkah	peach
päärynä	**pää**rewnæ	pear
raparperi	**rah**pahrpayri	rhubarb
rusinat	**roos**sinaht	raisins
saksan|pähkinät	**sahk**sahnpæhkinæt	walnuts
sitruuna	**sit**rōōnah	lemon
sulttaani-rusinat	**soolt**taaniroosinaht	sultanas
taatelit	**taa**taylit	dates
vadelmat	**vah**daylmaht	raspberries
vesi|meloni	**vays**simayloani	water melon
viikunat	**vee**koonaht	figs
viini|rypäleet	**vee**nirewpælāyt	grapes

Finns are keen on berries. A few species are found nowhere else; others are more common berries, widely appreciated.

lakka (**lahk**kah)	Arctic cloudberry; yellow berry growing on the marshes in northern Finland, regarded as the 'queen of berries' in Finland, used in desserts and for making *Lakka* liqueur
karpalo (**kahr**pahloa)	cranberry; also used for making *Polar* liqueur
mesi|marja (**may**ssimahryah)	Arctic bramble; *Mesimarja* liqueur is well known
mustikka (**moos**tikkah)	bilberry, or whortleberry; one of the commonest berries in Finland, used for a variety of desserts and pastries
puolukka (**p**°°**oa**lookkah)	lingonberry; used for many desserts and often served as jam or jelly with meat dishes

Desserts—Pastries *Jälki|ruokia—Leivonnaisia*

The most popular Finnish desserts are fruit soups (*kiisseli—keessayli*), pancakes, and ice-cream. Pies and pastries are usually eaten at coffee time, not as dessert. And as for puddings, Finns just don't care for them.

I'd like a dessert, please.	**Haluaisin jälkiruokaa.**	hahlooah¦sin yælkir°°oakaa
What do you recommend?	**Mitä suosittelette?**	mittæ s°°oassittaylayttay
Something light, please.	**Jotain kevyttä, kiitos.**	yoatah¦n kayvewttæ keetoass
Just a small portion.	**Vain pieni annos.**	vah¦n p¦ayni ahnnoass

jäätelö	**yæætaylur**	ice-cream
mansikka	**mahn**sikkah	strawberry
suklaa	**sook**laa	chocolate
vadelma	**vah**daylmah	raspberry
vanilja	**vah**nilyah	vanilla
kakku	**kahk**koo	cake
hedelmä|kakku	**hay**daylmæ**kahk**koo	fruit cake
sokeri|kakku	**soa**kayri**kahk**koo	sponge cake
suklaa|kakku	**sook**laa**kahk**koo	chocolate cake
täyte|kakku	**tæ**ᵉʷ**tay**kahk**koo	layer cake
kerma|vaahto	**kayr**mah**vaah**toa	whipped cream
kohokas	**koa**hoakahss	soufflé
leivos	**lay**¦voass	pastry
marengit	**mah**rayngit	meringues
ohukaiset	**oa**hookah¦sayt	small pancakes
omena|piirakka	**oa**maynah**pee**rahkah	apple pie
omena|torttu	**oa**maynah**tort**too	apple tart
suklaa|kastike	**sook**laa**kahs**tikkay	chocolate sauce
torttu	**tort**too	tart
vaahto	**vaah**toa	mousse
vanilja|kastike	**vah**nilyah**kahs**tikkay	custard
vanukas	**vah**nookahss	pudding
vohvelit	**voah**vaylit	waffles

kiisseli (**kees**sayli)	dish made of any fruit or berries and their juice, thickened with potato flour, usually served cold, often with sugar and/or cream and milk
köyhät ritarit (**kur**ᵉʷhæt **rit**tahrit)	'poor knights'; dough soaked in milk and then fried, served with jam, berries and whipped cream
luumu|keitto (l̄ōomookay̍ttoa)	prune soup; dessert soup made with prunes and thickened with potato flour, served cold or hot
mustikka|keitto (**moos**tikkah**kay̍**ttoa)	bilberry soup
mustikka|piirakka (**moos**tikkah**peer**ahkkah)	bilberry pie
mämmi (**mæm**mi)	an Easter speciality; made of rye-malt, rye meal, treacle, sugar and orange peel, served cold with sugar and cream
piimä|piirakka (**pee**mæ**peer**ahkkah)	a pie made with curdled milk, eggs, vanilla and raisins
puolukka|puuro (pᵖᵒoa**look**kah**poo**roa)	porridge made with semolina and lingonberries, served cold with milk
seka|hedelmä|keitto (**say**kah**hay**daylmæ **kay̍**ttoa)	dessert soup made with prunes and raisins, thickened and served hot or cold

Drinks *Juomia*

Beer *Olut*

Beer has been a part of Finnish culture in some form or another for over 1,000 years. Indeed, Finland's national epic covered the creation of the world in 200 verses but it took 400 verses to describe the invention of beer.

The niceties of Finland's beer classification system may be too complicated for the less enthusiastic drinker. Briefly, category 'A' (Export) beer, often more than five per cent alcohol, is only obtainable at a liquor store or in a licensed restaurant. Weaker beers called I and III are sold at supermarkets. Many foreign lagers, ales and stouts are available at both state liquor stores and supermarkets.

A-olut	ah-**oa**loot	export beer
keskiolut	kayskio**a**loot	medium-strong beer
portteri	**poart**tayri	porter
tumma olut	**toom**maa **oa**loot	dark beer
vehnäolut	**vayh**næo**a**loot	wheat beer

I'd like a beer.	**Haluaisin oluen.**	hah**loo**ah'sin **oa**looayn
a dark beer	**tumma olut**	**toom**mah **oa**loot
a light beer	**vaalea olut**	**vaa**layah **oa**loot
a bottle of beer	**pullo olutta**	**pool**loa oa**loot**tah
a draught beer	**tynnyri|olut**	**tewn**newrioa**loot**
half a litre of beer	**puoli litraa olutta**	p**°°**ali **li**traa oa**loot**tah
I'll have another.	**Saisinko toisen.**	sah'sinkoa **toa**'sayn

KIPPIS
(**kip**piss)
CHEERS

Wine *Viini*

Surprisingly, Finland has a wine industry. Most of the home-grown product is dessert wine. Some cheaper imported wines are bottled in Finland as well. You'll also find a good selection of French, Italian, German, Spanish and other known wines but these are very expensive and only available at the state-run *Alko* stores.

May I please have the wine list?	**Saisinko viini|listan?**	sah'sinkoa **vee**nilistahn

I would like a bottle of white/red wine.	**Voisinko saada pullon valko|viiniä/ puna|viiniä.**	voa'sinkoa saadah poolloan vahlkoaveeniæ/ poonahveeniæ
I'd like a glass of...	**Saisinko lasillisen...**	sah'sinkoa lahsillissayn
Waiter/waitress, bring me another..., please.	**Tarjoilija, toisitteko minulle toisen..., kiitos.**	tahryoa'liyah toa'sittekoa minnoollay toa'sayn... keettoass

red	**puna**	poonah
white	**valko**	vahlkoa
rosé	**rose**	roassay
sparkling	**kuohu**	k°°oahoo
dry	**kuiva**	koo'vah
sweet	**makea**	mahkayah

musta|herukka|viini	moostahhayrookkah veeni	blackcurrant wine
puna|herukka|viini	poonahhayrookkah veeni	redcurrant wine
omena|viini	oamaynahveeni	apple wine

Schnapps *Snapsi*

This strong colourless spirit, sometimes flavoured, is the traditional accompaniment to appetizers, especially herring. This traditional Scandinavian firewater comes in several varieties:

akvaviitti (**ahk**vahveeetti)	aquavit, flavoured with caraway seed; originally Danish, now also made in Finland
Kosken|korva (**koas**kaynkoarvah)	grain-based unflavoured spirit; fierce and fiery and inexpensive
Pöytä|viina (**pur**ᵉʷ**tæveenah**)	perhaps the most popular of the cheaper varieties; distilled from grain
vodka (**voad**kah)	competing with Russian and Polish vodka, the Finns make *Dry Vodka* and, in a special bottle, *Finlandia Vodka*

Liqueurs *Likööri*

Karpi
(kahrpi)
red liqueur made of different berries and fruit

Lakka
(lahkkah)
cloudberry liqueur, dark yellow, full-bodied

Mesi|marja
(mayssimahryah)
made of Arctic bramble, deep red, rather sweet

Polar
(poalahr)
cranberry liqueur, red, with slightly pungent flavour

Other alcoholic drinks *Muita alkoholi|juomia*

glögi
(glurgi)
a heated Christmas and winter drink of berry juice, red wine, almonds, raisins and spices

pontikka
(poantikkah)
illicitly distilled spirit, mountain dew

sahti
(sahhti)
a beer-like home brew with a bitter taste sold legally in certain parts of the province of Häme

I'd like a/an …	**Saisinko** …	**sah¦sinkoa**
aperitif	**aperitiivin**	ahpayritteevin
cognac	**konjakin**	koanyahkin
gin	**ginin**	ginnin
liqueur	**liköörin**	likkūrrin
rum	**rommin**	roammin
vermouth	**vermutin**	vayrmootin
vodka	**vodkan**	voadkahn
whisky	**viskin**	viskin
neat (straight)	**sekoittamattomana**	saykoa¦ttah- mahttoamahnah
on the rocks	**jäillä**	yæillæ
with a little water	**ja hieman vettä**	yah h¦aymahn vayttæ
Give me a gin and tonic, please.	**Saisinko gin|ton- icin, kiitos.**	sah¦sinkoa gintoanikin keetoass
Just a dash of soda, please.	**Vain tilkka soodaa, kiitos.**	vah¦n tilkkah sōadaa keetoass

Nonalcoholic drinks *Alkoholittomia juomia*

At mealtimes most Finns prefer to drink milk. Buttermilk (*piimä*—**pee**mæ) is also popular. Beer and mineral water are common too.

Finland is a nation of coffee-drinkers. At any time of day you're likely to see the pot boiling. Coffee (*kahvi*—**kahh**vi) is what is served when Finns invite friends home; coffee parties rather than dinner parties are the rule.

In many restaurants you can also get stronger *espresso* coffee, though it's not necessarily authentic. A glass of iced water is often served with coffee in restaurants.

Tea is also popular but not nearly so fanatically consumed as coffee.

apple juice	**omena|mehu**	oamaynahmayhoo
fruit juice	**hedelmä|mehu**	haydaylmæmayhoo
grapefruit juice	**greippi|mehu**	gray'ppimayhoo
herb tea	**yrtti|tee**	urtti**tay**
lemon juice	**sitruuna|mehu**	siroonahmayhoo
lemonade	**limonaadi**	limmoanaadi
milk	**maito**	mah'to
milkshake	**pirtelö**	peertaylur
mineral water	**mineraali|vesi**	minnayraalivaysi
fizzy (carbonated)	**hiili|happo**	heelihahpoa
still	**hiili|hapoton**	heelihahpoatoan
orange juice	**appelsiini|mehu**	ahppaylseenimayhoo
orangeade	**appelsiini|limonaa-di**	ahppaylseenili-mmoanaadi
tomato juice	**tomaatti|mehua**	toamaattimayhooah
tonic water	**tonic-vesi**	toanikvaysi

sima (**si**mmah)	a usually non-alcoholic home-made or commercially brewed sparkling drink made with brown sugar, lemon, honey (sometimes), hops and yeast; popular around May Day

Hot beverages *Kuumia juomia*

(hot) chocolate	**kaakao**	kaahkahoa
coffee	**kahvi**	kahhvi
black	**mustana**	**moos**tahnah
with cream	**kerman kanssa**	**kayr**mahn **kahns**sah
with milk	**maidon kanssa**	mah'doan **kahns**sah
caffeine-free	**kaffeiinitonta**	**kahff**fayeenitoantah
espresso coffee	**espresso-kahvi**	**ays**prayssoa-**kahh**vi
tea	**tee**	tāȳ
cup of tea	**kuppi teetä**	**koop**pi **tāy**tæ
with milk/lemon	**maidon/sitruu-**	mah'doan/**sit**rōōnahn
	nan kanssa	**kahns**sah
iced tea	**jää|teetä**	**yā͞tay**tæ

Complaints *Valituksia*

There's a plate/glass missing.	**Yksi lautanen/lasi uupuu.**	**ewk**si lah°°tahnayn **ōōpōō**
I don't have a knife/fork/spoon.	**Minulla ei ole veistä/haarukkaa/lusikkaa.**	minoollah ay' oalay vay'stæ/**haah**rookkaa/**loo**sikkaa
That's not what I ordered.	**Tämä ei ole sitä, mitä tilasin.**	**tæ**mæ ay' oalay **sit**tæ, **mit**tæ **til**lahsin
I asked for ...	**Pyysin ...**	**pēw**sin
There must be some mistake.	**On sattunut joku erehdys.**	oan **saht**toonoot **yoa**koo **ay**rayhdewss
May I change this?	**Voinko vaihtaa tämän?**	**voa'n**koa **vah'**taa **tæ**mæn
I asked for a small portion (for the child).	**Pyysin pientä (las-ten) annosta.**	**pēw**sin p'**ay**nayn (**lahs**tayn) **ahn**noastah
The meat is ...	**Liha on ...**	**lih**ah oan
overdone	**yli|kypsää**	**ew**likewpsǣ
underdone	**puoli|kypsää**	**p°°**oalikewpsǣ
too rare	**(liian) raakaa**	(**lee**ahn) **raa**kaa
too tough	**(liian) sitkeää**	(**lee**ahn) **sit**kayǣ

This is too...	Tämä on liian ...	tæmæ oan leeahn
bitter/salty/sweet	kitkerää/suolaista/makeaa	kitkayrǣ/s°°alah'stah/mahkayaa
I don't like this.	En pidä tästä.	ayn piddæ tæstæ
The food is cold.	Ruoka on kylmää.	r°°oakah oan kewlmǣ
This isn't fresh.	Tämä ei ole tuoretta.	tæmæ ay' oalay t°°aorayttah
What's taking you so long?	Miksi tämä kestää näin kauan?	miksi tæmæ kaystǣ næin kah°°ahn
Have you forgotten our drinks?	Oletteko unohtanut juomamme?	oalayttaykoa oonoahtahnoot y°°oamahmmay
The wine doesn't taste right.	Viinissä ei ole oikea maku.	veenissæ ay' oalay oa'kayah mahkoo
This isn't clean.	Tämä ei ole puhdas.	tæmæ ay' oalay poohdass
Would you ask the head waiter to come over?	Pyytäisittekö hovimestarin tänne.	pēwtæisittaykur haovimaystahrin tænnay

The bill (check) *Lasku*

I'd like to pay.	Haluaisin maksaa.	hahlooah'sin mahksaa
We'd like to pay separately.	Haluaisimme maksaa kukin erikseen.	hahlooah'mmay mahksaa kookin ayriksāyn
I think there's a mistake in this bill.	Tässä laskussa taitaa olla virhe.	tæssæ lahskoossah tah'taa oallah veerhay
What's this amount for?	Mihin tämä summa liittyy?	mihin tæmæ soommah leettēw
Is service included?	Sisältyykö tarjoilu|palkkio tähän?	sissæltēwkur tahryoa'loopahlkkioa tæhæn
Is everything included?	Sisältyykö siihen kaikki?	sissæltēwkur seehayn kah'kki
Do you accept traveller's cheques?	Otatteko matka|sekkejä?	oatattaykoa mahtkahshaykkayyæ
Can I pay with this credit card?	Voinko maksaa tällä luotto|kortilla?	voa'nkoa mahksaa tællæ l°°attoakoartilla

TIPPING, see inside back-cover

Please round it up to...	**Pyöristäkää se...-n.**	p^{ew}urristækæ say ...-n
Keep the change.	**Pitäkää vaihto|raha.**	pittækæ **vah**'htoarahhah
That was delicious.	**Se oli herkullista.**	say oali **hayrk**oollistah
We enjoyed it, thank you.	**Kiitos, pidimme siitä kovasti.**	**kee**toass piddimmay **seet**æ **koa**vahsti

---

TARJOILU(\|PALKKIO) SISÄLTYY HINTOIHIN
SERVICE INCLUDED

Snacks—Picnic *Väli\|palat—Piknik*

Open sandwiches are found in all bars, cafés and restaurants. Hot sandwiches are also a popular light snack.

Give me two of these and one of those.	**Saisinko kaksi tällaista ja yhden tuollaisen.**	**sah**'sinkoa **kahk**si **tæl**lah'stah yah **ewh**dayn t^{oo}**oal**lah'sayn
to the left/right	**vasemmalle/ oikealle**	**vah**saymmahllay/ **oak**ayahllay
above/below	**ylä|puolella/ ala|puolella**	**ewl**æp^{oo}oalayllah/ **ah**lahp^{oo}oalayllah
It's to take away.	**Se tulee mukaan.**	say too**lay** **moo**kaan
I'd like a/some...	**Saisinko...**	**sah**'sinkoa
chicken	**kanaa**	**kah**naa
half a roasted chicken	**puolikkaan grillattua kanaa**	p^{oo}**oal**ikkaan **gril**lahttooah **kah**naa
chips (french fries)	**ranskalaisia (perunoita)**	**rahns**kahlah'siah (**payr**oonoa'tah)
frankfurters	**nakkeja**	**nahk**kayyah
fried sausage	**paistetun makkaran**	**pah**'staytoon **mahk**kahrahn
omelet	**munakkaan**	**moon**ahkkaan

open sandwich	voi|leivän	voa'lay'væn
with ham	kinkku|voi|leivän	kinkkoo voa'lay'væn
with cheese	juusto|voi|leivän	yōōstoavoa'lay'væn
piece of cake	palan kakkua	pahlahn kahkkooah
potato salad	peruna|salaattia	payroonahsahlaattiah
sandwich	voi|leivän	voa'lay'væn
scrambled eggs	muna|kokkelia	moonahkoakkayliah
sweetcorn	maissia	mah'ssiah
toasted sandwich	lämpimän voi|lei-vän	læmpimæn voa'lay'væn

kappeli|voi|leipä (kahppaylivoa'-lay'pæ)	'chapel sandwich': fried French bread, bacon, topped with a fried egg
ooppera|voi|leipä (ōapayrahvoa'-lay'pæ)	'opera sandwich': fried French bread, hamburger patty, egg
muna-anjovis|leipä (moonah-ahnyoavis-lay'pæ)	dark bread, slices of hard-boiled egg, anchovy fillets, tomato
silli|voi|leipä (sillivoa'lay'pæ)	herring sandwich: dark bread, and herring, often egg and tomato

Here's a basic list of food and drink that might come in useful when shopping for a picnic.

I'd like a/an/some ...	**Saisinko**	sah'sinkoa
apples	**omenia**	oamayniah
bananas	**banaaneja**	bahnaanayyah
biscuits (Br.)	**keksejä**	kayksayyæ
beer	**olutta**	oaloottah
bread	**leipää**	lay'pǣ

butter	**voita**	**voa'**tah
cheese	**juustoa**	**yōo**stoah
chips (Am.)	**peruna|lastuja**	**pay**roonah**lahs**tooyah
chocolate bar	**suklaa|patukan**	**sook**laa**pah**tookahn
coffee	**kahvia**	**kahh**viah
cold cuts	**leikkeleitä**	**lay'**kkaylay'tæ
cookies	**keksejä**	**kayk**sayyæ
crackers	**voi|leipä|keksejä**	**voa'**lay'pæ**kayk**sayyæ
eggs	**munia**	**moo**niah
gherkins (pickles)	**suola|kurkkua**	**s°°oa**lah**koork**kooah
grapes	**viini|rypäleitä**	**vee**nirew**pæ**lay'tæ
ice-cream	**jäätelöä**	**yǣæ**tayluræ
milk	**maitoa**	**mah'**toah
mustard	**sinappia**	**sin**nahppiah
oranges	**appelsiineja**	**ahp**payl**see**nayyah
pepper	**pippuria**	**pip**pooriah
rolls	**sämpylöitä**	**sæm**pewlur'tæ
salt	**suolaa**	**s°°oa**laa
sausage	**makkaraa**	**mahk**kahraa
soft drink	**(alkoholittomia) juomia**	**(ahl**koahoalittoamiah) **y°°oa**miah
sugar	**sokeria**	**soa**kayriah
tea	**teetä**	**tāy**tæ
yoghurt	**jogurttia**	**yoa**koorttiah

Travelling around

Plane *Lento*

Is there a flight to Ivalo?	**Onko lentoa Iva-loon?**	oankoa **layn**toah ivvahlōan
Is it a direct flight?	**Onko se suora lento?**	oankoa say s°°oarah layntoa
When's the next flight to Jyväskylä?	**Milloin on seuraava lento Jyväskylään?**	milloa'n oan say°°raahvah layntoa yewvæskewlǣn
Is there a connection to Kajaani?	**Onko yhteyttä Kajaaniin?**	oankoa ewhhtayᵉ°ttæ kahyaahneen
I'd like to book a ticket to Oulu.	**Varaisin lipun Ouluun.**	vahrah'sin lippoon oa°°lōon
single (one-way)	**meno|lippu**	maynoalippoo
return (round trip)	**meno|paluu**	maynoapahlōō
business class	**business-luokka**	bisnis-l°°oakkah
aisle seat	**käytävä-paikka**	kæᵉ°tævæ-pah'kkah
window seat	**ikkuna-paikka**	ikkoonahpah'kkah
What time do we take off?	**Mihin aikaan kone lähtee?**	mihin ah'kaahn koanay læhtāy
What time should I check in?	**Mihin aikaan minun on ilmoit-tauduttava?**	mihin ah'kaahn oan ilmoa'ttah°°doottahvah
Is there a bus to the airport?	**Onko lentoase-malle bussia?**	oankoa layntoaahsaymahllah boossiah
What's the flight number?	**Mikä on lennon numero?**	mikkæ oan laynnoan noomayroa
What time do we arrive?	**Mihin aikaan olemme perillä?**	mihin ah'kaahn oalaymmay payrillæ
I'd like to... my reservation.	**Haluaisin... varaukseni.**	hahlooa'siin... vahrahooksayn
cancel	**peruuttaa**	payrōōttaa
change	**muuttaa**	mōōttaa
confirm	**vahvistaa**	vahhvistaa

| **SAAPUVAT** ARRIVAL | **LÄHTEVÄT** DEPARTURE |

Train *Juna*

Trains in Finland are operated by Finnish State Railways. Most long-distance trains are modern diesel trains. Electric trains make only certain short-distance runs from Helsinki.

Train travel is fast, comfortable and cheap. Long-distance trains usually have dining-cars and also sleeping-cars when necessary. First- and second-class seats may be reserved for a small extra charge; seat reservations are obligatory for special fast trains marked EP or IC. Children aged 6-17 travel half-price, under 6 free. The *Finnrail Pass* entitles to you to unlimited travel for periods of 8, 15 or 22 days.

kiito|juna (**kee**toayoonah)	long-distance express train between larger cities, stops only at main stations; luxury coaches; seat reservations required
pika|juna (**pikkah**yoonah)	long-distance train, stops at larger stations
paikallis|juna (**kah**ʲ**kahllis**yoonah)	local train, stops at all stations
kisko|bussi (**kiskoaboossi**)	small diesel train used on short runs
sähkö|juna (**sæhkur**yoonah)	electric train, used on short runs
makuu|vaunu (**mahkōōvah**°°noo)	sleeping car with individual compartments
lepo|vaunu (**laypoavah**°°noo)	berths with blankets and pillows
ravintola|vaunu (**rah**vintoalah**vah**°°noo)	dining-car
kahvila|vaunu (**kahh**villah**vah**°°noo)	buffet car
junailijan|vaunu (**yoo**nahʲliyahn**vah**°°noo)	guard's van or baggage car; only registered luggage permitted

To the railway station *Rauta\|tie\|asemalle*

Where's the railway station?	**Missä on rauta|tie|asema?**	missæ oan rahⁿⁿtahtiayah**say**mah
Taxi!	**Taksi!**	**tahk**si
Take me to the ...	**Viekää minut ...**	vʲay**kææ** minnoot
railway station	**rauta|tie|asemalle**	rah°°tahtiaah**say**mahllay

| What's the fare? | **Mitä maksaa?** | mittæ **mahk**saa |

SISÄÄN	ENTRANCE
ULOS	EXIT
LAITUREILLE	TO THE PLATFORMS
NEUVONTA	INFORMATION

Where's the...? *Missä on...?*

Where is/are (the)...?	**Missä on/ovat...?**	missæ oan/oavaht
bar	**baari**	baari
booking office	**lipun|myynti**	lippoon**mēwn**ti
currency exchange office	**valuutan|vaihto**	vahl$\overline{oo}$tahnvah'htoa
left-luggage office (baggage check)	**matka|tavara|säily-tys**	**maht**kahtahvahrah-sæilewtewss
lost property (lost and found) office	**löytö|tavara|toi-misto**	lur^{ew}turtahvahrahtoa'-mistoa
luggage lockers	**säilytys|lokerot**	sæ'lewtewsloakayroat
newsstand	**lehti|kioski**	layhtikioaski
platform 7	**laituri 7**	lah'toori say'tsaymæn
reservations office	**paikan|varaus**	pah'kahnvahrah^{oo}s
restaurant	**ravintola**	rahvintoalah
snack bar	**pika|baari**	pikkahbaari
ticket office	**lippu|toimisto**	lippootoa'mistoa
waiting room	**odotus|huone**	oadoatoosh^{oo}oanay
Where are the toilets?	**Missä ovat WC:t?**	missæ oavaht v$\overline{ay}$ss$\overline{ay}$t

Inquiries *Tiedusteluja*

When is the... train to Tampere?	**Milloin Tampe-reelle lähtee... juna?**	milloa'n tampayr$\overline{ay}$llay læht$\overline{ay}$... yoonah
first/last/next	**ensimmäinen/ viimeinen/seuraava**	aynsimmæ'nayn/ veemay'nayn/**say**^{oo}raavah
What time does the train to Turku leave?	**Mihin aikaan Tur-kuun lähtee juna?**	mihin ah'kaan toork$\overline{oo}$n læht$\overline{ay}$ yoonah
What's the fare to Savonlinna?	**Mitä maksaa lippu Savonlinnaan?**	mittæ mahksaa lippoo sahvoanlinnaan
Is it a through train?	**Onko se suora yhteys?**	oankoa say s^{oo}oarah ewhtay^{ew}ss
Is there a connection to...?	**Onko yhteyttä... -n/...-lle?**	oankoa ewhtay^{ew}ttæ...-n/ ...-llay

TAXI, see page 21

Do I have to change trains?	**Onko minun vaihdettava junaa?**	oankoa minnoon vah‖hdayttahvah yoonaa
Is there enough time to change?	**Onko junan|vaihtoon tarpeeksi aikaa?**	oankoa yoonahnvah‖htōan tahrpāyksi ah‖kaa
Is the train running on time?	**Onko juna aika|taulussa?**	oankoa yoonah ah‖kahtah°°loossah
What time does the train arrive in Mikkeli?	**Mihin aikaan juna saapuu Mikkeliin?**	mihin ah‖kaan yoonah saapōō mikkayleen
Is there a dining car/ sleeping car on the train?	**Onko junassa ravintola|vaunua/ makuu|vaunua?**	oankoa yoonassah rahvintoalahvah°°nooah/ mahkōōvah°°nooah
Does the train stop in Kouvola?	**Pysähtyykö juna Kouvolassa?**	pewsæht°ʷkur yoonah koa°°voalahssah
Which platform does the train to Lahti leave from?	**Miltä laiturilta juna Lahteen lähtee?**	miltæ lah‖tooriltan yoonah lahhtāyn læhtāy
Which platform does the train from Vaasa arrive at?	**Mille laiturille juna Vaasasta saapuu?**	millay lah‖toorillay yoonah vaassahstah saapōō
I'd like a time-table.	**Saisinko aika|taulun.**	sah‖sinkoa ah‖kahtah°°loon

---

Teidän täytyy vaihtaa...-ssa/... -lla.	You have to change at...
Vaihtakaa...-ssa/...-lla paikallis|junaan.	Change at... and get a local train.
Laituri 7 on...	Platform 7 is...
tuolla/ylhäällä	over there/upstairs
vasemmalla/oikealla	on the left/on the right
Juna... lähtee kello...	There's a train to... at...
Junanne lähtee laiturilta 8.	Your train will leave from platform 8.
Juna on... minuuttia myöhässä.	There will be a delay of... minutes.
Ensimmäinen luokka on edessä/ keskellä/takana.	First class at the front/in the middle/at the rear.

Tickets *Liput*

I'd like a ticket to Pori.	**Saisinko lipun Poriin.**	sah'sinkoa lippoon **poa**reen
single (one-way)	**meno|lippu**	**may**noalippoon
return (round trip)	**meno|paluu**	**may**noapah$\overline{oo}$
first/second class	**ensimmäinen/ toinen luokka**	**ayn**simmæ'nayn/**toa**nayn l$\overline{oo}$oakkah
for a child	**lasten lippu**	**lahs**tayn **lip**poo

Reservation *Varaus*

I'd like to reserve a...	**Haluaisin varata...**	hah**looah**'sin **vah**rahtah
seat (by the window)	**(ikkuna|)paikan**	(**ikk**oonah)pah'kahn
berth	**makuu|paikan**	mah**k$\overline{oo}$**pah'kahn
upper	**ylä|vuoteessa**	**ew**læv^{oo}oatæessah
middle	**keski|vuoteessa**	**kay**skiv^{oo}oatæyssah
lower	**ala|vuoteessa**	**ah**lahv^{oo}oatæyssah
berth in the sleeping car	**makuu|paikan makuu|vaunussa**	mah**k$\overline{oo}$**pah'kahn mah**k$\overline{oo}$**vah°noossah

All aboard *Kaikki vaunuihin*

Is this the right platform for the train to Pori?	**Onkohan tämä oikea laituri?**	**oan**koa tæmæ oa'kayah **lah**'toori
	Määrä|asema|ni on Pori.	**mæ**ræahsaymahni oan **poa**ri
Is this the right train to Tampere?	**Onko tämä Tampereen juna?**	**oan**koa tæmæ tahm**pay**rāyn **yoo**nah
Excuse me. Could I get past?	**Anteeksi. Pääsisinkö ohi?**	ahn**tāy**ksi pæ**sis**sinkur **oa**hi
Is this seat taken?	**Onko tämä paikka varattu?**	**oan**koa tæmæ **pah**'kkah **vah**rahttoo

TUPAKOITSIJOILLE SMOKER	**TUPAKOINTI KIELLETTY** NONSMOKER

I think that's my seat.	**Tämä taitaa olla minun paikka|ni.**	**tæ**mæ **tah**'taa **oal**lah **min**noon **pah**'kkahni
Would you let me know before we get to Lahti?	**Ilmoittaisitteko minulle kun tulemme Lahteen.**	**il**moa'ttah'sittaykoa **min**noollay koon **too**laymmay **lahh**tāyn
What station is this?	**Mikä asema tämä on?**	**mik**kæ **ah**saymah tæmæ oan

| How long does the train stop here? | Kuinka kauan juna seisoo täällä? | koo'nkah ka°°ahn yoonah say'soa tællæ |
| When do we arrive in Vaasa? | Milloin saavumme Vaasaan? | milloa'n saavoommay vaassaan |

Sleeping Nukkua

Are there any free compartments in the sleeping car?	Onko makuu|vaunussa vapaita paik-koja?	oankoa mahkoovah°°noossah vahpah'tah pah'kkoayah
Where's the sleeping car?	Missä on makuu|vaunu?	missæ oan mahkoovah°°noo
Where's my berth?	Missä on minun vuode|paikka|ni?	missæ oan minnoon v°°oadaypah'kkahni
I'd like a lower berth.	Voisinko saada ala|petin?	voa'sinkoa saadah ahlahpaytin
Would you make up our berths?	Laittaisitteko vuoteemme kuntoon?	lah'ttah'sittaykoa v°°oatāymmay koontōan
Would you wake me at 7 o'clock?	Herättäisittekö minut kello 7?	hayrættæ'sittaykur minnoot kaylloa say'tsaymæn

Eating Ruokailu

If you want a full meal in the dining-car (*ravintola\|vaunu*—**rah**vintoalah**vah**°°noo), you may have to get a ticket from the attendant who'll come to your compartment.

| Where's the dining-car? | Missä on ravintola\|vaunu? | missæ oan rahvintoalah vah°°noo |

Baggage—Porters Matkatavarat—Kantajat

Porter!	Kantaja!	kahntahyah
Can you help me with my luggage?	Voitteko auttaa kantamisessa?	voa'ttaykoa ah°°ttaa kahntahmisayssah
Where are the luggage trolleys (carts)?	Missä on työntö|kärryjä?	missæ oan tew"rnturkærrewyæ
Where are the luggage lockers?	Missä on säilytys|lokeroita?	missæ oan sæ'lewtewsloakayroa'tah
Where's the left-luggage office (baggage check)?	Missä on matka|tavaran säilytys?	missæ oan mahtkahtahvahrahn sæ'lewtews
I'd like to leave my luggage, please.	Jättäisin matka|tavara|ni säilöön.	yættæ'sin mahtkahtahvahrahni sæ'lūrn

I'd like to register (check) my luggage.	**Lähettäisin matka|tavara|ni.**	læhhayttæ'sin mahtkahtahvahrahni

> **LÄHTEVÄ MATKA\|TAVARA**
> REGISTERING (CHECKING) BAGGAGE

Underground (subway) *Metro*

Helsinki is the only city in Finland with an underground service. The network is fairly limited with the trains running from the city centre to some of the eastern suburbs of Helsinki. The underground service is called the Metro and the city centre metro station may be entered from the main railway station.

Where's the nearest underground station?	**Missä on lähin metro|asema?**	missæ oan læhin maytroaahsaymah
Does this train go to…?	**Meneekö tämä juna…-n/…-lle?**	maynāykur tæmæ yoonah…-n/…-llay
Is the next station…?	**Onko seuraava asema…?**	oankoa say°°raavah ahsaymah

Coach (long-distance bus) *Linja-auto*

Finland's extensve coach network is especially important in northern regions where there are no railways. Modern, comfortable coaches run frequent, fast services. The fares are higher than for trains. Information on routes and timetables are available during office hours from travel information desks at coach stations.

When's the next coach to…?	**Milloin lähtee seuraava bussi…-n/ …-lle?**	milloa'n læhtāy say°°raavah boossi…-n/ …-llay
Does this coach stop at…?	**Pysähtyykö tämä auto…-ssa/…-lla?**	pewsæhtēwkur tæmæ ah°°toa …ssah/…llah
How long does the journey (trip) take?	**Kuinka kauan matka kestää?**	koo'nkah kah°°ahn mahtkah kaystēæ

Note: Most of the phrases on the previous pages can be used or adapted for travelling on local transport.

PORTERS, see also page 18

Kulkuneuvot

Bus—Tram (streetcar) *Bussi—Raitiovaunu*

There are local bus services in all cities and towns, and trams run in the major cities.

In Helsinki local buses serve the city centre and the various suburbs, but the trams operate only in the central area. Both bus and tram tickets may be purchased from the driver, and passengers must stamp their ticket after purchase in a special machine provided in the bus or tram. A ticket inspector may levy an instant fine on a passenger who has not stamped a ticket for the journey. A single ticket or a multiple journey card may be obtained from the driver. A single ticket is valid for an hour and it can be used within this time limit for an unrestricted number of journeys. The tickets are valid for both buses and trams.

Buses should always be boarded at the front. However you may enter the trams through any door - front, back or middle - if you have a ticket ready, but use the front door if you need to buy a ticket.

Taking a round-trip on a tram in Helsinki is a good way to see the city.

I'd like a booklet of tickets for Helsinki.	**Saisinko kymmenen matkan lipun Helsinkiä varten.**	sah|sinkoa kewmmaynayn mahtkahn lippoon haylsinkiæ vahrtayn
Which tram (streetcar) goes to the town centre?	**Mikä raitiovaunu menee kaupungin keskustaan?**	mikkæ rah|tioavah°°noo maynāy kah°°poongin kayskoostaan
Where can I get a bus/a tram (streetcar) to the opera?	**Missä pääsen bussiin/raitiovaunuun, joka menee oopperan luo?**	missæ pāēsayn boosseen/ rah|tioavah°°nōōn, yoakah maynāy ōāppayrahn looah
Which bus do I take to Tapiola?	**Millä bussilla pääsen Tapiolaan?**	millæ boossillah pāēsayn tahp|oalaan
Where's the bus stop?	**Missä on bussi|pysäkki?**	missæ oan boossipewsækki
When is the... bus to Otaniemi?	**Milloin lähtee... bussi Otaniemeen?**	milloa|n læhtāy... boossi oatahn|aymāyn
first/last/next	**ensimmäinen/ viimeinen/seuraava**	aynsimmæ|nayn/ veemay|nayn/say°°raavah

How much is the fare to...?	**Mitä on maksu... -n/...-lle?**	mittæ oan **mahks**oo...-n/...-llay
Do I have to change buses?	**Täytyykö minun vaihtaa bussia?**	tæ^{ew}kur minnoon vah'htaa **boos**siah
How many bus stops are there to...?	**Montako pysäkkiä on...-n/...-lle?**	**mo**antahkoa pewsækkiæ oan...-n/...-llay
Will you tell me when to get off?	**Sanoisitteko, kun minun täytyy nousta pois?**	**sah**noa'sittaykoa koon minnoon tæ^{ew}t<del>ew</del> noa^{oo}stah **poais**
I want to get off at Finlandia Hall.	**Haluaisin pois Finlandia|talon kohdalla.**	hahl**ooah**'sin **poais** finlahndiah**tah**loan **koah**dahllah

---

PYSÄKKI   BUS STOP

Boat service Vesi\|liikenne

There are superb car-ferry services all year round between Germany, Sweden and Finland. These car-ferries are like floating luxury hotels and tax-free shopping centres combined, and in addition they have first class restaurants and night-clubs, swimming-pools and saunas. There are also day-cruises from Helsinki to Tallin, Estonia.

Inland, Finland is a country of thousands of lakes and during the summer both modern pleasure boats and old-fashioned steamers sail them.

When does the next boat for... leave?	**Milloin lähtee seuraava lautta...-n/...-lle?**	milloa'n læht<del>ay</del> say^{oo}raavah lah^{oo}ttah...-n/...-llay
Where's the embarkation point?	**Missä noustaan laivaan?**	mistæ noa^{oo}staan lah'vaan
How long does the crossing take?	**Kauanko ylitys kestää?**	kah^{oo}ahnkoa **ew**littews kayst<del>æ</del>
Which port(s) do we stop at?	**Mihin satamiin poikkeamme?**	mihin **sat**tahmeen poa'kkayahmmay
I'd like to take a cruise/tour of the harbour.	**Haluaisin risteilylle/satama|risteilylle.**	hahl**ooah**'sin ristay'lewllay/sahtahmahristay'lewllay
boat (small)/(large)	**vene/alus**	**vay**nay/**ah**loos

cabin	hytti	hewtti
single/double	yhden hengen/ kahden hengen	ewhhdayn/kahhdayn hayngayn
deck	kansi	kahnsi
ferry	lautta	lah°°ttah
hydrofoil	kanto|siipi|alus	kahntoaseepiahloos
life belt/boat	pelastus|liivit/ pelastus|vene	paylahstoosleevit/ paylahstoosvaynay
port	satama	sahtahmah
river cruise	joki|risteily	yoakiristay¹lew
ship	laiva	lah¹vah
steamer	höyry|laiva	hurᵉʷrewlah¹vah
reclining seat	lepo|tuoli	laypoat°°oali

Other means of transport *Muita kulku|välineitä*

The land area of Finland is large and the total population is small. You will find plenty of quiet country roads where cycling and walking is enjoyable. In addition, most cities and towns have special paths reserved for cyclists. During the winter long-distance skiing treks are organised.

There are no legal restrictions on hitchhiking, but like everywhere else in the world, it carries its own risks.

helicopter	helikopteri	haylikoaptayri
moped	mopo	moapoa
motorbike/scooter	moottori|pyörä/ skooteri	mōattoaripewᵘʳræ/ skōatayri

Or perhaps you prefer:

to hitchhike	mennä peukalokyy- dillä/liftata	maynnæ payᵒkahloakēwdillæ/ liftahtah
to walk	kävellä	kævayllæ

Bicycle hire *Pyörän vuokraus*

I'd like to hire a... bicycle.	Haluaisin vuok- rata...-pyörän	hahlooah¹sin vᵒᵒoakrahtah...-pewᵘʳræn
5-gear	vaihde|	vahʰday
mountain	maasto|	maastoa

Car *Auto*

Cars drive on the right in Finland. Outside built-up areas all vehicles must have dipped headlights switched on at all times, even in broad daylight. Main roads are good throughout the country, but many secondary roads are unsurfaced. The use of both front and rear seat belts is compulsory.

Where's the nearest (self-service) filling station?	Missä on lähin (itse|palvelu)|bensini|asema?	missæ oan læhin (itsaypahlvayloo) baynseeniahsaymah
Fill it up, please.	Tankki täyteen, kiitos.	tahnkki tæ°wtāȳn keetoass
Give me... litres of petrol (gasoline).	Saanko... litraa bensiiniä.	saankoa... litraa baynseeniæ
super (premium)/ regular/unleaded/ diesel	Korkea|oktaanista/ matala|oktaanista/ lyijytöntä/die-sel|öljyä	koarkayahoaktaahnistah/ mahtahlahoaktaahnistah/ lew^{i}yewturntæ/ d'aysaylurlyewæ
Please check the...	... Voisitteko tarkistaa sen.	voa'sittaykoa tahrkistaa sayn
anti-freeze	jäähdytys|neste	yǣhdewtewsnaystay
battery	akku	ahkkoo
brake fluid	jarru|neste	yarroonaystay
oil/coolant/ windscreen water	öljy/jäähdy-tys|neste/ tuuli|lasin|pesu| neste	urlyew/ yǣadewtewsnnaystay/ tōolilahsinpay soonaystay
Would you check the tyre pressures?	Tarkistaisitteko ilman|paineet?	tahrkistah'sittaykoa ilmahnpah'nāyt
1.6 front, 1.8 rear.	Yksi pilkku kuusi edessä, yksi pilkku kahdeksan takana.	ewksi pilkkoo kōosi aydayssæ ewksi pilkkoo kahhdayksahn tahkahnah
Please could you check the spare tyre too?	Tarkistaisitteko myös vara|renkaan?	tahrkistah'sittaykoa mew^urs vahrahraynkaahn
Can you mend this puncture (fix this flat)?	Voitteko korjata tämän renkaan?	voa'ttaykoa koaryahtah tæmæn raynkaahn
Would you change the... please?	Voisitteko vaihtaa ...	voa'sittaykoa vah'htaa
bulb	lampun	lamppoon
fan belt	tuulettimen hihnan	tōolayttimayn hihnahn
snow chains	lumi|ketjut	loomikaytyoot

CAR HIRE, see page 20

spark(ing) plugs	**sytytys|tulpat**	sewtewtewstoolpaht
tyre	**renkaan**	raynkaahn
wipers	**pyyhkijän sulat**	pēwhkiyæn soolaht
Would you clean the windscreen (windshield)?	**Puhdistaisitteko tuuli|lasin.**	poohdistah'sittaykoa tōōlilahsin

Asking the way—Street directions *Kysyä tietä—Kulku\|ohjeet*

Can you tell me the way to…?	**Voitteko neuvoa tien…-n/…-lle?**	voa'ttaykoa nay°°voah tiayn…-n/…-llay
In which direction is…?	**Missä suunnassa on…?**	missæ sōōnnahssah oan
How do I get to…?	**Miten pääsen…-n/…-lle?**	mitayn pǣsayn…-n/…-llay
Are we on the right road for…?	**Viekö tämä tie…-n/…-lle?**	v'aykur tæmæ t'ay…-n/…-llay
How far is the next village?	**Kuinka kaukana on seuraava kylä?**	koo'nkah kah°°kahnah oan say°°raahvah kewlæ
How far is it to… from here?	**Kuinka kaukana täältä on…?**	koo'nkah kah°°kahnah tæltæ oan
Is there a motorway (expressway)?	**Onko moot-tori|tietä?**	oankoa mōattoarit'aytæ
How long does it take by car/on foot?	**Kauanko kestää mennä autolla/jalan?**	ka°°ahnkoa kaystǣ maynnæ ah°°toallah/yahlahn
Can I drive to the centre of town?	**Voinko ajaa kaupungin keskus-taan?**	voh'nkoa ahyaa kah°°poongin kayskoostaan
Is traffic allowed in the town centre?	**Onko autolla ajo sallittu kaupungin keskustassa?**	oankoa ah°°toallah ahyoa sahllittooah kah°°poongin kayskoostahssah
Can you tell me where… is?	**Voitteko kertoa, missä… on?**	voa'ttaykoa kayrtoah missæ… oan
How can I find this place/address?	**Kuinka löydän tämän paikan/osoitteen?**	koo'nkah lur°°dæn tæmæn pah'kahn/oasoa'ttæyn
Where's this?	**Missä tämä on?**	missæ tæmæ oan
Can you show me on the map where I am?	**Voitteko näyttää kartalta, missä olen?**	voa'ttaykoa næ°°ttǣ kahrtahltah missæ oalayn
Where are the nearest public toilets?	**Missä on lähin yleinen käymälä?**	missæ oan læhin ewlay'nayn kæ°°mælæ

Olette väärällä tiellä.	You're on the wrong road.
Ajakaa suoraan eteenpäin.	Go straight ahead.
Se on tuolla vasemmalla/oikealla.	It's down there on the left/right.
Vasta|päätä (...-a/...-ta/...-tta)/ ...-n takana	opposite/behind...
...-n vieressä/...-n jälkeen	next to/after...
pohjoisessa/etelässä idässä/lännessä	north/south east/west
Ajakaa ensimmäiseen/toiseen tien|haaraan/risteykseen.	Go to the first/second crossroads (intersection).
Kääntykää liikenne|valoissa vasemmalle.	Turn left at the traffic lights.
Kääntykää seuraavassa kulmassa oikealle.	Turn right at the next corner.
Ajakaa...tietä/...-n katua.	Take the... road.
Se on yksi|suuntainen katu.	It's a one-way street.
Teidän täytyy palata...-n luo.	You have to go back to...
Seuratkaa Hämeen|linnan viittoja/merkkejä.	Follow signs for Hämeen|linna.

Parking *Pysäköinti*

Park in the direction of moving traffic, on the right side of the road. Obey the posted parking restrictions. You may be fined for parking less than three metres from a pedestrian crossing.

Where can I park?	Minne voin pysä-köidä?	minay voa'n pewsækur'dæ
Is there a car park nearby?	Onko lähellä pysä-köinti|aluetta?	oankoa læhayllæ pewsækur'ntiahloo^{ey}ttah
May I park here?	Voinko pysäköidä tähän?	voa'nkoa pewsækur'dæ tæhæn
How long can I park here?	Kuinka kauan voin pysäköidä tässä?	koo'nkah kah^{oo}vahn voa'n pewsækur'dæ tæssæ
What's the charge per hour?	Mitä maksu on tunnilta?	mittæ oan mahksoo toonniltah
Do you have some change for the parking meter?	Olisiko teillä koli-koita pysä-köinti|mittariin?	oalisikoa tay'llæ koalikkoa'tah pewsækur'ntimittahreen

Breakdown—Road assistance *Konerikko—Tie|palvelu*

The Automobile and Touring Club of Finland (*Auto-liitto*) operates a 24-hour service telephone number in Helsinki that will give you information on garages anywhere in the country which can come out to your vehicle in case of breakdown.

Where's the nearest garage?	**Missä on lähin korjaamo?**	missæ oan læhin koaryaamoa
My car has broken down.	**Autoni meni epä|kuntoon.**	aˤˤtoani mayni aypækoontōͣan
Where can I make a phone call?	**Mistä voin soittaa?**	mistæ voaⁱn soaⁱttaa
I've had a break-down at...	**Autoni meni epä|kuntoon...-n kohdalla.**	aˤˤtoani mayni aypækoontōͣan...-n koahdahllah
Can you send a mechanic?	**Voitteko lähettää korjaajan?**	voaⁱttaykoa læhayttǣ koaryaayahn
My car won't start.	**Autoni ei käyn-nisty.**	ahˤˤtoani ayⁱ kæⁿʷnnistew
The battery is dead.	**Akku on tyhjä.**	ahkkoo oan tewhyæ
I've run out of petrol (gasoline)/diesel.	**Minulta on bensa/dieselöljy lopussa.**	minnooltah oan baynsah/deessaylurlyew loapoossah
I have a flat tyre.	**Minulla on rengas tyhjä.**	minoollah oan rayngahs tewhyænæ
The engine is over-heating.	**Moottori yli|kuu-menee.**	mōͣattoari ewlikōͣomaynāy
There's something wrong with the...	**... ei toimi kun-nolla.**	ayⁱ toami koonnoallah
brakes	**jarrut**	yarroot
carburettor	**kaasutin**	kaasootin
exhaust pipe	**pako|putki**	pahkoapootki
radiator	**jäähdyttäjä**	yǣhdewttæyæ
wheel	**pyörä**	pewʷʳræ
Can you send a breakdown van (tow truck)?	**Voitteko lähettää hinaus|auton?**	voaⁱttaykoa læhayttǣ hinnahˤˤsahˤˤtoan
How long will you be?	**Kuinka pian voitte olla täällä?**	kooⁱnkah pⁱahn voaⁱttay oallah tǣllæ
Can you give me an estimate?	**Voitteko antaa arvion?**	voaⁱttaykoa ahntaa ahrvⁱoan

Accident—Police *Onnettomuus—Poliisi*

Please call the police.	**Kutsukaa poliisi.**	kootsookaa **poa**leessi
There's been an accident. It's about 2 km. from Tampere.	**On sattunut onnettomuus. Se on noin 2km Tampereelta.**	oan **saht**toonoot oannayttoamōōss say oan noain 2km tahmpayr**ay**ltah
Where's there a telephone?	**Missä on puhelin?**	missæ oan **poo**haylin
Call a doctor/an ambulance quickly.	**Kutsukaa nopeasti lääkäri/ambulanssi.**	kootsookaa **noa**payahsti l**æ**kæri/**ahm**boolahnssi
There are people injured.	**Ihmisiä on loukkaantunut.**	**ih**missiæ oan **loa°°**kkaantoonoot
Here's my driving licence.	**Tässä on ajokorttini.**	**tæ**ssæ oan ahyoa**koart**tini
What's your name and address?	**Mikä on nimenne ja osoitteenne?**	mikkæ oan **nim**maynnay yah oassoa**ttay**nnay
What's your insurance company?	**Mikä on vakuutusyhtiönne?**	mikæ oan vah**kōō**toos**ewht**urnnay

Road signs *Liikennemerkkejä*

AJA HITAASTI	Drive slowly
AJO SALLITTU OMALLA VASTUULLA	Drive at own risk
AJO SALLITTU TONTEILLE	Access to residents only
ALUERAJOITUS	Local speed limit
HEIKKO TIENREUNA	Soft shoulders
IRTOKIVIÄ	Loose stones
KAPEA SILTA	Narrow bridge
KELIRIKKO	Frost damage
KOKEILE JARRUJA	Test your brakes
KOULU	School
LINJA-AUTOKAISTA	Bus has priority
LIUKAS TIE	Slippery road
LOSSI	Ferry
NOPEUSRAJOITUS	Speed limit... km
NÄHTÄVYYS	Lookout point
PYSÄKÖINTIPAIKKA	Parking
PYÖRÄILIJÄ	Cycle path
RYHMITYSMERKKI	Get in lane
SUOSITELTU NOPEUSRAJOITUS	Recommended speed limit
TIE SAVETTU	Newly-surfaced road
TIETYÖ	Road works
TULLI	Customs
YKSITYISTIE	Private road

Sightseeing

Where's the tourist office?	**Missä on matka-|toimisto?**	missæ oan **mahtkah-**toa**i**mistoa
What are the main points of interest?	**Mitä nähtävyyksiä täällä on?**	mittæ næhtævewksiæ tællæ oan
We're here for...	**Olemme täällä ....**	oalaymmay tællæ
only a few hours	**vain muutaman tunnin**	vah**i**n **mōō**tahmahn toonnin
a day	**päivän**	pæ**i**væn
a week	**viikon**	veekoan
Can you recommend a sightseeing tour/an excursion?	**Voitteko suositella nähtävyys|kierrosta/retkeä?**	voa**i**ttaykoa s**ºº**assittayllah næhtævew̄sk**i**ayrroastah/raytkayæ
Where do we leave from?	**Mistä on lähtö?**	mistæ oan læhtur
Will the bus pick us up at the hotel?	**Hakeeko bussi meidät hotellilta?**	hahk**āy**koa boossi maydæt hoatayllilta
How much does the tour cost?	**Paljonko kierros maksaa?**	pahlyoankoa k**i**ayrroass mahksaa
What time does the tour start?	**Mihin aikaan kierros alkaa?**	mihin ah**i**kaan k**i**ayrroass ahlkaa
Is lunch included?	**Sisältyykö lounas hintaan?**	sissæltew̄kur loa**ºº**nahs hintaan
What time do we get back?	**Mihin aikaan olemme takaisin?**	mihin ah**i**kaan oalaymmay tahkah**i**sin
Do we have free time in...?	**Onko meillä varan aikaa...?**	oankoa may**i**llæ vahrahn ah**i**kaa
Is there an English-speaking guide?	**Onko siellä englantia puhuva opas?**	oankoa s**i**ayllæ aynglahntiah poohoovah oapahss
I'd like to hire a private guide for...	**Haluaisin palkata yksityisen oppaan...**	hahlooah**i**ssin pahlkahtah ewkssittew**i**sayn oappaann
half a day	**puoleksi päiväksi**	p**ºº**oalayksi pæ**i**væksi
a day	**päiväksi**	pæ**i**væksi
Where is/Where are the...?	**Missä on/Missä ovat...?**	missæ oan/missæ oavaht
abbey	**luostari**	l**ºº**oastahri
art gallery	**taide|galleria**	tah**i**daygahllayriah
botanical gardens	**kasvi|tieteellinen puutarha**	kahsvit**i**aytēȳllinnayn pōōtahrhah

building	rakennus	rahkaynnooss
business district	liike|keskus	leekaykayskooss
castle	linna	linnah
cathedral	tuomio|kirkko	t°°amioakeerkkoa
cemetery	hautaus|maa	hah°°tah°°smaa
city centre	(kaupungin) kes-kusta	(kah°°poongin) kayskkoostah
chapel	kappeli	kahppayli
church	kirkko	keerkkoa
concert hall	konsertti|sali/|talo	koansayrttisahli/tahloa
convent	nunna|luostari	noonnahlᴏ̄ᴏoastahri
court house	oikeus|talo	oaᵏkay°°stahloa
downtown area	keskusta	kayskoostah
embankment	ranta|penger	rahntahpayngayr
exhibition	näyttely	næᵉʷttaylew
factory	tehdas	tayhdahss
fair	messut/markkinat	mayssoot/mahrkkinnaht
flea market	kirppu|tori	keerppootoari
fortress	linnoitus	linnoaⁱtooss
fountain	(suihku)lähde	(soo'hkoo)læhday
gardens	puu|tarha	pᴏ̄ᴏtahrah
harbour	satama	sahtahmah
lake	järvi	yærvi
library	kirjasto	keeryahstoa
market	(kauppa|)tori	(kah°°ppah)toari
memorial	muisto|merkki	mooⁱstoamayrkki
monastery	munkki|luostari	moonkkil°°oastahri
monument	monumentti	moanoomayntti
museum	museo	moossayoa
old town	vanha kaupunki	vahnhah kah°°poonki
opera house	ooppera|talo	ᴏ̄āppayrah
palace	palatsi	pahlahtsi
park	puisto	pooⁱstoa
parliament building	edus|kunta|talo	aydooskoontahtahloa
planetarium	planetaario	plahnaytahrioa
presidential palace	presidentin|linna	prayssidayntinlinnah
ruins	rauniot	rah°°nⁱoat
shopping area	ostos|keskus	oastoaskayskooss
square	tori	toari
stadium	stadion	stahdⁱoan
statue	patsas	pahtsahs
stock exchange	pörssi	purssi
theatre	teatteri	tayahttayri
theme park	tiede|puisto/|kes-kus	tᵃaydaypooⁱstoa/kayskooss
tomb	hauta	hah°°tah
tower	torni	toarni

town hall	**kaupungin|talo/ raati|huone**	kah°°poongintahloa/ raattih°°oanay
university	**yli|opisto**	ewlioapistoa
zoo	**eläin|tarha**	aylæ'ntahrhah

Admission *Sisään\|pääsy*

Is... open on Sundays?	**Onko... avoinna sunnuntaisin?**	oankoa... ahvoa'nnah soonnoontah'sin
What are the opening hours?	**Mitkä ovat auki|olo|ajat?**	mitkæ oavaht ah°°kioaloaahyaht
When does it close?	**Milloin se sulje-taan?**	milloa'n say soolyaytaan
How much is the entrance fee?	**Mikä on pääsy|maksu?**	mikkæ oan pæ̈sewmahksoo
Is there any reduc-tion for (the)...?	**Onko heille alen-nuksia...?**	oankoa hay'llay ahlaynnooksiah
children	**lapsille**	lahpsillay
disabled	**vammaisille**	vahmmah'sillay
groups	**ryhmille**	rewhmillay
pensioners	**eläkeläisille**	aylækaylæ'ssillay
students	**opiskelijoille**	oapiskayliyoa'llay
Do you have a guide-book (in English)?	**Onko teillä opas|kirjaa (englan-niksi)?**	oankoa tay'llæ oapahskeeryaa
Can I buy a catalogue?	**Voinko ostaa luet-telon?**	voa'nkoa oastaa looayttayloan
Is it all right to take pictures?	**Saako valo|kuvata?**	saakoa vahloakoovahtah

| VAPAA PÄÄSY | ADMISSION FREE |
| VALOKUVAAMINEN KIELLETTY | NO PHOTOGRAPHS |

| Is there easy access for the disabled? | **Onko vammaisille omaa sisään\|käyn-tiä?** | oankoa vahmmah'ssillay oamaa sissæ̈nkæ'ᵛⁿtiæ |
| Are there facilities/ activities for children? | **Onko lapsille omia tiloja/omaa toimin-taa?** | oankoa lahpsillay oamiah tiloayah/oamaa toa'mintaa |

Who—What—When? *Kuka—Mikä—Milloin?*

| What's that building? | **Mikä tuo rakennus on?** | mikkæ t°°oa rahkaynnooss |
| Who was the...? | **Kuka oli...** | kookah oali |

architect	**arkkitehti**	**ahrk**kitayhti
artist	**taiteilija**	**tah**'tay'liyah
painter	**taide|maalari**	**tah**'daymaalahri
sculptor	**kuvan|veistäjä**	**koo**vahnvay'stæyæ
Who built it?	**Kenen rakentama se on?**	**kay**nayn **rah**kayntahmah say oan
Who painted that picture?	**Kenen maalaama tuo taulu on?**	**kay**nayn **maa**laamah t°°oa **tah**°°loo oan
When did he live?	**Milloin hän eli?**	**mill**oa'n hæn **ay**li
When was it built?	**Milloin se on rakennettu?**	**mill**oa'n say oan **rah**kaynnayttoo
Where's the house where ... lived?	**Missä on talo, jossa ... asui?**	**missæ** oan **tah**loa **yoa**ssah ... **ah**soo'
We're interested in ...	**Meitä kiinnostaa/ kiinnostavat ...**	**may**'tæ **keen**noastaa/ **keen**noastahvaht
antiques	**antiikki**	**ahn**teekki
archaeology	**arkeologia**	**ahr**kayoaloagiah
art	**taide**	**tah**'day
botany	**kasvi|tiede**	**kahs**vit'ayday
ceramics	**keramiikka**	**kay**rahmeekkah
coins	**(metalli|)rahat**	**(may**tahlli)rahhaht
fine arts	**taide-esineet**	**tah**'dayaysinnæyt
furniture	**huone|kalut**	**h**°°oanaykahloot
geology	**geologia**	**g**ⁿᵛoaloagiah
handicrafts	**käsi|työ(|tuotteet)**	**kæ**sitewᵘᶦt°°oattæyt)
history	**historia**	**hist**oariah
medicine	**lääke|tiede**	**læ**kayt'ayday
music	**musiikki**	**moo**seekki
natural history	**luonnon|historia**	**l**°°oannoan**hist**oariah
ornithology	**lintu|tiede**	**lintoo**t'ayday
painting	**maalaus(|taide)**	**maa**lah°°s(**tah**'day)
pottery	**saven|valanta**	**sah**vaynvahlahntah
religion	**uskonto**	**oos**koantoa
sculpture	**kuvan|veisto (|taide)**	**koo**vahnvay'stoa(**tah**'day)
zoology	**eläin|tiede**	**ay**læ'nt'ayday
Where's the ... department?	**Missä on ...osasto?**	**missæ** oan ... **oa**ssahstoa
It's ...	**Se on ...**	say oan
amazing	**hämmästyttävä**	**hæm**mæstewttævæ
awful	**kaamea**	**kaa**mayah
beautiful	**kaunis**	**kah**°°niss
gloomy	**synkkä**	**sewnk**kæ
impressive	**vaikuttava**	**vah**'koottavah
interesting	**mielen|kiintoinen**	**m**'aylaynkeentoa'nayn

magnificent	**komea**	**koa**mayah
pretty	**sievä**	s'**ayvæ**
strange	**outo**	**oa**°°**toa**
superb	**erinomainen**	**ay**rinoamah'**nayn**
terrifying	**pelottava**	**pay**loattahvah
tremendous	**valtava**	**vahl**tahvah
ugly	**ruma**	**roo**mah

Churches—Religious services *Jumalan|palvelus*

The vast majority of Finns are Protestants (Evangelical Luth-
eran). Churches are usually open for visiting. In Helsinki there
are also two Roman Catholic churches, a Greek Orthodox
cathedral, an Anglican church, American (Protestant) services
and a synagogue.

Is there a... near here?	**Onko täällä ...?**	**oan**koa **tæll**læ
Catholic church	**katolista kirkkoa**	**kah**toallistah **keerk**koaah
Protestant church	**protestanttista kirkkoa**	**proa**taystahnttistah **keerk**koaah
mosque	**moskeijaa**	**moas**kay'yaa
synagogue	**synagoogaa**	**sew**nahgōāgaa
What time is...?	**Mihin aikaan on...?**	**mi**hin ah'**kaan oan**
mass/the service	**messu/jumalan-|palvelus**	**may**ssoo/ **yoo**mahlahn**pahl**vayllooss
Where can I find a... who speaks English?	**Mistä löytyisi..., joka puhuu englantia?**	**mis**tæ lur°°tew'si... **yoa**kah poohōō **ayng**lahntian
priest/minister/rabbi	**katolinen pappi/ (protestanttinen) pappi/rabbi**	**kah**toallinayn **pahp**pi/ (**proa**taystahnttinayn) **pahp**pi/**rahb**bi
I'd like to visit the church.	**Haluaisin käydä kirkossa.**	**hah**looah'sin **kæew**dæ **keer**koassah
I'd like to go to confession.	**Haluaisin mennä ripittäytymään.**	**hah**looah'sin **mayn**næ **rip**pittæ°°tewmæn

In the countryside *Maaseudulla*

Is there a scenic route to...?	**Onko kaunista reittiä...?**	**oan**koa **kah**°°nistah **ray'**ttiæ
How far is it to...?	**Kuinka kaukana on...?**	**koo'**nkah **kah**°°kahnah **oan**

Can we walk there?	**Voiko sinne kävellä?**	**voa'koa sinn**ay kævayllæ
How high is that mountain?	**Kuinka korkea tuo vuori on?**	**koo'nn**kah **koark**ayah t°°oa v°°oari oan
What kind of... is that?	**Minkä lajin... tuo on?**	**mink**æ **lah**yin... t°°oa oan
animal	**eläin**	**ayl**æin
bird	**lintu**	**lin**too
flower	**kukka**	**kook**kah
tree	**puu**	p$\overline{oo}$

Landmarks *Maa|merkkejä*

bridge	**silta**	**silt**ah
cliff	**jyrkänne**	**yewr**kænnay
farm	**maa|talo**	**maa**tahloa
field	**pelto**	**payl**toa
fjord	**vuono**	**v°°**oanoa
footpath	**polku**	**poal**koo
forest	**metsä**	**mayt**sæ
garden	**puu|tarha**	$\overline{poo}$**tahr**hah
glacier	**jäätikkö**	**yæt**ikkur
hill	**mäki**	**mæk**i
house	**talo**	**tah**loa
island	**saari**	**saa**ri
lake	**järvi**	**yær**vi
meadow	**niitty**	**neet**tew
mountain	**vuori**	**v°°**oari
(mountain) pass	**sola**	**soa**lah
path	**polku**	**poal**koo
peak	**huippu**	**hoo'p**poo
pond	**lampi**	**lahm**pi
river	**joki**	**yoa**ki
road	**tie**	t'ay
sea	**meri**	**may**ri
spring	**lähde**	**læh**day
valley	**laakso**	**laak**soa
village	**kylä**	**kew**læ
vineyard	**viini|tarha**	**veen**itahrhah
wall	**muuri**	$\overline{moo}$ri
waterfall	**vesi|putous**	**vays**ipootoa^{uu}ss
wood	**metsä**	**mayt**sæ

ASKING THE WAY, see page 76

Relaxing

Cinema (movies)—Theatre *Elo|kuvat—Teatteri*

All films are shown in the original version with Finnish and Swedish subtitles. There are ususally two showings at 7 and 9 p.m. You can buy tickets in advance.

In theatres curtain time is normally 7.30 p.m. Advance booking is advisable.

The newspapers list the day's stage and screen schedules.

What's on at the cinema tonight?	**Mitä elo|kuvissa on tänä iltana?**	mittæ **ay**loa**koo**vissah oan **tæ**næ **il**tahnah
What's playing at the... Theatre?	**Mitä... -teatterissa esitetään?**	mittæ... **tay**ahttayrissah **ay**ssittayt**ǣ**n
What sort of play is it?	**Millainen näytelmä se on?**	millah'nayn nǣ**ew**taylmæ say oan
Who's it by?	**Kenen kirjoittama se on?**	kaynayn **keer**yoattahmah say oan
Can you recommend a good...?	**Mikä olisi hyvä...?**	mikkæ **o**alissi **hew**væ
film	**filmi**	**fil**mi
comedy	**komedia**	**koa**mayd'ah
musical	**musikaali**	**moo**ssikkaali
Where's that new film directed by... being shown?	**Missä esitetään sitä uutta filmiä, jonka on ohjannut...?**	missæ **ay**ssitayt**ǣ**n sittæ **oo**ttah filmiæ **yon**kah oan **oah**yahnnoot
Who's in it?	**Kuka siinä näyttelee?**	kookah **see**næ nǣ**ew**ttayl**ay**
Who's playing the lead?	**Kuka on pää|osassa?**	kookah oan **pǣo**assahssah
Who's the director?	**Kuka on ohjaaja?**	kookah oan **oah**yaayah
At which theatre is that new play by... being performed?	**Missä teatterissa esitetään sitä uutta näytelmää, jonka on kirjoittanut...?**	missæ **tay**ahttayrissah **ay**ssittayt**ǣ**n sittæ **oo**ttah nǣ**ew**taylm**ǣ yoan**kah oan **keer**yoattahnoot
What time does it begin?	**Mihin aikaan se alkaa?**	mihin ah'kaan say **ahl**kaa
Are there any seats for tonight?	**Onko täksi illaksi paikkoja?**	oankoa tæksi illahksi pah'**kkoa**yah
How much are the seats?	**Paljonko liput maksavat?**	pahl**yoan**koa **lip**poot **mahk**sahvaht

I'd like to reserve 2 seats for the show on Friday evening.	**Haluaisin varata 2 paikkaa perjantai-illan näytökseen.**	hahlooah'sin **vah**rahtaht **kah**ksi pah'kkaa payryahntai illahn næ°"turksāyn
Can I have a ticket for the matinée on Tuesday?	**Saisinko lipun tiistain varhais|näytäntöön.**	sah'sinkoa **li**ppoon **tees**tah'n vahrhah's**næ°"**tæntūrn
I'd like a seat in the stalls (orchestra).	**Haluaisin paikan etu|permannolta.**	hahlooah'sin pah'kahn aytoopayrmannoaltah
Not too far back.	**Ei liian takaa.**	ay' **lee**ahntahkaa
Somewhere in the middle.	**Jostain keskeltä.**	yoastah'n **kays**kayltæ
How much are the seats in the circle (mezzanine)?	**Paljonko maksavat parveke|paikat?**	pahlyoankoa **mahk**sahvaht pahrvaykaypah'kaht
May I have a programme, please?	**Saisinko ohjelman.**	sah'sinkoa **oah**yaylmahn
Where's the cloakroom?	**Missä on vaate|säilö?**	missæ oan **vaa**taysæ'liur

---

Valitettavasti näytös on loppuun|myyty.	I'm sorry, we're sold out.
Jäljellä on vain muutamia paikkoja parvekkeella.	There are only a few seats left in the circle (mezzanine).
Saanko nähdä lippunne?	May I see your ticket?
Tässä on paikkanne.	This is your seat.

Opera—Ballet—Concert *Ooppera—Baletti—Konsertti*

Finland is a country of music and architecture and both of these forms of art are combined in the new ultra modern opera house in the centre of Helsinki. Nearby there is also a large concert hall, Finlandia House, designed by Alvar Aalto, one of Finland's foremost architects.

Can you recommend a good...?	**Mikä olisi hyvä...?**	mikkæ **oa**lisi hewvæ
ballet	**baletti**	**bah**laytti
concert	**konsertti**	**koan**sayrtti

DAYS OF THE WEEK, see page 151

opera	**ooppera**	ōāppayrah
operetta	**operetti**	oapayraytti
Where's the opera house/the concert hall?	**Missä on ooppera|talo/konsertti|sali?**	missæ oan ōāppayrahtahloa/ koansayrttisahli
What's on at the opera tonight?	**Mitä oopperassa on tänä iltana?**	mittæ ōāppayrahssah oan tænæ iltahnah
Who's singing/ dancing?	**Kuka laulaa/tanssii?**	kookah lah°°laa/tahnssee
Which orchestra is playing?	**Mikä orkesteri soittaa?**	mikkæ oarkaystayri soa'ttaa
What are they playing?	**Mitä he esittävät?**	mittæ hay ayssittævæt
Who's the conductor/ soloist?	**Kuka on kapelli|mestari/ solisti?**	kookah oan kahpayllimaystahri

Nightclubs—Discos Yö\|kerho—Disko

In the larger towns there are nightclubs and discotheques. Some restaurants provide cabaret-type entertainment and most large restaurants have a dance-floor. Men are usually required to wear a jacket and tie.

During the summer open air dances are very popular. These are held on large, purpose-built covered platforms called *tanssilava* (**tahn**ssilavah), which are usually situated in a picturesque setting near a lake or in a forest clearing.

Can you recommend a good nightclub?	**Voitteko suositella hyvää yö|kerhoa?**	voa'ttaykoa s°°asittayllah hewvǣ ew°°kayrhoaah
Is there a floor show?	**Onko siellä ohjelmaa?**	oankoa s'ayllæ oahyaylmaa
What time does the show start?	**Mihin aikaan ohjelma alkaa?**	mihin ah'kaan oahyaylmah ahlkaa
Is evening dress required?	**Vaaditaanko ilta|puku?**	vaadittaankoa iltahpookoo
Where can we go dancing?	**Minne voimme mennä tanssimaan?**	minnay voa'mmay maynnæ tahnssimmaan
Is there a discotheque in town?	**Onko tässä kaupungissa diskoa?**	oankoa tæssæ kah°°poongissah diskoaah
Would you like to dance?	**Haluaisitteko tanssia?**	hahlooah'sittaykoa tahnssiah

Sports *Urheilu*

Is there a football (soccer) match anywhere this Saturday?	**Onko jossain jalka|pallo-ottelua tänä lauantaina?**	oankoa yoassah'n yalkahpahlloa-oattaylooah tænæ lah°°ahntah'nah
Which teams are playing?	**Mitkä joukkueet pelaavat?**	mitkæ yoa°°kkooāyt paylaavaht
Can you get me a ticket?	**Voitteko hankkia minulle lipun?**	voa'ttaykoa hahnkkiah minnoollay lippoon

basketball	**kori|pallo**	koaripahlloa
boxing	**nyrkkeily**	newrkkaylew
car racing	**kilpa-ajot**	kilpahahyoat
cycling	**pyöräily**	pew°°ræilew
cycle racing	**pyörä|kilpailut**	pew°°rækilpah'loot
football (soccer)	**jalka|pallo**	yahlkahpahlloa
ice hockey	**jää|hockey**	yæhoakkay'
(horse-back) riding	**ratsastus**	rahtsahstooss
mountaineering	**vuoristo|kiipeily**	v°°oaristoakeepay'lew
speed skating	**pika|luistelu**	pikkahloo'stayloo
ski jumping	**mäki|hyppy**	mækihewppew
skiing	**hiihto**	heehtoa
swimming	**uinti**	oo'nti
tennis	**tennis**	taynnis
trotting race	**ravi|kilpailut**	rahvikilpah'loot
volleyball	**lento|pallo**	layntoapahlloa

I'd like to see a boxing match.	**Haluaisin nähdä nyrkkeily|ottelun.**	hahlooah'sin næhdæ newrkkaylewoattayloon
What's the admission charge?	**Mitä on pääsy|maksu?**	mikkæ oan pāesewmahksoo
Where's the nearest golf course?	**Missä on lähin golf-rata?**	missæ oan læhin golf-rahtah
Where are the tennis courts?	**Missä on tennis-kenttiä?**	missæ oan taynniskaynttiæ
What's the charge per ...?	**Mitä on maksu ...?**	mikkæ oan mahksoo
day/round/hour	**päivältä/kierrok-selta/tunnilta**	pæ'væltæ/k'ayrroaksayltah/toonniltah
Can I hire (rent) rackets?	**Voinko vuokrata mailat?**	voa'nkoa v°°oakrahtah mah'laht
Where's the race course (track)?	**Missä on kilpa|rata?**	missæ oan kilpahrahtah

Is there any good fishing/hunting around here?	Onko täällä hyviä kalastus|/metsästys|paikkoja?	oankoa tællæ hewviæ kahlahstoos/maytsæstewspah'kkoayah
Do I need a permit?	Tarvitsenko luvan?	tahrvitsaynkoa loovahn
Where can I get one?	Mistä voin saada sellaisen?	mistæ voa'n saadah sayllah'sayn
Can one swim in the lake/river?	Voiko tuossa järvessä/joessa uida?	voa'koa t°°oassah yærvayssæ/yoa°ʸssah oo'dah
Is there a swimming pool here?	Onko täällä uimaallasta?	oankoa tællæ oo'mahahllahstah
Is it open-air or indoor?	Onko se ulko|allas vai sisä|allas?	oankoa say oolkoaahllahs vah' sissæahllahs
Is it heated?	Lämmitetäänkö sitä?	læmmittaytænkur sittæ
What's the temperature of the water?	Mikä on veden lämpö|tila?	mikkæ oan vayday̲n læmpurtillah
Is there a sandy beach?	Onko hiekka|rantaa?	oankoa h'aykkahrahntaa

On the beach *Rannalla*

Is it safe to swim here?	Onko täällä turvallista uida?	oankoa tællæ toorvahllista oo'dah
Is there a lifeguard?	Onko täällä hengen|pelastajaa?	oankoa tællæ hayngaynpaylahstahyaa
Is it safe for children?	Onko se turvallinen lapsille?	oankoa say toorvahllinayn lahpsillay
The sea is very calm.	Meri on hyvin tyyni.	mayri oan hewvin tē̲wni
There are some big waves.	Suuria aaltoja on jonkin verran.	sōō̲riah aaltoayah oan yoankin vayrrahn
Are there any dangerous currents?	Onko täällä vaarallisia virtoja?	oankoa tællæ vaarahllissiah virtoayah
I want to hire (rent) a/an/ some...	Olisiko... vuokrattavissa?	oalissikkoa... v°°oakrahttahvissa
bathing hut (cabana)	uima|koppia	oo'mahkoappiah
deck chair	kansi|tuolia/lepoa|tuolia	kahnsit°°oaliah/laypoat°°oaliah
motorboat	moottori|venettä	mōō̲ttoarivaynayttæ
rowing-boat	soutu|venettä	soa°°toovaynayttæ
sailing boat	purje|venettä	pooryayvaynayttæ
skin-diving equipment	sukellus|varusteita	sookaylloosvahroostay'tah
sunshade (umbrella)	aurinko|varjoa	ah°°rinkoavahryoaah

surfboard	laine|lautaa	lah'naylah°°taa
water-skis	vesi|suksia	vayssisooksiah
windsurfer	purje|lautaa	pooryaylah°°taa

| YKSITYINEN RANTA | PRIVATE BEACH |
| UIMINEN KIELLETTY | NO SWIMMING |

Winter sports *Talvi\|Urheilu*

Cross-country skiing is the number-one winter sport in Finland.
Every child learns to ski at the age of 3 or 4, and continues to
ski very often for the rest of his or her life. Slalom has also
become fashionable during the last few years, although Finnish
slopes are modest compared to the Alpine region, for instance.
The skiing season lasts from January to March in the southern
parts of the country, but in Lapland the best skiing period is in
April. Skating is also popular among younger people, and all
boys of school age play ice-hockey.

Is there a skating rink near here?	Onko täällä lähellä luistin|rataa?	oankoa tǣllæ læhayllæ loo'stinrahtaa
I'd like to ski.	Haluaisin hiihtää.	hahlooah'sin heehtǣ
downhill/cross-country skiing	laskettelu/ murto|maa|hiihto	lahskayttayloo/ moortoamaaheehtoa
Are there any ski runs for...?	Onko rinnettä ...?	oankoa rinnayttæ
beginners	aloittelijoille	ahloa'ttayliyoa'llay
average skiers	tavallisille hiihtäjille	tahvahllisillay heehtæyillay
good skiers	hyville hiihtäjille	hewvillay heehtæyillay
Can I take skiing lessons?	Voinko saada hiihto|tunteja?	voa'nkoa saadah heehtoatoontayyah
Are there any ski lifts?	Onko hiihto|his-sejä?	oankoa heehtoahissayyæ
Are there any floodlit ski runs?	Onko valaistuja hiihtomäkiä?	oankoa vahlah'stooyah heehtoamækiæ
I want to hire ...	Voinko vuok-rata ...?	voa'nkoa v°°oakrahtah
poles	sauvat	sah°°vaht
skates	luistimet	loo'stimmayt
ski boots	hiihto|kengät	heehtoakayngæt
skiing equipment	hiihto|varusteet	heehtoavahroostāȳt
skis	sukset	sooksayt

Making friends

Introductions *Esittely*

May I introduce...?	**Saanko esitellä...?**	saankoa ayssittayllæ
Esko, this is...	**Esko, tässä on...**	ayskoa tæssæ oan
My name is...	**Nimeni on...**	nimmayni oan
Pleased to meet you!	**Hauska tutustua.**	hah°°skah tootoostooah
What's your name?	**Mikä teidän nimenne on?/Mikä sinun nimesi on?**	mikkæ tay'dæn nimmaynnay oan/mikkæ sinnoon nimmayssi oan
How are you?	**Kuinka voitte?/Mitä kuuluu?**	koo'nkah voa'ttay/mittæ kooloo
Fine, thanks. And you?	**Kiitos, hyvin. Entä te?/Kiitos, hyvää. Entä sinulle?**	keetoass hewvin ayntæ tay/keetoass hewvææ ayntæ sinnoollay

Follow up *Jatko-osa*

How long have you been here?	**Kauanko olet(te) ollut täällä?**	kah°°ahnkoa oalayt(tay) oalloot tǣllæ
We've been here a week.	**Olemme olleet täällä viikon.**	oalaymmay oallāyt tǣllæ veekoan
Is this your first visit?	**Onko tämä teille/sinulle ensimmäinen käynti?**	oankoa tæmæ tay'llay/sinnoollay aynsimmæinayn kæ°ʷnti
No, we came here last year.	**Ei, tulimme tänne viime vuonna.**	ay' toolimmay tænnay veenay v°°oannah
Are you enjoying your stay?	**Viihdyt(te)kö täällä?**	veehdewt(tay)kur tǣllæ
Yes, I like it very much.	**Kyllä, minusta täällä on mukavaa.**	kewllæ minnoostah tǣllæ oan mookahvaa
I like the scenery a lot.	**Pidän maisemasta.**	piddæn mah'saymahstah
What do you think of the country/people?	**Mitä pidät(te) maasta/ihmisistä?**	mittæ piddæt(tay) maastah/ihmississtæ
Where do you come from?	**Mistä päin tulet (te)?**	mistæ pæ'n toolayttay
I'm from...	**Olen...-sta/...-lta**	oalayn...-stah/...-ltah

Finnish has two words for 'you': *te* and *sinä, te* being the polite form. Throughout this section we give the formal version of the phrase followed by the informal where appropriate. See GRAMMAR for more details.

What nationality are you?	**Mitä kansallisuutta olet(te)?**	mittæ **kahn**sallissōōttah **o**alayt(tay)
I'm...	**Olen...**	**o**alayn
American	**amerikkalainen**	ahmayrikkahlah'nayn
British	**britti**	**britti**
Canadian	**kanadalainen**	kahnahdahlah'nayn
English	**englantilainen**	aynglahntillah'nayn
Irish	**irlantilainen**	eerlahntillah'nayn
Where are you staying?	**Missä asut(te)?**	**mi**ssæ **a**hsoottay
Are you on your own?	**Olet(te)ko yksin?**	**o**alayt(tay)koa **ewk**sin
I'm with my...	**Minulla on mukana...**	**min**noollah **o**an **moo**kahnah
wife	**vaimo**	**vah'**moa
husband	**aviomies**	**ah**vioam'ays
family	**perhe**	**payr**hay
children	**lapset**	**lahp**sayt
parents	**vanhemmat**	**vahn**haymmaht
boyfriend/girlfriend	**poika|ystävä/ tyttö|ystävä**	**poa'**kahewstævæ/ **tewt**turewstævæ

father/mother	**isä/äiti**	**i**ssæ/**æ**iti
son/daughter	**poika/tytär**	**poa'**kah/**tew**tær
brother/sister	**veli/sisko**	**vay**li/**sis**koa
uncle/aunt	**setä/täti**	**say**ttæ/**tæ**tti
nephew (brother's son)/niece (brother's daughter)	**veljen|poika/ veljen|tytär**	**vay**lyaynpoa'kah/ **vay**lyayntewtær
nephew (sister's son)/niece (sister's daughter)	**sisaren|poika/ sisaren|tytär**	**sis**sahraynpoa'kah/ **sis**sahrayntewtær
cousin	**serkku**	**sayrk**koo

Are you married/ single?	**Olet(te)ko naimi- sissa/naimaton?**	**o**alayt(tay)koa **nah'**mississah/ **nah'**mahtoan
Do you have children?	**Onko teillä/sinulla lapsia?**	**oan**koa **tay'**llæ/sinnoollah **lahp**siah
What do you do?	**Mitä teet(te) täällä?**	mittæ **tāyt**(tay) **tæl**læ
I'm a student.	**Olen opiskelija.**	**o**alayn **o**apiskayliyah

COUNTRIES, see page 146

	Mitä opiskelet(te)?	mittæ oapiskaylayt(tay)
...e on a ...ess trip/on ...ay.	Olen täällä liike|matkalla/ lomalla.	oalayn tǣllæ leekaymahtkahllah/ loamahllah
Do you travel a lot?	Matkustat(te)ko paljon?	mahtkoostaht(tay)koa pahlyoan

The weather Sää

What a lovely day!	Ihana päivä!	ihhahnah pæˈvæ
What awful weather!	Kaamea ilma!	kaamayah ilmah
Isn't it cold/ hot today?	Eikö olekin kylmä/ kuuma tänään?	ayˈkur oalaykin kewlmæ/ kōomah tænǣn
Is it usually as warm as this?	Onko tavallisesti näin lämmintä?	oankoa tahvahllissaysti næˈn læmmintæ
Do you think it's going to... tomorrow?	Luulet(te)ko, että huomenna...?	lōolayt(tay)koa ayttæ hˣˣoamaynnah
be a nice day	on kaunis päivä	oan kahˣˣnis pæˈvæ
rain	sataa	sahtaa
snow	sataa lunta	sahtaa loontah
What's the weather forecast?	Mikä on sää|ennuste?	mikkæ oan sǣaynnoostay

cloud	pilvi	pilvi
fog	sumu	soomoo
frost	pakkanen	pahkkahnayn
hail	rae	rahay
ice	jää	yǣ
lightning	salama	sahlahmah
moon	kuu	kōo
rain	sade	sahday
sky	taivas	tahˈvahs
snow	lumi	loomi
star	tähti	tæhti
sun	aurinko	ahˣˣrinkoa
thunder	ukkonen	ookkoanayn
thunderstorm	ukkos|myrsky	ookkoasmewrskew
wind	tuuli	tˣˣli

DAYS OF THE WEEK, see page 151

Ystävät ja tuttavat

Invitations *Kutsuja*

Would you like to have dinner with us on...?	**Haluaisit(te)ko syödä päivällistä kanssamme...na?**	hahlooah'sit(tay)koa s^{ew}urdæ pæ^{i}vællistæ kahnssahmmay...nah
May I invite you to lunch?	**Tulisit(te)ko kanssani lounaalle?**	toolissit(tay)koa kahnssahni loa^{oo}naallay
Can you come round for a drink this evening?	**Tulisit(te)ko kanssani drinkille tänä iltana?**	toolissit(tay)koa kahnssahni drinkillay tænæ iltahnah
There's a party. Are you coming?	**On kutsut. Olet(te)ko tulossa?**	oan kootsoot oalayt(tay)koa tooloassah
That's very kind of you.	**Hyvin ystävällistä.**	hewvin ewstævællistæ
Great. I'd love to come.	**Hienoa. Tulen mielelläni.**	h^{i}aynoah toolayn m^{i}aylaylllæni
What time shall we come?	**Mihin aikaan voimme tulla?**	mihin ah^{i}kaan voa^{i}mmay toollah
May I bring a friend?	**Voinko tuoda erään ystäväni?**	voa^{i}nkoa t^{oo}adah ayrææn ewstævæni
I'm afraid we have to leave now.	**Nyt meidän täytyy lähteä.**	newt may^{i}dæn tæ^{ew}t$\overline{ew}$ læhtayæ
Next time you must come to visit us.	**Ensi kerralla teidän/sinun täytyy tulla käymään meillä.**	aynsi kayrrahllah tay^{i}dæn/ sinnoon tæ^{ew}t$\overline{ew}$ toollah kæ^{ew}m$\overline{ææ}$n may^{i}llæ
Thanks for the evening. It was great.	**Kiitos illasta. Oli oikein mukavaa.**	keetoass illahstah oali oa^{i}kay^{i}n mookahvaa

Dating *Treffit*

Do you mind if I smoke?	**Häiritseekö, jos poltan?**	hæ^{i}ritsayk^{ew} yoas poaltahn
Would you like a cigarette?	**Haluaisit(te)ko savukkeen?**	haahlooah'sit(tay)koa sahvookkäyn
Do you have a light, please?	**Saisinko tulta?**	sah^{i}sinkoa tooltah
Why are you laughing?	**Miksi naurat(te)?**	miksi nah^{oo}raht(tay)
Is my Finnish that bad?	**Onko suomen|kieleni niin kehnoa?**	oankoa s^{oo}oamaynk^{i}aylayni neen kayhnoah
Do you mind if I sit here?	**Häiritseekö, jos istun tähän?**	hæ^{i}ritsayk^{ew} yoas istoon tæhæn
Can I get you a drink?	**Saanko tarjota drinkin?**	saankoa tahryoatah drinkin

Are you waiting for someone?	Odotat(te)ko jotak-uta?	oadoataht(tay)koa yoatahkootah
Are you free this evening?	Olet(te)ko vapaa tänä iltana?	oalayttaykoa vahpaa tænæ iltahnah
Would you like to go out with me tonight?	Lähtisit(te)kö kans-sani ulos tänä iltana?	læhtissit(tay)kur kahnssahni ooloass tænæ iltahnah
Would you like to go dancing?	Lähtisit(te)kö tans-simaan?	læhtissit(tay)kur tahnssimmaan
I know a good discotheque.	Tiedän hyvän dis-kon.	t'aydæn hewvæn diskoan
Shall we go to the cinema (movies)?	Menisimmekö elo-kuviin?	maynissimmaykur ayloakooveen
Would you like to go for a drive?	Lähtisit(te)kö aje-lulle?	læhtissit(tay)kur ahyayloollay
Where shall we meet?	Missä tapaamme?	missæ tahpaammay
I'll pick you up at your hotel.	Haen teidät/sinut hotellilta.	hahayn tay'dæt/sinnoot hoataylliltah
I'll call for you at 8.	Tulen kello 8.	toolayn kaylloa kahdayksahltah
May I take you home?	Saanko saattaa teidät/sinut kotiin?	saankoa saattaa tay'dæt/sinnoot koateen
Can I see you again tomorrow?	Voimmeko tavata huomenna uudel-leen?	voa'mmaykoa tahvahtah h°°amaynnah ōōdayllāyn
I hope we'll meet again.	Toivon, että tapaamme uudel-leen.	toa'voan ayttæ tahpaammay ōōdayllāyn

... and you might answer:

I'd love to, thank you.	Kiitos, mielelläni.	keetoass m'aylayllæni
Thank you, but I'm busy.	Kiitos, mutta minulle ei sovi.	keetoass moottah minnoollay ay' soavi
No, I'm not inter-ested, thank you.	Ei kiitos. Ei kiin-nosta.	ay' keetoass ay' keennoastah
Leave me alone, please!	Jättäkää minut rauhaan!	yættækāē minnoot rah°°haan
Thank you, it's been a wonderful evening.	Kiitos, on ollut ihana ilta.	keetoass oan oalloot ihhahnah iltah
I've enjoyed myself.	Minulla on ollut hauskaa.	minnoollah oan oalloot hah°°skaa

Shopping Guide

This shopping guide is designed to help you find what you want with ease, accuracy and speed. It features:

1. A list of all major shops, stores and services (p.98).

2. Some general expressions required when shopping to allow you to be specific and selective (p.100).

3. Full details of the shops and services most likely to concern you. Here you'll find advice, alphabetical lists of items and conversion charts listed under the headings below.

LAUNDRY, see page 29/HAIRDRESSER'S, see page 30

Ostosopas

Shops, stores and services *Myymälät, tavara|talot ja palvelut*

Shops are usually open from 9 a.m. to 5 or 6 p.m. on weekdays, closing at 3 p.m. on Saturday and all day Sunday. Some large stores stay open until 8 p.m. one or two nights, usually Mondays and Fridays. During June, July and August, however, shopping hours are somewhat limited.

Where's the nearest...?	**Missä on lähin...?**	missæ oan læhin
antique shop	**antiikki|kauppa**	ahnteekkikah°°uppah
art gallery	**taide|galleria**	tah'daygahllayriah
baker's	**leipomo**	laypoamoa
bank	**pankki**	pahnkki
barber's	**parturi**	pahrtoori
beauty salon	**kauneus|hoitola**	kah°°nay°°shoa'toalah
bookshop	**kirja|kauppa**	keeryuaka°°uppah
butcher's	**liha|kauppa**	lihahka°°uppah
camera shop	**valo|kuvaus|liike**	vahloakoovah°°usleekay
chemist's	**apteekki**	ahptāykki
dairy	**maito|kauppa**	mah'toka°°uppah
delicatessen	**herkku|myymälä**	hayrkkoomewmælæ
dentist	**hammas|lääkäri**	hahmmahslǣkæri
department store	**tavara|talo**	tahvahrahtaloa
drugstore	**apteekki**	ahptāykki
dry cleaner's	**pesula**	payssoolah
electrical goods shop	**sähkö|liike**	sæhkurleekay
fishmonger's	**kala|kauppa**	kahlahka°°uppah
florist's	**kukka|kauppa**	kookkahka°°uppah
furrier's	**turkis|liike**	toorkisleekay
greengrocer's	**vihannes|myymälä**	vihahnnaysmewmælæ
grocer's	**seka|tavara|kauppa**	saykahtahvahrahka°°uppah
hairdresser's (ladies/ men)	**kampaaja/parturi**	kahmpaayah/pahrtoori
hardware store	**kodin|kone|myy- mälä**	koadinkoaneymēwmælæ
health food shop	**luon- tais|tuote|myy- mälä**	l°°oantah'st°°oataymēw mælæ
hospital	**sairaala**	sah'raahlah
ironmonger's	**rauta|kauppa**	rah°°tahkah°°ppah
jeweller's	**kulta|seppä**	kooltahsayppæ
launderette	**itse|palvelu|pesula**	itsaypahlvayloopayssoolah
laundry	**pesula**	payssoolah

library	kirjasto	keeryahstoa
market	tori	toari
newsagent's	lehti|myymälä	layhtimewmælæ
newsstand	lehti|kioski	layhtikioaski
optician	optikko	oaptikkoa
pastry shop	konditoria	koanditoariah
photographer	valo|kuvaamo	vahloakoovaamoa
police station	poliisi|asema	poaleesiahsaymah
post office	posti	poasti
second-hand shop	osto- ja myynti|liike	oasto- yah mewntileekey
shoemaker's (repairs)	suutari	sootahri
shoe shop	kenkä|kauppa	kaynkækah°°ppah
shopping centre	ostos|keskus	oastoaskayskooss
souvenir shop	matka|muisto|myymälä	mahtkamoo'stoamewmælæ
sporting goods shop	urheilu|väline|kauppa	oorhayloovælinaykah°°pah
stationer's	paperi|kauppa	pahpayrikah°°ppah
supermarket	valinta|myymälä	vahlintahmewmælæ
sweet shop	makeis|kauppa/ karkki|kauppa	mahkayskah°°ppah/ kahrkkikah°°ppah
tailor's	räätäli	rætæli
telegraph office	lennätin	laynnætin
tobacconist's	tupakka|kauppa	toopahkkahkah°°ppah
toy shop	lelu|kauppa	laylookah°°ppah
travel agency	matka|toimisto	mahtkahtoa'mistoa
vegetable store	vihannes|kauppa	vihahnnayskah°°ppah
veterinarian	eläin|lääkäri	elæ'nlækæri
watchmaker's	kello|seppä	kaylloasayppæ
wine merchant	alko	ahlkoa

SISÄÄN	ENTRANCE
ULOS	EXIT
HÄTÄ|ULOS|KÄYNTI	EMERGENCY EXIT

General expressions *Yleisiä ilmauksia*

Where? *Missä?*

Where's there a good...?	**Missä on hyvä ...?**	missæ oan **hew**væ
Where can I find a...?	**Mistä löytyy ...?**	mistæ lur^{ew}tēw
Where's the main shopping area?	**Missä on tärkein ostos|alue?**	missæ oan **tær**kay'n **o**astoasahlooay
Is it far from here?	**Onko se kaukana täältä?**	oankoa say kah^{oo}kahnah **tǣ**ltæ
How do I get there?	**Miten sinne pää-see?**	mittayn sinnay **pǣ**sāy

ALE/ALENNUS\|MYYNTI   SALE

Service *Palvelu*

Can you help me?	**Voitteko auttaa minua?**	voa'ttaykoa ah^{oo}ttaa minnooah
I'm just looking.	**Minä vain katselen.**	minnæ vah'n **kaht**saylayn
Do you sell...?	**Myyttekö ...-a?**	**mēw**ttaykur ...-a
I'd like to buy...	**Ostaisin ...-n/-a**	oastah'sin ...-n/-a
I'd like...	**Haluaisin ...-n/-a**	hahlooah'sin ...-n/-a
Can you show me some...?	**Voitteko näyttää minulle ...-n/-a?**	voa'ttaykoa næ^{ew}ttǣ minnoollay ...-n/-a
Do you have any...?	**Onko teillä ...-a?**	oankoa tay'llæ ...-a
Where's the... department?	**Missä on ... -osasto?**	missæ oan ...-oasahstoh
Where is the lift (elevator)?	**Missä on hissi?**	missæ oan **hissi**
Can you show me...?	**Voitteko näyttää minulle ...?**	voa'ttaykoa næ^{ew}ttǣ minnoollay
this/that	**tätä/tuota**	tætæ/t^{oo}oatah
the one in the window/in the display case	**sitä, joka on ikkunassa/ näytteillä olevaa**	sittæ **yoa**kah oan ikkoonahssah/ næ^{ew}ttay'llæ oalayvaa

Defining the article *Tavaran määrittely*

I'd like a... one.	Minulle saisi olla...	minnullay sah'si oallah
big	iso	issoa
cheap	halpa	hahlpah
dark	tumma	toommah
good	hyvä	hewvæ
heavy	painava	pah'nahvah
large	suurta kokoa	soortah koakoah
light (weight)	kevyt	kayvewt
light (colour)	vaalea	vaalayah
oval	soikea	soa'kayah
rectangular	suora|kulmainen	s⁰⁰oarahkoolmah'nayn
round	pyöreä	pᵉʷurrayæ
small	pieni	p'ayni
square	nelis|kulmainen	nayliskoolmah'nayn
sturdy	tanakka	tahnahkkah
I don't want anything too expensive.	En halua mitään liian kallista.	ayn hahlooah mittæn leeahn kahllistah

Preference *Mieltymykset*

Can you show me some others?	Voitteko näyttää jotain muita?	voa'ttaykkoa næᵉʷttæ yoatah'n moo'tah
Don't you have anything...?	Eikö teillä olisi jotain...?	aykur tay'llæ oalissi yoatah'n
cheaper/better	halvempaa/parempaa	hahlvaympaa/pahraympaa
larger/smaller	suurempaa/pienempää	sōoraympaa/p'aynympǣ

How much? *Paljonko?*

How much is this?	Paljonko tämä maksaa?	pahlyoankoa tæmæ mahksaa
How much are they?	Paljonko nämä maksavat?	pahlyonkoa næmæ mahksavaht
I don't understand.	En ymmärrä.	ayn ewmmærræ
Please write it down.	Voisitteko kirjoittaa.	voa'sittayko keeryoattaa
I don't want to spend more than... marks.	En halua maksaa enempää kuin... markkaa.	ayn hahlooah mahksaa aynaympǣ koo'n... mahrkkaa

COLOURS, see page 112

Decision *Päätös*

It's not quite what I want.	**Se ei ole aivan sitä, mitä haluan.**	say ayⁱ **o**alay ahⁱvahn **sit**tæ mittæ **hah**looahn
No, I don't like it.	**Ei, en pidä siitä.**	ayⁱ ayn piddæ **see**tæ
I'll take it.	**Otan sen.**	**oa**tahn sayn

Ordering *Tilaaminen*

Can you order it for me?	**Voitteko tilata sen minulle?**	voaⁱttaykoa **til**lahtah sayn **min**noollay
How long will it take?	**Kauanko se kestää?**	kah^{oo}ahnkoa say **kays**tǣ

Delivery *Toimitus*

I'll take it with me.	**Otan sen mukaan.**	**oa**tahn sayn **moo**kaan
Deliver it to the... Hotel.	**Hotelli.... Toimittakaa se sinne.**	hoataylli... **toa**ⁱmittahkaa say **sin**nay
Please send it to this address.	**Lähettäisittekö sen tähän osoitteeseen.**	læhayttæⁱsittaykur sayn **tæ**hæn **oa**ssoaⁱttǣsayn
Will I have any difficulty with the customs?	**Onko minulla vaikeuksia tullissa?**	**oan**koa **min**noollah vahⁱkay^{oo}ksiah **tool**lissah

Paying *Maksaminen*

How much is it?	**Paljonko se maksaa?**	**pahl**yoankoa say **mahk**saa
Can I pay by traveller's cheque?	**Voinko maksaa matka|shekillä?**	voaⁱnkoaⁱ **mahk**saa **mahtk**ahshaykillæ
Do you accept dollars/pounds?	**Hyväksyttekö dollareita/puntia?**	hewvæksewttaykur **doal**lahraytah/**poon**tiah
Do you accept credit cards?	**Hyväksyttekö luotto|kortteja?**	hewvæksewttaykur l^{oo}**oat**toakoarttayyah
Do I have to pay the VAT (sales tax)?	**Täytyykö minun maksaa liike|vaihto|vero?**	tæ^{ew}**tew**kur minnoon **mahk**saa **lee**kayvahⁱhtoavayroa
I think there's a mistake in the bill.	**Laskussa taitaa olla virhe.**	**lahs**koossah tahⁱtaa **oal**lah **veer**hay

Anything else? *Saako olla muuta?*

No, thanks, that's all.	Ei, kiitos. Siinä kaikki.	ay¹ **kee**toass **see**næ **kah**¹kki
Yes, I'd like...	Kyllä. Haluaisin...	**kewl**læ **hah**looah¹sin
Can you show me...?	Voitteko näyttää minulle...-n/-a?	**voa**¹ttaykoa **næ**ᵉʷtæ **min**noolle...-n/-a
May I have a bag, please?	Saisinko kassin, kiitos.	**sah**¹sinkoa **kahs**sin **kee**toass
Could you wrap it up for me, please?	Panisitteko sen pakettiin.	**pah**nissittaykoa sayn **pah**kaytteen
May I have a receipt?	Saisinko kuitin.	**sah**¹sinkoa **koo**¹tin

Dissatisfied? *Tyytymätön?*

Can you exchange this, please?	Voisitteko vaihtaa tämän.	**voa**¹sittaykoa **vah**¹htaa **tæ**mæn
I want to return this.	Palauttaisin tämän.	**pah**lah°°ttah¹sin **tæ**mæn
I'd like a refund. Here's the receipt.	Saisinko rahat takaisin. Tässä on kuitti.	**sah**¹sinkoa **rah**haht **tah**kah¹sin **tæ**ssæ oan**koo**¹tti

---

Voinko auttaa?	Can I help you?
Mitä saisi olla?	What would you like?
Mitä... saisi olla?	What... would you like?
väriä/muotoa/laatua	colour/shape/quality
Valitettavasti meillä ei ole sellaista.	I'm sorry, we don't have any.
Tällä hetkellä meillä ei ole sitä varastossa.	We're out of stock at the moment.
Tilaammeko teille sellaisen?	Shall we order it for you?
Otatteko sen mukaanne vai lähetämmekö sen?	Will you take it with you or shall we send it?
Entä muuta?/Saako olla muuta?	Anything else?
... markkaa, olkaa hyvä.	That's... marks, please.
Kassa on tuolla.	The cash desk is over there.

Bookshop—Stationer's Kirja|kauppa—Paperi|kauppa

In Finland bookshops and stationers' are usually combined, but separate stationers' also exist. Newspapers and magazines are sold at newsstands.

Where's the nearest...?	Missä on lähin...?	missæ oan læhin
bookshop	kirja|kauppa	keeryahkah°°ppah
stationer's	paperikauppa	pahpayrika°°ppah
newsstand	lehtikioski	layhtikioaski
Where can I buy an English-language newspaper?	Mistä voi ostaa englannin|kielisiä sanoma|lehtiä?	mistæ voai oastaa aynglahnnink'aylissiæ sahnoamahlayhtiæ
Where's the guide-book section?	Missä on opas|kirja|osasto?	missæ oan oapahskeeryahoassahstoa
Where do you keep the English books?	Missä teillä on englannin|kielisiä kirjoja?	missæ tay'llæ oan aynglahnnink'aylissiæ keeryoayah
Have you any of...'s books in English?	Onko teillä... kir-joja englanniksi?	oankoa tay'llæ keeryoayah aynglahnniksi
Do you have second-hand books?	Onko teillä antik-variaatti-osastoa?	oankoa tayllæ ahnteekvahriaatti-oasahstoa
I want to buy a/an/some...	Saisinko....	sah'sinkoa
address book	osoite|kirjan	oassoa'taykeeryahn
adhesive tape	teippi|rullan	tay'ppiroollahn
ball-point pen	kuula|kärki|kynän	koolahkærkikewnæn
book	kirjan	keeryan
calendar	kalenterin	kahlayntayrin
carbon paper	hiili|(jäljen-nös)|paperia	heeli(yælyaynnurs) pahpayriah
crayons	väri|kyniä	værikewniæ
dictionary	sana|kirjan	sahnahkeeryan
Finnish-English	suomi-englanti	s°°oami-aynglahnti
pocket	tasku|kokoa	tahskookoakoah
drawing paper	piirustus|paperia	peeroostoospahpayriah
drawing pins	piirustus|neuloja	peeroostoosnay°°loayah
envelopes	kirje|kuoria	keeryayk°°oariah
eraser	pyyhe|kumin	pewhaykoomin
exercise book	kirjoitus|vihon	keeryoa'toosvihhoan
felt-tip pen	huopa|kärki|kynän	h°°oapahkærkikewnæn
fountain pen	täyte|kynän	tæ ͤ ͫ ͫ taykewnæn
glue	liimaa	leemaa

grammar book	kieli|opin	k'aylioapin
guidebook	opas|kirjan	oapahskeeryahn
ink	mustetta	moostayttah
black/red/blue/	mustaa/ punaista/sinistä	moostaa /poonnah'stah/ sinnistæ
(adhesive) labels	(itse|liimautuvia) nimi|lappuja	(ittseleemah°°tooviah) nimmilahppooyah
magazine	aika|kaus|lehden	ah'kahkah°°slayhdayn
map	kartan	kahrtahn
street map	kaupungin kartan	ka°°poongin kahrtahn
road map of...	tie|kartan, jossa näkyy...	t'aykahrtahn yoassa nækew̄
mechanical pencil	lyijy|täyte|kynän	lew'yewtæ°ʷtaykewnæn
newspaper	sanomalehden	sahnoamahlayhdayn
American/English	amerikkalaisen/ englantilaisen	ahmayrikkahlah'sayn/ aynglantillah'sen
notebook	muisti|kirjan	moo'stikeeryahn
note paper	kirjoitus|paperia	keeryoa'toospahpayriah
paintbox	vesi|väri|rasian	vayssiværirahsiahn
paper	paperia	pahpayriah
paperback	tasku|kirjan	tahskookeeryan
paperclips	(paperi|)liittimiä	(pahpayri)leettimmiæ
paper napkins	paperi|lautas|lii- noja	pahpayrilah°°tahslee- noayah
paste	liimaa	leemaa
pen	kynän	kewnæn
pencil	lyijy|kynän	lew'yewkewnæn
pencil sharpener	kynän|teroittimen	kewnæntayroa'ttimmayn
playing cards	peli|kortit	paylikoartit
pocket calculator	tasku|laskimen	tahskoolahskimmayn
postcard	posti|kortin	poastikoartin
propelling pencil	(kierrettävän) lyijy|täyte|kynän	(k'ayrrayttævæn) lew'yewtæ°ʷtaykewnæn
refill (for a pen)	säiliön (kynään)	sæ'liurn (kewnǣn)
rubber	pyyhe|kumin	pew̄haykoomin
ruler	viivottimen	veevoattimmayn
staples	niittejä	neettayyæ
string	narua	nahrooah
thumbtacks	piirustus|nastoja	peeroostoosnahstoayah
travel guide	matka|oppaan	mahtkahoappaan
typewriter ribbon	kirjoitus|koneen väri|nauhan	keeryoa'tooskoanāȳn værinah°°hahn
typing paper	kone|kirjoi- tus|paperia	koanaykeeryoa'toospah- payriah
writing pad	lehtiön	layhtiurn

Camping and sports equipment *Leirintä ja urheilu|varusteita*

I'd like to hire a(n)/ some...	**Haluaisin vuok-rata ...-n/-a**	hahlooah'sin v°°oakrahtah...-n/-a
air bed (mattress)	**ilma|patjan**	ilmahpaht'yahn
butane gas	**nestekaasua (butaania)**	naystaykaassooah (bootaahniah)
campbed	**teltta|sängyn**	taylttahsæsngewn
(folding) chair	**(kokoon|pantavan) tuolin**	(koakōōanpahntahvahn) t°°oalin
charcoal	**grilli|hiiliä**	grilliheeliæ
compass	**kompassin**	koampahssin
cool box	**kylmä|kassin**	kewlmæskahssin
fire lighters	**sytykkeitä**	sewtewkkay'tæ
fishing tackle	**kalastus|välineitä**	kahlahstoosvælinnay'tæ
flashlight	**tasku|lampun**	tahskoolahmpoon
groundsheet	**teltta|patjan**	taylttahpaht'yahn
hammock	**riippu|maton**	reeppoomahtoan
ice pack	**jää|pussin**	yæpoossin
insect spray (killer)	**hyönteis|suihkeen**	h°wurntay'ssoo'hkayn
kerosene	**valo|petrolia**	vahloapaytroaliah
lamp	**lampun**	lahmpoon
lantern	**lyhdyn**	lewhdewn
mallet	**nuijan**	noo'yahn
matches	**tuli|tikkuja**	toolitikkooyah
(foam rubber) mattress	**(vaahto|muovi|) patjan**	(vaahtoam°°oavi)pahtyahn
mosquito net	**hyttys|verkkoa**	hewttewsvayrkkoah
paraffin	**valo|petrolia /(lamppu|öljyä)**	vahloapaytroaliah /(lahmppoourlyewæ)
picnic basket	**eväs|korin**	ayvæskoarin
pump	**pumpun**	poompoon
rope	**köyttä**	kur°wttæ
rucksack	**repun**	raypoon
skiing equipment	**hiihto|välineet**	heehtoavælinnāyt
skin-diving equipment	**sukellus|välineet**	sookaylloosvælinnāyt
sleeping bag	**makuu|pussin**	mahkōōpoossin
(folding) table	**(kokoon|taitetta-van) pöydän**	(koakōāntah'tayttahvahn) pur°wdæn
tent	**teltan**	tayltahn
tent pegs	**teltta|puikkoja**	taylttahpoo'kkoayah
tent pole	**teltta|seipään**	taylttahsay'ppæn
torch	**tasku|lampun**	tahskoolahmpoon
windsurfer	**purje|laudan**	pooryaylah°°dahn
water flask	**kenttä|pullon**	kaynttæpoolloan

CAMPING, see page 32

Chemist's (drugstore) *Apteekki*

Finnish chemists' don't stock the great range of goods you'll find in Britain or the U.S. They only sell medicines. Because of strict Finnish regulations, it's difficult to buy anything much stronger than aspirin without a prescription. This means that, although what you're looking for may be on the chemist's shelf, you may not be able to obtain it. For perfume, cosmetics etc., you must go to a *kemikaali|kauppa* (**kay**mikkaali-kah°°ppah).

A notice in the window of any chemist's shop lists the address of the nearest all-night chemist's.

This section has been divided into two parts:

1. Pharmaceutical—medicine, first-aid etc.
2. Toiletry—toilet articles, cosmetics

General *Yleistä*

Where's the nearest (all-night) chemist's?	**Missä on lähin (yö)apteekki?**	missæ oan læhin (^{ew}ur) ahptāykki
What time does the chemist's open/ close?	**Mihin aikaan apteekki aukeaa/ menee kiinni?**	mihin ah¦kaan ahptāykki ah°°kayaa/maynāy keenni

1—Pharmaceutical *Lääkkeitä*

I'd like something for...	**Saisinko jotain . . .**	sah¦sinkoa yoatah¦n
a cold/a cough	**vilustumiseen/ yskään**	viloostoomissāyn/ewskǣn
hay fever	**heinä|nuhaan**	hay¦nænoohaahn
insect bites	**hyönteisen pistok-siin**	h^{ew}urntay¦sayn pistoakseen
sunburn	**auringon poltta-maan ihoon**	ah°°ringoan poalttahmaan ihhōan
travel/altitude sickness	**matka-/lento-pahoin|vointiin**	mahtkah-/layntoa-pahhoa¦nvoa¦nteen
an upset stomach	**vatsa|vaivoihin**	vahtsahvah¦voa¦hin
Can you prepare this prescription for me?	**Saisinko lääkkeen tällä reseptillä.**	sah¦sinkoa lǣkkayn tællæ rayssayptillæ
Can I get it without a prescription?	**Saako sen ilman reseptiä?**	saakoa sayn ilmahn rayssayptiæ
Shall I wait?	**Odotanko?/Saako sen odotettaessa?**	oadoatahnkoa/saakoa sayn oadoattahayssah

DOCTOR, see page 137

Can I have a/an/ some...?	Saisinko...	sah'sinkoa
adhesive plaster	laastaria	laastahriah
analgesic	jotain kipua lievit- tävää	yottah'n kippooah l'ayvittævāē
antiseptic cream	antiseptistä voi- detta	ahntissayptistæ voa'dayttah
aspirin	aspiriinia	aahspireeniah
bandage	siteen	sittāyn
elastic bandage	kimmo|siteen/ ideaali|siteen	kimmoasittāyn/ iddayaallisittāyn
Band-Aids®	laastaria	laastahriah
condoms	kondomeja	koandoamayyah
contraceptives	ehkäisy|välineitä	ayhkæ'sewvælinnay'tæ
corn plasters	liika|varvas|laasta- ria	leekahvahrvahslaastahriah
cotton wool (absorbent cotton)	vanua	vahnooah
cough drops	yskän|lääkettä	ewskænlāēkayttæ
disinfectant	desifiointi|ainetta	dayssinfioa'ntiah'nayttah
ear drops	korva|tippoja	koarvahtippoayah
eye drops	silmä|tippoja	silmætippoayah
first-aid kit	ensi|apu|pakkauk- sen	aynsiahpoopahkkah°°ksayn
gauze	side|harsoa	siddayhahrsoaah
insect repellent/spray	hyttys|öljyä/hyön- teis|suihketta	hewttewsurlyewæ/ h°ʷurntay'ssoo'hkayttah
iodine	jodia	yoadiah
laxative	ulostus|lääkettä	ooloastooslāēkayttæ
mouthwash	suu|vettä	soovayttæ
nose drops	nenä|tippoja	naynætippoayah
sanitary towels (napkins)	terveys|siteitä	tayrvayewssittay'tæ
sleeping pills	uni|tabletteja	oonitahblayttayyah
suppositories	perä|puikkoja	payræpoo'kkoayah
... tablets	...-tabletteja	-tahblayttayyah
tampons	tampooneja	tahmpoanayyah
thermometer	lämpö|mittarin	læmpurmittahrin
throat lozenges	kurkku|tabletteja	koorkkootahblayttayyah
tranquillizers	rauhoittavaa lää- kettä	rah°ohoa'ttahvaa lāēkayttæ
vitamin pills	vitamiini|pillereitä	vittahmeenipillayray'tæ

MYRKKYÄ	POISON
VAIN ULKOISEEN KÄYTTÖÖN	FOR EXTERNAL USE ONLY

2—Toiletry *Kosmetiikka*

I'd like a/an/some ...	**Saisinko ...**	sah'sinkoa
after-shave lotion	**parta|vettä**	pahrtahvayttæ
astringent	**kasvo|vettä**	kahsvoavayttæ
bath salts	**kylpy|suolaa**	kewlpews°°oalaa
blusher (rouge)	**poski|punaa**	poaskipoonaa
bubble bath	**kylpy|vaahtoa**	kewlpewvaahtoah
cream	**voidetta**	voa'dayttah
cleansing cream	**puhdistus|voidetta**	poohdistoosvoa'dayttah
foundation cream	**alus|voidetta**	ahloosvoa'dayttah
moisturizing cream	**kosteus|voidetta**	koastay°°svoa'dayttah
night cream	**yö|voidetta**	°ᵚurvoa'dayttah
cuticle remover	**kynsi|nauha|vettä**	kewnsinah°°hahvayttæ
deodorant	**deodoranttia**	dayoadoarahnttiah
emery board	**hiekka|paperi|viilan**	h'aykkahpahpayriveelahn
eyebrow pencil	**kulma|kynän**	koolmahkewnæn
eyeliner	**silmän|rajaus|väriä/rajaus|kynän**	silmænrahyahoosværiæ/ rahyahooskewnæn
eye shadow	**luomi|väriä**	l°°oamiværiæ
face powder	**kasvo|puuteria**	kahsvoapootayriah
foot cream	**jalka|voidetta**	yahlkahvoa'dayttah
hand cream	**käsi|voidetta**	kæsivoa'dayttah
lipsalve	**huuli|rasvaa**	hoolirahsvaa
lipstick	**huuli|punaa**	hōōlipoonaa
make-up remover pads	**meikin|poisto|-vanua**	may'kin poa'stoa-vahnooah
nail brush	**kynsi|harjan**	kewnsihahryahn
nail clippers	**kynsi|leikkurin**	kewnsilay'kkoorin
nail file	**kynsi|viilan**	kewnsiveelahn
nail polish	**kynsi|lakkaa**	kewnsilahkkaa
nail polish remover	**kynsi|lakan|poisto|ainetta**	kewnsilahkahnpoa'stoaah'nayttah
nail scissors	**kynsi|sakset**	kewnsisahksayt
perfume	**haju|vettä**	hahyoovayttæ
powder	**puuteria**	pōōtayriah
powder puff	**puuteri|huisku**	pōōtayrihoo'skoo
razor	**parta|kone**	pahrtahkoanay
razor blades	**parta|koneen teriä**	pahrtahkoanayn tayriæ
rouge	**poski|punaa**	poaskipoonaa
safety pins	**haka|neuloja**	hahkahnay°°loayah
shaving brush	**parta|sudin**	pahrtahsoodin
shaving cream	**parta|vaahdoketta**	pahrtahvaahdoakayttah

soap	**saippuaa**	sa'ppooaa
sponge	**pesu|sienen**	payssoos'aynayn
sun-tan cream	**aurinko|voidetta**	ah°°rinkoavoa'dayttah
sun-tan oil	**aurinko|öljyä**	ah°°rinkoaurlyewæ
talcum powder	**talkkia**	talkkiah
tissues	**paperi|pyyhkeitä**	pahpayripewhkay'tæ
toilet paper	**vessa|paperia**	vayssahpahpayriah
toilet water	**eau de toilette**	ur day tooahlayt
toothbrush	**hammas|harjan**	hahmmahshahryahn
toothpaste	**hammas|tahnaa**	hahmmahstahhnaa
towel	**pyyhkeen**	pewhkāyn
tweezers	**pinsetit**	pinsaytit

For your hair *Hiuksia varten*

bobby pins	**hius|neuloja**	hi°°snay°°loayah
colour shampoo	**väri|shampoota**	værishahmpōatah
comb	**kamman**	kahmmahn
curlers	**papiljotteja**	pahpillyoattayyah
dry shampoo	**kuiva|shampoota**	koo'vahshahmpōatah
dye	**hius|väriä**	hi°°sværiæ
hairbrush	**hius|harjan**	hi°°shahryahn/
hair gel	**hius|geeliä**	hi°°sghāylliæ
hairgrips	**hius|solkia**	hi°°ssoalkiah
hair lotion	**hius|vettä**	hi°°svayttæ
hairpins	**(hius|)pinnejä**	(hi°°s)pinnayyæ
hair slide	**hius|soljen**	hi°°ssoalyayn
hair spray	**hius|lakkaa**	hi°°slahkkaa
setting lotion	**kampaus|nestettä**	kahmpah°°snaystayttæ
shampoo	**shampoota/hius-ten|pesu|ainetta**	shahmpoatah/ hi°°staynpaysooah'- nayttah
for dry/greasy (oily) hair	**kuiville/rasvai-sille hiuksille**	koo'villay/rahsvah'sillay hi°°ksillay
tint	**hius|väriä**	hi°°sværiæ
wig	**peruukin**	payrōōkin

For the baby *Vauvalle*

baby food	**vauvan|ruokaa**	vah°°vahnr°°ahkaa
dummy (pacifier)	**(huvi|)tutin**	(hoovi)tootin
feeding bottle	**tutti|pullon**	toottipoolloan
nappies (diapers)	**vaippoja**	vah'ppoayah

Clothing *Vaatetus*

If you want to buy something specific, prepare yourself in advance. Look at the list of clothing on page 115. Get some idea of the colour, material and size you want. They're all listed on the next few pages.

General *Yleistä*

Do you have...	**Löytyisikö teiltä...?**	lur°wtew'sikur tay'ltæ
Do you have... for a 10-year-old boy/girl?	**Löytyisikö teiltä... 10-vuotiaalle pojalle/tytölle?**	lur°wtew'sikur tay'ltæ... kewmmaynv°°oatiaallay poayallay/tewturllay
I'd like something like this.	**Haluaisin jotain tällaista.**	hahlooah'sin yotah'n tællah'stah
I like the one in the window.	**Haluaisin sen joka on ikkunassa.**	hahlooah'sin sayn joakah oan ikkoonassah
How much is that per metre?	**Mitä tuo maksaa metriltä?**	mitæ t°°oa mahksaa maytriltæ

1 centimetre (cm)	= 0.39 in.	1 inch	= 2.54 cm
1 metre (m)	= 39.37 in.	1 foot	= 30.5 cm
10 metres	= 32.81 ft.	1 yard	= 0.91 m.

Colour *Väri*

I'd like something in...	**Haluaisin jotain...**	hahlooah'sin yotah'n
I'd like a darker/lighter shade.	**Haluaisin tummem-paa/vaaleampaa sävyä.**	hahlooah'sin toommaympaa/vaalayahmpaa sævewæ
I'd like something to match this.	**Haluaisin jotain tämän kanssa yhteen|sopivaa.**	hahlooah'sin yotah'n tæmæn kahnssah ewhhtāynsoapivaa
I don't like the colour.	**En pidä väristä.**	ayn pidæ væristæ

beige	**beigeä**	**bay**shiæ
black	**mustaa**	**moos**taa
blue	**sinistä**	**sin**nistæ
brown	**ruskeata**	**roos**kayahtah
fawn	**vaalean|ruskeaa**	**vaa**layahan**roos**kayah
golden	**kullan|väristä**	**kool**lahnværistæ
green	**vihreää**	**vih**rayǣ
grey	**harmaata**	**hahr**maahtah
mauve	**malvan|väristä**	**mahl**vahnværistæ
	(**hailakan|punaista**)	(hah'lahkahn**poo**nah'stah)
orange	**oranssia**	**oa**rahnssiah
pink	**vaalean|punaista**	**vaa**layahn**poo**nah'stah
purple	**sini|punaista**	**sini**poonah'stah
red	**punaista**	**poo**nah'stah
scarlet	**helakan|punaista**	**hay**lahkahn**poo**nah'stah
silver	**hopean|väristä**	**hoa**payahnværistæ
turquoise	**turkoosia**	**toor**koassiah (**sini**vih-
	(**sini|vihreää**)	rayæ)
white	**valkoista**	**vahl**koa'stah
yellow	**keltaista**	**kayl**tah'stah
light...	**vaalean|...**	**vaa**layahn
dark...	**tumman|...**	**toom**mahn

| yksiväristä | ruudullista | kuvioitua | raidallista | (iso\|)pilkullista |
| (ewksiværistæ) | (r°°doollistah) | (koovioa'tooa) | (rah'dahllistah) | ((iisoa) pilkoollistah) |

Fabric *Kangas*

Do you have any-thing in...?	**Onko teillä mitään...?**	**oan**koa **tay'**llæ mittæn
Is that...?	**Onko tämä...?**	**oan**koa tæmæ
handmade	**käsin|tehtyä**	**kæ**sintayhtewæ
imported	**maahan|tuotua**	**maa**hahnt°°oatooah
made here	**kotimaista**	**kot**timah'stah
I'd like something thinner.	**Haluaisin jotain ohuempaa.**	hahl**ooah'**sin yotah'n **oa**hooaympaa
Do you have anything of better quality?	**Onko teillä mitään parempi|laatuista?**	**oan**koa **tay'**llæ mittæn pah**ray**mpilaatoo'stah
What's it made of?	**Mistä se on tehty?**	mistæ say oan **tayh**tew
It's made of...	**Se on...**	say oan

cambric	hienoa palttinaa	h'aynoah pahlttinaa
camel-hair	kamelin|karvaa	kahmaylinkahrvaa
chiffon	shifonkia	shiffoankiah
corduroy	vako|samettia	vahkoasahmayttiah
cotton	puu|villaa	poovillaa
crepe	kreppiä	krayppiæ
denim	farkku|kangasta	fahrkkookahngahstah
felt	huopaa	h°°oapaa
flannel	flanellia	flahnaylliah
gabardine	gabardiinia	gahbahrdeeniah
lace	pitsiä	pitsiæ
leather	nahkaa	nahhkaa
linen	pellavaa	payllahvaa
poplin	popliinia	poapleeniah
satin	satiinia	sahteeniah
silk	silkkiä	silkkiæ
suede	mokkaa	moakkaa
towelling	pyyhe|kangasta	pewhaykahngahstah
velvet	samettia	sahmayttiah
velveteen	puu|villa|samettia	poovillahsahmayttiah
wool	villaa	villaa
worsted	kampa|lankaa	kahmpahlahnkaa

Is it…?	Onko se…?	oankoa say
pure cotton/wool	täyttä (puhdasta) puuvillaa/villaa	tæewttæ (poohhdahstah) poovillaa/villaa
synthetic	teko|kuitua	taykoakoo'tooah
colourfast	väriä|päästämätön	væriæpæstæmæturn
crease (wrinkle) resistant	rypistymätöntä	rewpistewmæturntæ
Is it hand washable/ machine washable?	Onko se käsin|pestävä/kone|pestävä?	oanko say kæsinpaystævæ/ koanaypaystævæ
Will it shrink?	Kutistuuko se?	kootistookoa say

Size *Koko*

I take size 38.	Otan kokoa 38.	oatahn koakoah 38
Could you measure me?	Voisitteko tarkistaa kokoni?	voa'sittaykoa tahrkistaa koakoani
I don't know the Finnish sizes.	En tunne suomalai- sia kokoja.	ayn toonnay s°°oamahlah'ssiah koakoayah

Women

Sizes can vary somewhat from one manufacturer to another, so be sure to try on shoes and clothing before you buy.

Dresses/Suits						
American	8	10	12	14	16	18
British	10	12	14	16	18	20
Continental	36	38	40	42	44	46

Stockings						Shoes			
American British	8½	9	9½	10	10½	6	7	8	9
						4½	5½	6½	7½
Continental	0	1	2	3	4 5	37	38	40	41

Men

Suits/overcoats							Shirts			
American British	36	38	40	42	44	46	15	16	17	18
Continental	46	48	50	52	54	56	38	40	42	44

Shoes										
American British	5	6	7	8	8½	9	9½	10	11	
Continental	38	39	40	41	42	43	44	44	45	

A good fit? *Sopiva?*

Can I try it on?	**Voinko sovittaa sitä?**	voa'nkoa soavittaa sittæ
Where's the fitting room?	**Missä on sovitus|koppi?**	missæ oan soavittooskoappi
Is there a mirror?	**Onko siellä peiliä?**	oankoa s'ayllæ pay'liæ
It fits very well.	**Se istuu oikein hyvin.**	say istoo oa'kayin hewvin
It doesn't fit.	**Se ei istu.**	say ay istoo
It's too...	**Se on liian...**	say oan leeahn
short/long	**lyhyt/pitkä**	lewhhewt/pitkæ
tight/loose	**tiukka/väljä**	ti°°kkah/vælyæ
How long will it take to alter?	**Kauanko sen korjaus kestää?**	kah°°ahnkoa sayn koaryaoos kaystǣ

NUMBERS, see page 147

Clothes and accessories *Vaatteita ja asusteita*

I'd like a/an/ some ...	Haluaisin ...	hahlooah¹sin
anorak	anorakin	ahnoarahkin
bathing cap	uima|lakin	oo¹mahlahkin
bathing suit	uima|puvun	oo¹mahpoovoon
bathrobe	kylpy|takin	kewlpewtahkin
blouse	puseron	poosayroan
bow tie	rusetin	roosaytin
bra	rinta|liivit	rintahleevit
braces	henkselit	haynksaylit
cap	lakin	lahkin
cardigan	neule|takin/	nay°°laytahkin/villahtahkin
	villa|takin	
coat	takin	tahkin
dress	leningin	layningin
with long sleeves	pitkä|hihaisen ...	pitkæhihhah¹sayn
with short sleeves	lyhyt|hihaisen ...	lewhewthihhah¹sayn
sleeveless	hihattoman ...	hihhahttoamahn
dressing gown	aamu|takin	aamootahkin
evening dress (woman's)	ilta|puvun	iltahpoovoon
girdle	(naisten) liivit	(nah¹stayn) leevit
gloves	hansikkaat	hahnsikkaat
handbag	käsi|laukun	kæsilah°°koon
handkerchief	nenä|liinan	naynæleenahn
hat	hatun	hahtoon
jacket	(lyhyen) takin/	(lewhewayn) tahkin/
	pusakan	poosahkahn
jeans	farmari|housut/	fahrmahrihoa°°soot/
	farkut	fahrkoot
jersey	villa|takin	villahtahkin
jumper (Br.)	villa|puseron	villahpoosayroan
kneesocks	polvi|sukat	poalvisookaht
nightdress	yö|paidan	ᵉʷurpah¹dahn
overalls	haalarit	haalahrit
pair of...	parin ...	pahrin
panties	pikku|housut	pikkoohoa°°soot
pants (Am.)	housut	hoa°°soot
panty girdle	housu|liivit	hoa°°sooleevit
panty hose	sukka|housut	sookkahhoa°°soot
parka	sade|pusakan	sahdaypoosahkahn
pullover	villa|paidan	villahpah¹dahn
polo (turtle)-neck	jossa on poolo-	yoassah oan poaloa-
	kaulus	kah°°loos
round-neck	jossa on pyöreä	yoassah oan pᵉʷurayæ
	kaula-aukko	kah°°lahah°°kkoa

V-neck	**jossa on V-aukko**	yoassah oan V-ah°°kkoa
with long/short sleeves	**jossa on pitkät/ lyhyet hihat**	yoassah oan pitkæt/ lewhhewayt hihhaht
without sleeves	**joka on hihaton**	yoakah oan hihhahtoan
pyjamas	**pyjaman**	pewyahmahn
raincoat	**sade|takin**	sahdaytahkin
scarf	**huivin**	hoo'vin
shirt	**paidan**	pah'dahn
shorts	**shortsit**	shoartsit
skirt	**hameen**	hahmāyn
slip	**alus|hameen**	ahlooshahmāyn
socks	**(nilkka|)sukat**	(nilkkah)sookaht
stockings	**(naisten) sukat**	(nah'stayn) sookaht
suit (man's)	**puvun**	poovoon
suit (woman's)	**kävely|puvun/ jakku|puvun**	kævaylewpoovoon/ yahkkoopoovoon
suspenders (Am.)	**henkselit**	haynksaylit
sweater	**neule|puseron/ villa|paidan**	nay°°laypoosayroan/ villahpah'dahn
sweatshirt	**college-paidan**	koallaygay-pah'dahn
swimming trunks	**uima|housut**	oo'mahhoa°°soot
swimsuit	**uima|puvun**	oo'mahpoovoon
T-shirt	**T-paidan**	tāypah'dahn
tie	**solmion/kravatin**	soalmioan/krahvahtin
tights	**sukka|housut**	sookkahhoa°°soot
tracksuit	**verryttely|puvun**	vayrrewttaylewpoovoon
trousers	**(pitkät) housut**	(pitkæt) hoa°°soot
umbrella	**sateen|varjon**	sahtaynvahryoan
underpants	**(miesten) alus|housut**	(m'aystayn) ahlooshoa°°soot
undershirt	**alus|paidan**	ahloospah'dahn
vest (Am.)	**(miesten) liivit**	(m'aystayn) leevit
vest (Br.)	**alus|paidan**	ahloospah'dahn
waistcoat	**liivin/hihattoman (villa|)takin**	leevin/hihhahttoamahn (villah)tahkin

belt	**vyö**	v^ewur
buckle	**solki**	soalki
button	**nappi**	nahppi
collar	**kaulus**	kah°°looss
hood	**huppu**	hooppoo
pocket	**tasku**	tahskoo
press stud (snap fastener)	**paino|nappi**	pah'noanahppi
zip (zipper)	**veto|ketju**	vaytoakaytyoo

Shoes *Kengät*

I'd like a pair of...

	Haluaisin...	hahlooah'sin
boots	**saappaat**	saappaat
moccasins	**mokkasiinit**	moakkahseenit
plimsolls (sneakers)	**kumi|tossut**	koomitoassoot
sandals	**sandaalit**	sahndaalit
shoes	**kengät**	kayngæt
flat	**matala|korkoi-set...**	mahtahlahkoarkoa'sayt
with a heel	**..., korolliset**	koaroallisayt
with leather soles	**..., joissa on nahka|pohja**	yoa'ssah oan nahhkahpoahyah
with rubber soles	**..., joissa on kumi|pohja**	yoa'ssah oan koomipoahyah
slippers	**tohvelit**	toahvaylit
These are too...	**Nämä ovat liian...**	næmæ oavaht leeahn
narrow/wide	**kapeat/leveät**	kahpayaht/layvayæt
big/small	**isot/pienet**	issoat/p'aynayt
Do you have a larger/smaller size?	**Onko teillä suurempaa/pienempää kokoa?**	oankoa tay'llæ sooraympaa/p'aynympǣ koakoah
Do you have the same in black?	**Onko teillä tätä mustana?**	oankoa tay'llæ tætæ moostahnah
cloth	**kangasta**	kahngahstah
leather	**nahkaa**	nahhkaa
rubber	**kumia**	koomiah
suede	**mokka|nahkaa**	moakkahnahhkaa
Is it real leather?	**Onko se aitoa nahkaa?**	oankoa say ah'toaah nahhkaa
I need some shoe polish/shoelaces.	**Tarvitsen kengän|kiilloketta/kengän|nauhat**	tahrvitsayn kayngænkeelloakayttah/kayngænnah°°haht

Repairs *Korjaukset*

Can you repair these shoes?	**Voitteko korjata nämä kengät?**	voa'ttaykoa koaryahtah næmæ kayngæt
Can you stitch this?	**Voitteko ommella tämän?**	voa'ttaykoa oammmayllah tæmæn
I want new soles and heels.	**Haluaisin uudet pohjat ja korot.**	hahlooah'sin ōōdayt poahyat yah koaroat
When will they be ready?	**Milloin ne ovat valmiit?**	milloa'n nay oavaht vahlmeet

COLOURS, see page 112

Electrical appliances Sähkö|koneet

Voltage in Finland is 220 AC 60 cycle. Plugs are of the 2-pin (round hole) type, for which adaptors are available.

What's the voltage?	**Mikä on jännite?**	mikkæ oan **y**æn**n**ittay
Do you have a battery for this?	**Olisiko teillä paristoa tähän?**	oalisikoa tay'llæ pahristoaah tæhæn
This is broken. Can you repair it?	**Tämä on rikki. Voitteko korjata sen?**	tæmæ oan **rikki** voa'ttaykoa **koar**yahtah sayn
Can you show me how it works?	**Voitteko näyttää, miten se toimii?**	voa'ttaykoa næ**ew**ttæ mittayn say toa'mee
I'd like to hire/to buy a video cassette.	**Haluaisin vuokrata/ostaa video|kasetin.**	hahlooah'sin v°°oakrahtah/oastaa viddayoakahsaytin
I'd like a/an/ some...	**Haluaisin...**	hahlooah'sin
adaptor	**adapterin/sovittimen**	ahdahptayrin/ soavittimmayn
amplifier	**vahvistimen**	vahhvistimmayn
bulb	**(hehku|)lampun**	(hayhkoo)lahmpoon
CD player	**CD-soittimen**	saȳdaȳ-soa'ttimmayn
clock-radio	**kello|radion**	kaylloarahdioan
electric toothbrush	**sähkö|hammas|harjan**	sæhkurhahmmahshahryahn
extension lead (cord)	**jatko|johdon**	yahtkoayoahdoan
hair dryer	**hiusten|kuivaajan**	hi°°staynkoo'vaayahn
headphones	**kuulokkeet**	kōōloakkaȳt
(travelling) iron	**(matka|)silitys|raudan**	(mahtkah) sillittewsra°°dahn
lamp	**lampun**	lahmpoon
plug	**pistokkeen**	pistoakkaȳn
portable...	**kannettavan...**	kahnnayttahvahn
radio	**radion**	rahd'oan
car radio	**auto|radion**	ah°°toarahd'oan
(cassette) recorder	**(kasetti|)nauhurin**	(kahsaytti)nah°°hoorin
record player	**levy|soittimen**	layvewsoa'ttimmayn
shaver	**parran|ajo|koneen**	pahrrahnahyoakoanaȳn
speakers	**kaiuttimet**	kah'oottimmayt
(colour) television	**(väri|)television**	(værri)taylayvissioan
transformer	**muuntajan**	moontahyahn
video-recorder	**video|nauhurin**	vidayoanah°°hoorin

Grocer's *Elin|tarvike|myymälä*

I'd like some bread, please.	Haluaisin leipää.	hahlooah'sin lay'pæ
What sort of cheese do you have?	Mitä eri juusto|laatuja teillä on?	mittæ ayri yoostoalaatooya tay'llæ oan
A piece of...	Pala...	pahlah
that one	tuota	t°°oatah
the one on the shelf	tuota hyllyllä olevaa	t°°oatah hewllewllæ oalayvaa
I'll have one of those, please.	Saisinko yhden noita.	sah'sinko ewhdayn noa'tah
May I help myself?	Voinko ottaa itse?	voa'nkoa oattaa itsay
I'd like...	Saisinko...	sah'sinko
a kilo of apples	kilon omenia	killoan oamayniah
half a kilo of tomatoes	puoli kiloa tomaatteja	p°°oali killoah toamaattayyah
100 grams of butter	100 grammaa voita	sahtah grahmmaa voa'tah
a litre of milk	litran maitoa	litrahn mah'toah
half a dozen eggs	puoli tusinaa munia	p°°oali toosinaa mooniah
4 slices of ham	4 siivua kinkkua	naylyæ seevooah kinkkooah
a packet of tea	paketin teetä	pahkaytin tāytæ
a jar of jam	purkin hilloa	poorkin hilloaah
a tin (can) of peaches	tölkin persikoita	turlkin payrsikoa'tah
a tube of mustard	putkilon sinappia	pootkiloan sinnahppiah
a box of chocolates	suklaa|rasia	sooklaarahsiah

---

1 kilogram or kilo (kg.) = 1000 grams (g.)		
100 g. = 3.5 oz.	½ kg. = 1.1 lb.	
200 g. = 7.0 oz.	1 kg. = 2.2 lb.	
1 oz. = 28.35 g.		
1 lb. = 453.60 g.		

1 litre (l.) = 0.88 imp. quarts = 1.06 U.S. quarts	
1 imp. quart = 1.14 l.	1 U.S. quart = 0.95 l.
1 imp. gallon = 4.55 l.	1 U.S. gallon = 3.8 l.

FOOD, see also page 62

Household articles *Talous|tarvikkeita*

aluminium foil	**alumiini|folio**	ahloomeeni**foa**lioa
bottle opener	**pullon|avaaja**	poolloanah**vaa**yah
bucket	**ämpäri**	**æmp**pæri
can opener	**purkin|avaaja**	poorkinah**vaa**yah
candles	**kynttilät**	**kewnt**tilæt
clothes pegs (pins)	**pyykkipojat**	pew**kki**poayaht
frying pan	**paistin|pannu**	pah'**stin**pahnnoo
matches	**tuli|tikut**	**too**litikkoot
paper napkins	**paperi|lautas|liinat**	pahpayri**lah**°°tahslee-naht
paper towel	**paperi|pyyhe**	pahpayri**pew**hay
plastic bags	**muovi|kassi**	m°°**oa**vikahssi
saucepan	**kattila**	**kaht**tilah
tea towel	**astia|pyyhe**	ahstiah**pew**hay
vacuum flask	**termos|pullo**	tayrmoas**pool**loa
washing powder	**pesu|pulveri**	paysoo**pool**vayri
washing-up liquid	**nestemäinen**	naystaymæinayn
	pesu|aine	paysooah'nay

Tools *Työ|kaluja*

hammer	**vasara**	**vah**sahrah
nails	**naulat**	nah°°laht
penknife	**kynä|veitsi**	kewnævay'tsi
pliers	**pihdit**	**pih**dit
scissors	**sakset**	**sahk**sayt
screws	**ruuveja**	**roo**vayyah
screwdriver	**ruuvi|meisseli**	roovimay'ssayli
(adjustable) spanner	**jako|avain**	yakoaah**vah'**n

Crockery *Astiat*

cups	**kupit**	**koo**pit
mugs	**mukit**	**moo**kit
plates	**lautaset**	lah°°tahsayt
saucers	**tee|vadit/kahvi|lau-taset**	tayvahdit/ kahhvilah°°tahsayt
tumblers	**(juoma|)lasit**	(y°°oamah)lahsit

Cutlery (flatware) *Ruokailu|välineet*

forks	**haarukat**	**haa**rookat
knives	**veitset**	vay'tsayt
spoons	**lusikat**	**loo**sikkaht
teaspoons	**tee|lusikat**	tayloosikkaht
plastic	**muovista**	m°°**oa**vistah
stainless steel	**ruostumattomasta teräksestä**	r°°oastoomahttoah-mahstah tayræksaystæ

Jeweller's—Watchmaker's *Kulta|seppä—Kello|seppä*

Could I see that, please?	**Saisinko katsoa tuota?**	sah'sinkoa kahtsoah t°°oatah
Do you have anything in gold?	**Onko teillä mitään, joka on kultaa?**	oankoa tay'llæ mittǣn yoakah oan kooltaa
How many carats is this?	**Montako karaattia tässä on?**	moantahkoa kahraattiah tæssæ oan
Is this real silver?	**Onko tämä aitoa hopeaa?**	oankoa tæmmæ ah'toah hoapayaa
Can you repair this watch?	**Voitteko korjata tämän kellon?**	voa'ttaykoa koaryahtah tæmæn kaylloan
I'd like a/an/some...	**Haluaisin...**	hahlooah'sin
alarm clock	**herätys|kellon**	hayrætewskayllon
bangle	**ranne|renkaan**	rahnnayraynkaan
battery	**pariston**	pahristoan
bracelet	**ranne|korun**	rahnnaykoaroon
chain bracelet	**ranne|ketjun**	rahnnaykaytyoon
charm bracelet	**amu-letti|ranne|ketju**	ahmoolayttirahnnay kaytyoon
brooch	**rinta|korun**	rintahkoaroon
chain	**ketjun**	kaytyoon
charm	**amuletin**	ahmoolaytin
cigarette case	**savuke|kotelon**	sahvookaykoatayloan
cigarette lighter	**tupakan|sytyttimen**	toopahkahnsew-tewttimmayn
clock	**kellon**	kaylloan
cross	**ristin**	ristin
cuckoo clock	**käki|kellon**	kækikaylloan
cuff links	**kalvosin|napit**	kahlvoassinnahpit
cutlery	**ruokailu|välineet**	r°°oakah'loovælināyt
earrings	**korva|korut**	koarvahkoaroot
gem	**jalokiven**	yahloakivayn
jewel box	**koru|lippaan**	koaroolippaan
mechanical pencil	**lyijy|täyte|kynän**	lew'yewtæ°ᵂtaykewnæn
music box	**soitto|rasian**	soa'ttoarahsiahn
necklace	**kaula|korun**	kah°°lahkoaroon
pendant	**riipuksen**	reepooksayn
pin	**neulan**	nay°lahn
pocket watch	**tasku|kellon**	tahskookaylloan
powder compact	**puuteri|rasian**	pōōtayrirahsiahn
propelling pencil	**(kierrettävän) lyijy|täyte|kynän**	(k'ayrrayttævæn) lew'yewtæ°ᵂtaykewnæn

ring	**sormuksen**	**soar**mooksayn
engagement ring	**kihla|sormuksen**	**kihh**lah**soar**mooksayn
signet ring	**sinetti|sormuk-sen**	**sinn**aytti**soar**mooksayn
wedding ring	**vihki|sormuksen**	**vihh**ki**soar**mooksayn
rosary	**rukous|nauhan**	**rook**oa°°**snah**°°hahn
silverware	**hopea|esineitä**	**hoap**aya**hay**ssinnay't**æ**
tie clip	**solmion pidikkeen**	**soal**mioan **piddik**k**āy**n
tie pin	**solmio|neulan**	**soal**mioanay°°lahn
watch	**kellon**	**kayll**oan
automatic	**automaatti|**	ah°°toamaatti
digital	**digitaali|**	**diggi**taali
quartz	**kvartsi|**	**kvahrt**si
with a second hand	**..., jossa on sekunti|viisari**	**yoass**ah oan **say**koontti**vees**ahri
waterproof	**veden|pitävän**	**vayd**aynpitt**æ**v**æ**
watchstrap	**kellon hihnan**	**kayll**oan **hihn**ahn
wristwatch	**ranne|kellon**	**rahn**nay**kayll**oan

amber	**meri|pihka**	**mayr**ipihkah
amethyst	**ametisti**	**ah**maytisti
chromium	**kromi**	**kroa**mi
copper	**kupari**	**koo**pahri
coral	**koralli**	**koar**ahlli
crystal	**kristalli**	**krist**ahlli
cut glass	**hiottu lasi**	**hioa**ttoo **lah**si
diamond	**timantti**	**timm**ahntti
emerald	**smaragdi**	**smahr**ahgdi
enamel	**emali**	**ay**mahli
gold	**kulta**	**kool**tah
gold plate	**kullattu**	**kooll**ahttoo
ivory	**norsun|luu**	**noar**soonloo
jade	**jade**	**yah**day
onyx	**onyks**	**oa**newks
pearl	**helmi**	**hayl**mi
pewter	**tina**	**tinn**ah
platinum	**platina**	**plah**tinnah
ruby	**rubiini**	**roo**beeni
sapphire	**safiiri**	**sah**feeri
silver	**hopea**	**hoap**ayah
silver plate	**hopeoitu**	**hoap**ayoa'too
stainless steel	**ruostumaton teräs**	r°°oastoomahtoan **tayr**æs
topaz	**topaasi**	**toa**paassi
turquoise	**turkoosi**	**toork**o̅a̅ssi

Optician *Optikko*

I've broken my glasses.	Silmä|lasini menivät rikki.	silmælahsinni maynivæt rikki
Can you repair them for me?	Voitteko korjata ne?	voaittaykoa koaryahtah nay
When will they be ready?	Milloin ne ovat valmiit?	milloaᶦn nay oavaht vahlmeet
Can you change the lenses?	Voitteko vaihtaa linssit?	voaittaykoa vahⁱhtaa linssit
I'd like tinted lenses.	Haluaisin värjätyt linssit.	hahlooahisin væryætewt linssit
The frame is broken.	Sangat ovat rikki.	sahngaht oavaht rikki
I'd like a spectacle case.	Haluaisin silmä|lasi|kotelon.	hahlooahisin silmælahsikoatayloan
I'd like to have my eyesight checked.	Haluaisin näkö|tarkastuksen.	hahlooahisin nækurtahrkahstooksayn
I'm short-sighted/long-sighted.	Olen liki|näköinen/kauko|näköinen	oalayn likkinækurᶦnayn/kahᵒᵒkoanækurᶦnayn
I'd like some contact lenses.	Haluaisin kontakti|linssit .	hahlooahisin koantahktilinssit
I've lost one of my contact lenses.	Olen hukannut toisen kontakti|linssini.	oalayn hookahnnoot toaisayn koantahktilinssini
Could you give me another one?	Voitteko antaa minulle toisen?	voaittaykoa ahntaa minnoollay toaisayn
I have hard/soft lenses.	Minulla on kovat/pehmeät linssit.	minnoollah oan koavaht/payhmayæt linssit
Do you have any contact-lens fluid?	Onko teillä kontakti|linssi|nestettä?.	oankoa tayⁱllæ koantahktilinssinaystayttæ
I'd like to buy a pair of sunglasses.	Haluaisin ostaa aurinko|lasit.	hahlooahisin oastaa ahᵒᵒrinkoalahsit
May I look in a mirror?	Voinko katsoa peiliin?	voaⁱnkoa kahtsoah payⁱleen
I'd like to buy a pair of binoculars.	Haluaisin ostaa kiikarin.	hahlooahisin oastaa keekahrin

Photography *Valokuvaus*

I'd like a(n)... camera.	Haluaisin... kameran.	hahlooah¦sin... kahmayrahn
automatic	automaatti¦	ah°°toamaatti
inexpensive	huokean	h°°oakayahn
simple	yksinkertaisen	ewksinkayrtah¦sayn
Can you show me some video cameras please?	Voisitteko näyttää minulle video¦kameroita.	voa¦sittaykoa næewttæ minnoollay vidayoakahmayroa¦tah
I'd like to have some passport photos taken.	Haluaisin passi¦kuvaan.	hahlooah¦sin pahssikoovahn

Film *Filmi*

I'd like a film for this camera.	Haluaisin filmin tähän kameraan.	hahlooah¦sin filmin tæhæn kahmayraan
black and white	musta¦valkoista	moostahvahlkoa¦stah
colour	värillistä	værillistæ
colour negative	väri¦negatiivi	værinaygahteevi
colour slide	väri¦dia	væridihah
cartridge	kasetti	kahsaytti
disc film	filmi¦kiekko	filmik¦aykkoa
roll film	filmi¦rulla	filmiroollah
video cassette	video¦kasetti	videokahsaytti
24/36 exposures	kahden¦kymmenen ¦neljän/kolmen ¦kymmenen¦ kuuden kuvan	kahhdaynkewmmaynayn naylyæn/koalmayn kewmmaynayn kōōdayn koovahn
this size	tätä kokoa	tætæ koakoah
this ASA/DIN number	tätä ASA/DIN numeroa	tætæ ASA/DIN noomayroah
artificial light type	keino¦valoon sopivaa	kay¦noavahlōōn soapivaa
daylight type	päivän¦valoon sopivaa	pæ¦vænvahlōōn soapivaa
fast (high-speed)	herkkää (nopeaa)	hayrkkææ (noapayaa)
fine grain	hieno¦rakeista	h¦aynoarahkay¦stah

Processing *Kehitys*

How much do you charge for processing?	Paljonko kehittäminen maksaa?	pahlyoankoa kayhittæminayn mahksaa
I'd like ... prints of each negative.	Haluaisin ... kuvaa kustakin negatiivista.	hahlooah'sin ... koovaa koostahkin naygahteevistah
with a matt finish	matta|pintaisia	mahttahpintah'siah
with a glossy finish	kiiltävä|pintaisia	keeltævæpintah'siah
Will you enlarge this, please?	Suurentaisitteko tämän.	soorayntah'sittaykoa tæmæn
When will the photos be ready?	Milloin kuvat ovat valmiit?	milloa'n koovaht oavaht vahlmeet

Accessories and repairs *Lisä\|laitteet ja korjaukset*

I'd like a/an/some ...	Haluaisin ...	hahlooah'sin
battery	pariston	pahristoan
cable release	lanka|laukaisimen	lahnkahlah°°kah'simmayn
camera case	kamera|laukun	kahmayrahlah°°koon
(electronic) flash	(electronisen) salama|laitteen	(aylayktroanissayn) sahlahmahlah'ttayn
filter	suodattimen	s°°oadahttimayn
for black and white	musta|valkoiselle	moostahvahlkoa'sayllay
for colour	värille	værillay
lens	objektiivin	oabyaykteevin
telephoto lens	tele|objektiivin	taylayoabyaykteevin
wide-angle lens	laaja|kulma|objektiivin	laayahkoolmahoabyaykteevin
lens cap	linssin|suojuksen	linssis°°oayooksayn
Can you repair this camera?	Voitteko korjata tämän kameran?	voa'ttaykoa koaryahtah tæmæn kahmayrahn
The film is jammed.	Filmi on juuttunut kiinni.	filmi oan yōōttoonoot keenni
There's something wrong with the ...	... ei toimi kunnolla.	ay' toa'mi koonnoallah
exposure counter	kuva|laskuri	koovahlahskoori
film winder	filmin|kelaaja	filminkaylaayah
flash attachment	salama|laite	sahlahmahlah'tay
lens	objektiivi	oabyaykteevi
light meter	valotus|mittari	vahloatoosmittahri
rangefinder	etäisyys|mittari	aytæ'sewsmittahri
shutter	suljin	soolyin

NUMBERS, see page 147

Tobacconist's *Tupakka|kauppa*

A packet of cigarettes, please.	**Saisinko rasian savukkeita?**	sah'sinkoa rahsiahn sahvookkay'tah
Do you have any American/English cigarettes?	**Onko teillä amerikkalaisia/englantilaisia savukkeita?**	oankoa tay'llæ ahmayrikkahlah'siah/ aynglahntilah'siah sahvookkay'tah
I'd like a carton.	**Saisinko kartongin.**	sah'sinkoa kahrtoangin
Give me a/some..., please.	**Saisinko...**	sah'sinkoa
candy	**makeisia**	mahkay'siah
chewing gum	**puru|kumia**	poorookoomiah
chewing tobacco	**puru|tupakkaa**	poorootoopahkkaa
chocolate	**suklaata**	sooklaatah
cigarette case	**savuke|kotelon**	sahvookaykoatayloan
cigarette holder	**imukkeen**	immookkāyn
cigarettes	**savukkeita**	sahvookkay'tah
filter-tipped/ without filter	**suodatin|.../ ilman filtteriä**	s°°oadahtin|/ilmahn filttayriæ
light/dark tobacco	**vaaleaa/tummaa tupakkaa**	vaalayaa/toommaa toopahkkaa
mild/strong	**mietoja/väkeviä...**	m'aytoayah/vækayviæ
menthol	**mentholi|...**	mayntoali
king-size	**king-size-kokoa**	king-size-koakoah
cigars	**sikaareja**	sikkaarayyah
lighter	**sytyttimen**	sewtewttimmayn
lighter fluid/gas	**besiiniä/kaasua sytyttimeen**	baynseeniæ/kaasooah sewtewttimmāyn
matches	**tuli|tikkuja**	toolitikkooyah
pipe	**piipun**	peepoon
pipe cleaners	**piipun puhdistimia/piippu|rasseja**	poohdistimmiah/ peeppoorahssayyah
pipe tobacco	**piippu|tupakkaa**	peeppootoopahkkaa
pipe tool	**piippu|kalun**	peeppookahloon
postcard	**posti|kortin**	poastikoartin
snuff	**nuuskaa**	nooskaa
stamps	**posti|merkkejä**	poastimayrkkayyæ
sweets	**jotain makeaa**	joatah'n mahkayaa
wick	**sytyttimeen sydämen**	sewtewttimmāyn sewdæmmayn

Miscellaneous *Sekalaista*

Souvenirs *Muistoesineitä*

Souvenirs include objects made of wood, *puukko* hunting knives and reindeer skins and antlers. Lapp crafts are popular too. Look for carvings made from reindeer bones, felt items and dolls.

candles	**kyntillät**	kewnttilæt
candlesticks	**kyntillän|jalat**	kewnttilænjahlaht
ceramics	**keramiikka/posliini**	kayrahmeekkah/**poas**leeni
furs	**turkikset**	toorkiksayt
glass	**lasi**	lahsi
handicrafts	**käsi|työt**	kæsitᵉʷurt
jewellery	**korut**	koaroot
reindeer hide	**poron|talja**	poaroantahlyah
table linen	**pöytä|-ja lautas|lii-nat**	purᵉʷtæ-yah lah°otahsleenaht
textiles	**tekstiilit**	tayksteelit
wall rug	**ryijy**	rewⁱyew
wooden toys	**puu|lelut**	poolayloot

Records—Cassettes *Levyt—Kasetit*

I'd like a...	**Saisinko...**	sahⁱsinkoa
cassette	**kasetin**	kahsaytin
video cassette	**video|kasetin**	videokahsaytin
compact disc	**CD-levyn**	sāydāy-layvewn

L.P. (33 rpm)	**LP-levyn (kolme|kymmentä| kolme kierrosta minuutissa)**	ælpāy-layvewn (koalmaykewmmayntæ koalmay kⁱayrroastah minnootissah)
E.P. (45 rpm)	**EP-levy (neljä|kymmentä| viisi kierrosta minuutissa)**	āypāy-layvew (naylyækewmmayntæ veesi kⁱayrroastah minnootissah)
single	**single**	singayl

Do you have any records by...?	**Onko teillä levyjä?**	oan**koa** tay'**llæ lay**vewyæ
Can I listen to this record?	**Voinko kuunnella tämän levyn?**	voa'**nkoa koon**nayllah tæmæn **lay**vewn
chamber music	**kamari|musiikki**	**kah**mahri**moo**seekki
classical music	**klassinen musiikki**	**klahs**sinayn **moo**seekki
folk music	**kansan|musiikki**	**kahn**sahn**moo**seekki
folk song	**kansan|laulu**	**kahn**sahn**lah**°°loo
instrumental music	**soitin|musiikki**	soa'**tin**moo**seekki
jazz	**jatsi**	**yaht**si
light music	**kevyt musiikki**	**kay**vewt **moo**seekki
orchestral music	**orkesteri|musiikki**	**oar**kaystayri**moo**seekki
pop music	**pop-musiikki**	pop**moo**seekki

Toys *Leikki\|kalut*

I'd like a toy/game...	**Haluaisin leikki|kalun/pelin**	hah**loo**ah'sin lay'**kki**kahloon/**pay**lin
for a boy	**pojalle**	**poa**yahllay
for a 5-year-old girl	**5-vuotiaalle tytölle**	**veesi-v**°°**oa**tiaallay **tew**turllay
(beach) ball	**(ranta|)pallon**	(**rahn**tah)**pahl**loan
bucket and spade (pail and shovel)	**ämpärin ja lapion**	**æm**pærin yah **lah**pioan
building blocks (bricks)	**rakennus|palikoita**	**rah**kaynnoos**pah**likoa'tah
card game	**kortti|pelin**	**koart**tipaylin
chess set	**shakki|pelin**	**shahk**kipaylin
doll	**nuken**	**noo**kayn
electronic game	**elektronisen pelin**	**ay**layktroanissayn **pay**lin
roller skates	**rulla|luistimet**	**rool**lahloo'stimayt
snorkel	**snorkkelin**	**snoark**kaylin

Your money: banks—currency

Banks are open from Monday to Friday, 9.15 a.m. to 4.15 p.m., both summer and winter. There's certain to be someone who speaks English at any large bank. You can also change your money at most hotels, department stores and the larger shops. Though you will normally have to change your money at a bank, there are a few exchange offices in the large towns. Out of hours, try the exchange office at the Helsinki Railway Station. It remains open from 8.30 a.m. to 8 p.m., Monday to Saturday, and on Sundays from 12.30 p.m. to 7 p.m.

Remember to take your passport with you when changing money.

Major credit cards are accepted in most hotels and restaurants, service stations, department stores and shops. Internationally recognized traveller's cheques are easily cashed. Other traveller's cheques can only be cashed in banks or currency exchange offices.

The basic unit of the Finnish monetary system is the mark (*markka*), which is divided into 100 pennies (*penni, penniä*). The abbreviation for mark is *mk* and for penni *p*.

There are coins of 10 and 50 pennies and of 1, 5 and 10 marks. Banknotes are of 10, 50, 100, 500 and 1000 marks.

| Where's the nearest bank? | **Missä on lähin pankki?** | missæ oan læhin pahnkki |
| Where's the nearest currency exchange office? | **Missä on lähin valuu-tan\|vaihto\|paikka?** | missæ oan læhin vahlōotahnvah'htoa paihkkah |

At the bank *Pankissa*

I want to change some dollars/pounds.	**Haluaisin vaihtaa dollareita/puntia.**	hahlooah'sin **vah'h**taa **doall**ahray'tah/**poon**tiah
I want to cash a traveller's cheque.	**Haluaisin muuttaa matka|shekin rahaksi.**	hahlooah'sin mōōttaa **maht**kahshaykin **rah**haahksi
What's the exchange rate?	**Mikä on vaihto|kurssi?**	mikkæ oan **vah'h**toa**koors**si
How much commission do you charge?	**Mikä on väli- tys|palkkionne?**	mikkæ oan **væ**littews**pahlkk**'oannay
Can you cash a personal cheque?	**Otatteko vastaan henkilö|kohtaisen shekin?**	oatahttaykoa **vahs**taan **hayn**killur**koah**tah'sayn **shay**kin
Can you fax my bank in London?	**Voitteko lähettää faksin pankkiini Lontooseen?**	voa'ttaykoa læhayttǣ **fahk**sin **pahnk**keeni loan**tōas**sāyn
I have a/an/some ...	**Minulla on ...**	minnoollah oan
credit card Eurocheques letter of credit	**luotto|kortti euroshekkejä remburssi**	l'ooattoakoartti ayroashaykkayyæ **raym**boorssi
I'm expecting some money from New York. Has it arrived?	**Odotan rahaa New Yorkista. Onko se tullut?**	oadoatahn **rah**haa new **yoar**kistah **oan**koa say **tooll**loot
Please give me ... notes (bills) and some small change.	**Saisinko ... sete- leinä ja loput vaihto|rahana.**	sah'sinkoa ... **say**taylay'næ yah **loa**poot **vah'h**toa**rah**hahnah
Give me ... large notes and the rest in small notes.	**Saisinko ... suurina ja loput pieninä seteleinä.**	sah'sinkoa ... **sōō**rinnah yah **loa**poot p'**ay**ninnæ **say**taylay'næ

Deposits—Withdrawals *Panot—Otot*

I want to ...	**Haluaisin ...**	hahlooah'sin
open an account withdraw ... marks	**avata tilin nostaa ... markkaa.**	**ah**vahtah **t**illin **noas**taa ... **mahrk**kaa
Where should I sign?	**Mihin alle|kirjoi- tan?**	mihin **ahl**laykeery'oatahn
I'd like to pay this into my account.	**Tallettaisin tämän tililleni.**	**tahl**layttah'sin **tæ**mæn **t**ilillayni

NUMBERS, see page 147

Business terms *Liike|termejä*

My name is...	Nimeni on...	nimmayni oan
Here's my card.	Tässä on korttini.	tæssæ oan koarttini
I have an appointment with...	Minulla on tarnami-nen... kanssa.	minnoollah oan tahrnahminayn... kahnssah
Can you give me an estimate of the cost?	Voitteko antaa arvion kustannuk-sista?	voaʼttaykoa ahntaa ahrvʼoan koostahnnooksistah
What's the rate of inflation?	Mikä on inflaatio-taso?	mikkæ oan inflaatioa-tahsoa
Can you provide me with a(n)...?	Voitteko järjestää minulle...	voaʼttaykoa yæryaystæ minnoollay
interpreter	tulkin	toolkin
personal computer	henkilö|kohtaisen tieto|koneen	haynkillurkoahtahʼsayn tʼaytoakoanāyn
secretary	sihteerin	sihtāyrin
Where can I make photocopies?	Missä voin ottaa valo|kopioita?	missæ voaʼn oattaa vahloakoapioaʼtah

amount	summa	soommah
balance	saldo	saldoa
capital	pää|oma	pǣoamah
cheque	shekki	shaykki
contract	sopimus	soapimmoos
discount	alennus	ahlaynnoos
expenses	kulut	kooloot
interest	korko	koarkoa
investment	investointi	invaystoaʼnti
invoice	lasku	lahskoo
loss	tappio	tahppioa
mortgage	kiinnitys	keennittews
payment	maksu	mahksoo
percentage	prosentti	proasayntti
profit	voitto	voaʼttoa
purchase	osto	oastoa
sale	myynti	mēwnti
share	osake	oasahkay
transfer	siirto	seertoa
value	arvo	ahrvoa

At the post office

A symbolic hunting horn and the words *Posti—Post* identify post offices in Finland. Mailboxes are painted yellow. Business hours normally are from 9 a.m. to 5 p.m., Monday to Friday.

Out of hours, a limited-service post office operates at the Helsinki Railway Station. It is open from 7 a.m. to 9 p.m., Monday to Saturday, and on Sundays from 9 a.m. to 9 p.m.

At the Helsinki Airport the post office is open from 7 a.m. to 7 p.m., Monday to Saturday, and on Sundays from 9 am. to 3 p.m.

Where's the nearest post office?	Missä on lähin posti?	missæ oan læhin poasti
What time does the post office open/close?	Mihin aikaan posti aukeaa/suljetaan?	mihin ah¹kaan poasti ah°°kayaa/soolyaytaan
A stamp for this letter/postcard, please.	Saisinko posti|merkin tähän kirjeeseen/korttiin.	sah¹sinkoa poastimayrkin tæhæn keeryāysāyn/koartteen
A... penni stamp, please.	Saisinko... pennin posti|merkin.	sah¹sinkoa... paynnin poastimayrkin
What's the postage for a letter to London?	Mikä on kirje|maksu Lontooseen?	mikkæ oan keeryaymahksoo loantōāsāyn
What's the postage for a postcard to Los Angeles?	Mitä maksaa postikortti Los Angelesiin?	mittæ mahksaa poastikoartti loas ahngaylaysseen
Where's the letter box (mailbox)?	Missä on posti|laatikko?	missæ oan poastilaatikkoa
I want to send this parcel.	Haluaisin lähettää tämän paketin.	hahlooah¹sin læhyttǣ tæmæn pahkaytin
I'd like to send this (by)...	Lähettäisin tämän...	læhayttæisin tæmæn
airmail	lento|postissa	layntoapoastissah
express (special delivery)	pikana	pikkahnah
registered mail	kirjattuna	keeryahttoonah

At which counter can I cash an international money order?	Millä luukulla voin lunastaa kan‍sain	välisen maksu	määräyk‍sen?	millæ lōōkoollah voa‍'n loonahstaa kahnsah‍'nvælissayn mahksoomæ‍rǣ‍ew‍ksayn
Where's the poste restante (general delivery)?	Missä on poste restante?	missæ oan poastay raystahntay
Is there any post (mail) for me? My name is...	Onko minulle pos‍tia? Nimeni on...	oankoa minnoollay poastiah nimmayni oan

POSTIMERKIT	STAMPS
PAKETIT	PARCELS
MAKSU|ÄÄRÄYKSET	MONEY ORDERS

Telegrams—Telexes—Faxes *Sähkeet—Teleksit—Faksit*

Telegrams are accepted at Helsinki's main post office round the clock.

I'd like to send a telegram/telex.	Haluaisin lähettää sähkeen/teleksin.	hahlooah‍'sin læhayttǣ sæhkāyn/taylayksin
May I have a form, please?	Saisinko kaavak‍keen?	sah‍'sinkoa kaavahkkāyn
How much is it per word?	Mitä maksu on sanalta?	mittæ mahksoo oan sahnahltah
How long will a cable to Boston take?	Paljonko sähke Bostoniin vie aikaa?	pahlyoankoa sæhkae boastoaneen v‍'ay ah‍'kaa
How much will this (tele)fax cost?	Paljonko tämä faksi maksaa?	pahlyoankoa tæmæ fahksi mahksaa

Telephoning *Puhelut*

Finland has automatic telephone service within the country; consult a telephone directory for long-distance codes. Direct dialling also exists to most European networks: dial 990 followed by the code number of the country desired, local area code and subscriber's number. For non-European countries, dial 92022 and the operator will put you through. Street booths can be used for local and domestic long-distance calls.

Where's the telephone?	**Missä on puhelin?**	missæ oan **poo**haylin
Where's the nearest telephone booth?	**Missä on lähin puhelin|kioski?**	missæ oan læhin **poo**haylink'oaski
May I use your phone?	**Voinko käyttää puhelintanne?**	voa'nnkoa kæ°ᵂttæ **poo**haylintahnnay
Do you have a telephone directory for Helsinki?	**Onko teillä Helsingin puhelin|luetteloa?**	oankoa tayllæ **hayl**singin poohaylinl°°ayttayloah
I'd like to call... in England.	**Haluaisin soittaa... Englannissa.**	hahlooah'sin soa'ttaa... **ayng**lahnnissah
What's the dialling (area) code for Vaasa?	**Mikä on suunta|numero Vaasaan?**	mikkæ oan soōntah**noo**mayroa
How do I get the international operator?	**Miten pääsen ulkomaan|puhelu|keskukseen?**	mitayn **pāy**sayn oolkoamaan**poo**hayloo **kays**kooksāyn

Operator *Keskus*

I'd like Kuopio 234 567.	**Saisinko Kuopio 234567.**	sah'sinkoa k°°oapioa 234567
Can you help me get this number?	**Auttaisitteko minua soittamaan tähän numeroon?**	ah°°ttah'ssittaykoa minnooah soa'ttahmaan tæhæn noomayrōan
I'd like to place a personal (person-to-person) call.	**Saisinko henkilö|puhelun.**	sah'sinkoa haynkillur**poo**hayloon
I'd like to reverse the charges (call collect).	**Saisinko vastaan|ottaja maksaa-puhelun.**	sah'sinkoa vahstaanoattahyah mahksaa-**poo**hayloon

NUMBERS, see page 147

Speaking *Puhelimessa*

Hello. This is...	**Hei. Täällä...**	hay^i **tǣllæ**
I'd like to speak to...	**Onko... tavatta-vissa?**	oankoa... tahvahttahvissah
Extension...	**Saanko (ala|)nume-roon...**	saankoah (ahlah) noomayrōan
Speak louder/more slowly, please.	**Voisitteko puhua kovemmalla äänellä/hitaammin.**	voa^{i}sittaykoa poohooah koavaymmahllah ǣnayllæ/hittaammin

Bad luck *Huonoa onnea*

Would you try again later, please?	**Yrittäisittekö myö-hemmin uudelleen.**	ewrittæ^{i}sittaykur m^{ew}urhaymmin ōodayllāyn
Operator, you gave me the wrong number.	**Keskus, annoitte minulle väärän numeron.**	kayskooss ahno^{i}ttay minnoollay vǣræn noomayroan
Operator, we were cut off.	**Keskus, puhelu meni poikki.**	kayskoos poohayloo mayni poa^{i}kki

Finnish telephone alphabet *Suomalaiset puhelin\|aakkoset*

A	**Anna**	ahnnah	R	**Risto**	ristoa	
B	**Bertta**	bayrttah	S	**Sakari**	sahkahri	
C	**Cecilia**	saysilliah	T	**Tauno**	tah^{oo}noa	
D	**Daavid**	daavid	U	**Urho**	oorhoa	
E	**Erkki**	ayrkki	V	**Väinö**	vǣ^{i}nur	
F	**Faarao**	faarahoa	W	**kaksin|-kertainen**	kahksinkayr-tah^{i}nayn vāy	
G	**Gabriel**	gahbr^{i}ayl				
H	**Heikki**	hay^{i}kki		**v**		
I	**Iivari**	eevahri	X	**Xeres**	ksayrays	
J	**Jaakko**	yaakkoa	Y	**Yrjö**	uryur	
K	**Kalle**	kahllay	Z	**Zeppelin**	tsayppaylin	
L	**Lauri**	lah^{oo}ri	Å	**ruotsalainen**	r^{oo}oat-sahlah^{i}nayn	
M	**Mikko**	mikkoa		**o**	ōa	
N	**Niilo**	neeloa				
O	**Otto**	oattoa	Ä	**äiti**	ǣiti	
P	**Pekka**	paykkah	Ö	**öljy**	urlyew	
Q	**Quintus**	kvintoos				

Not there *Ei paikalla*

When will he/she be back?	**Milloin hän palaa?**	**milloa'**in hæn **pah**laa
Will you tell him/her I called? My name is…	**Kertoisitteko hänelle, että soitin. Nimeni on…**	**kayr**toa'sittaykoa **hæn**ayllaay **ayt**tæ **soa'**tin **nim**mayni oan
Would you ask him/her to call me?	**Pyytäisittekö häntä soittamaan minulle.**	**pēw**tæisittaykur **hæn**tæ **soa'**ttahmaan **min**noollay
Would you take a message, please?	**Voisinko jättää viestin?**	**voa'**sinkoa **yæt**tæ **v'**aystin

Charges *Maksut*

What was the cost of that call?	**Mitä tämä puhelu maksoi?**	**mi**tæ **tæ**mæ **poo**hayloo **mahk**soa'
I want to pay for the call.	**Haluaisin maksaa puhelun.**	**hah**looah'sin **mahk**saa **poo**hayloon

---

Teille on puhelu.	There's a telephone call for you.
Mihin numeroon soitatte?	What number are you calling?
Linja on varattu.	The line's engaged.
Numero ei vastaa.	There's no answer.
Teillä on väärä numero.	You've got the wrong number.
Puhelin on epä|kunnossa.	The phone is out of order.
Hetkinen.	Just a moment.
Hetkinen.	Hold on, please.
Hän on juuri nyt ulkona./Hän ei ole juuri nyt paikalla.	He's/She's out at the moment.

Doctor

You should ensure that your health insurance policy covers the cost of any accident or illness while on holiday. Finland has reciprocal health agreements with the Nordic countries, covering medical care and doctors' fees. There are also similar agreements with Britain. The quality of medical care in Finland is very high. All hospitals have doctors on duty 24 hours a day and many of them speak English.

General *Yleistä*

Can you get me a doctor?	**Voitteko hakea minulle lääkärin.**	voa'ttaykoa hahkayah minnoollay lǣkærin
Is there a doctor here?	**Onko täällä lääkäriä?**	oankoa tǣllæ lǣkæriæ
I need a doctor, quickly.	**Tarvitsen lääkärin, nopeasti.**	tahrvitsayn lǣkærin noapayahsti
Where can I find a doctor who speaks English?	**Mistä löytyisi lääkäri, joka puhuu englantia?**	mistæ lurᵉʷtewʾsi lǣkæri yoakah poohōō aynglahntiah
Where's the surgery (doctor's office)?	**Missä on lääkärin vastaan|otto?**	missæ oan lǣkærin vahstaanoattoa
What are the surgery (office) hours?	**Mitkä ovat vastaan|otto|ajat?**	mitkæ oavaht vahstaanoattoaahyaht
Could the doctor come to see me here?	**Voisiko lääkäri tulla katsomaan minua tänne?**	voa'sikoa lǣkæri toollah kahtsoamaan minnooah tænnay
What time can the doctor come?	**Mihin aikaan lääkäri voi tulla?**	mihin ahʾkaan lǣkæri voaʾ toollah
Can you recommend a/an ...?	**Voitteko suositella ...**	voa'ttaykoa sᵒᵒoasittayllah
general practitioner	**yleis|lääkäriä**	ewlayʾslǣkæriæ
children's doctor	**lasten|lääkäriä**	lahstaynlǣkæriæ
eye specialist	**silmä|lääkäriä**	silmælǣkæriæ
gynaecologist	**gynekologia**	gewnaykoaloagiah
Can I have an appointment ...?	**Voinko saada ajan ...?**	voaʾnkoah saadah ahyahn
tomorrow	**huomenna**	hᵒᵒoamaynnah
as soon as possible	**mahdollisimman pian**	mahhdoallissimmahn pʾahn

CHEMIST'S, see page 107

Parts of the body *Ruumiin|osia*

English	Finnish	Pronunciation
appendix	umpi|lisäke	oompilissækay
arm	käsi|varsi	kæsivahrsi
back	selkä	saylkæ
bladder	virtsa|rakko	virtsahrahkkoa
bone	luu	$\overline{loo}$
bowel	suoli	s°°oali
breast	rinta	rintah
chest	rinta|kehä	rintahkayhæ
ear	korva	koarvah
eye(s)	silmä(t)	silmæ(t)
face	kasvot	kahsvoat
finger	sormi	soarmi
foot	jalka	yahlkah
genitals	suku|elimet	sookooaylimmayt
gland	rauhanen	rah°°hahnayn
hand	käsi	kæsi
head	pää	pǣ
heart	sydän	sewdæn
jaw	leuka	lay°°kah
joint	nivel	nivvayl
kidney	munuainen	moonooah'nayn
knee	polvi	poalvi
leg	sääri	sǣri
ligament	nivel|side	nivvaylsidday
lip	huuli	h$\overline{oo}$li
liver	maksa	mahksah
lung	keuhko	kay°°hkoa
mouth	suu	s$\overline{oo}$
muscle	lihas	lihhahss
(back of the) neck	kaula (ja niska)	kah°°lah (yah niskah)
nerve	hermo	hayrmoa
nose	nenä	naynæ
rib	kylki|luu	kewlkill$\overline{oo}$
shoulder	olka|pää	oalkahpǣ
skin	iho	ihhoa
spine	selkä|ranka	saylkærahnkah
stomach (inside/ outside)	maha/vatsa	mahhah/vahtsah
tendon	jänne	yænnay
thigh	reisi	ray'si
throat	kurkku	koorkkoo
thumb	peukalo	pay°°kahloa
toe	varvas	vahrvahs
tongue	kieli	k'ayli
tonsils	kita|risat	kittahrissaht
vein	suoni	s°°oani

Accident—Injury *Onnettomuus—Vamma*

There's been an accident.	**On sattunut onnettomuus.**	oan **saht**toonoot oannayttoamōōss
My child has had a bad fall.	**Lapselleni sattui paha kaatuminen.**	lahpsayllayni **saht**tooi pahhah kaatoominnayn
He/She has hurt his/her head.	**Hän loukkasi päänsä.**	hæn loa°°**k**kahsi **pǣ**nsæ
He's/She's unconscious.	**Hän on tajuton.**	hæn oan **tah**yootoan
He's/She's bleeding (heavily).	**Hän vuotaa verta (runsaasti).**	hæn v°°**oa**taa **vay**rtaa (**roon**saasti)
He's/She's (seriously) injured.	**Hän on (vakavasti) loukkaantunut.**	hæn oan (**vah**kahvahsti) loa°°kkaantoonoot
His/Her arm is broken.	**Häneltä on käsi murtunut.**	**hæ**nayltæ oan **kæ**si **moor**toonoot
His/Her ankle is swollen.	**Hänen nilkkansa on turvoksissa.**	**hæ**nayn **nilk**kahnsah oan **toor**voaksissah
I've been stung.	**Olen saanut pistoksen.**	**oa**layn **saa**noot **pist**oaksayn
I've got something in my eye.	**Olen saanut jotain silmääni.**	**oa**layn **saa**noot **yoa**tahᶦn **sil**mǣni
I've got a/an ...	**Minulle on tullut ...**	**min**noollay oan **tool**loot
blister	**rakko**	**rahk**koa
boil	**paise**	**pah**ᶦsay
bruise	**mustelma**	**moost**aylmah
burn	**palo|haava**	**pahl**oa**haa**vah
cut	**(viilto|)haava**	(**veel**toa)**haa**vah
graze	**raapaisu/ veri|naarmu**	**raa**pahᶦsoo/**vay**rinaarmoo
insect bite	**hyönteisen purema**	h°°**urn**taysayn **poo**raymah
lump	**kyhmy**	**kewh**mew
rash	**ihottuma**	**ihh**oattoomah
sting	**pistos**	**pist**oass
swelling	**turvotusta**	**toor**voatoostah
wound	**haava**	**haa**vah
Could you have a look at it?	**Voisitteko katsoa sitä?**	**voa**ᶦsittaykoa **kaht**soah **sit**tæ
I can't move my ...	**En voi liikuttaa ...**	ayn voaᶦ **lee**koottaa
It hurts.	**Siihen koskee.**	**see**hayn **koas**kā̄y

Ilmoittautuminen	Reception
Seuraava!	Next!
Mihin koskee?	Where does it hurt?
Millaista kipua se on?	What kind of pain is it?
lievää/pistävää/tykyttävää	dull/sharp/throbbing
jatkuvaa/ajoittaista	constant/on and off
Se on . . .	It's . . .
murtunut/nyrjähtänyt	broken/sprained
pois sijoiltaan/revähtänyt	dislocated/torn
Täytyy ottaa röntgen|kuva.	I'd like you to have an X-ray.
Se täytyy laittaa kipsiin.	We'll have to put it in plaster.
Se on tulehtunut.	It's infected.
Oletteko saanut jäykkä|kouristus|rokotuksen?	Have you been vaccinated against tetanus?
Annan teille särky|lääkettä.	I'll give you a painkiller.

Illness *Tauti*

I'm not feeling well.	**En voi hyvin.**	ayn voaˈ **hew**vin
I'm ill.	**Olen sairas.**	**oa**layn sah'rahs
I feel . . .	**Minulla on . . .**	**min**noollah oan
dizzy	**huimausta**	hooˈmahᵒᵒstah
nauseous	**pahoin|vointia**	pahhoaˈnvoaˈntiah
shivery	**puistatuksia**	pooˈstahtooksiah
I have a temperature (fever).	**Minulla on kuu-metta.**	**min**noollah oan kōōmayttah
My temperature is 38 degrees.	**Minulla on 38 astetta kuumetta.**	**min**noollah oan 38 ahstayttah kōōmayttah
I've been vomiting.	**Olen oksentanut.**	**oa**layn **oak**sayntahnoot
I'm constipated/ I've got diarrhoea.	**Minulla on umme-tusta/ripuli.**	**min**noollah oan **oom**maytoostah/**rip**pooli
My . . . hurt(s).	**. . .-ni on kipeä.**	-ni oan **kip**payæ
I've got (a/an) . . .	**Minulla on . . .**	**min**noollah oan
asthma	**astma**	**ahst**mah
backache	**selkä|särkyä**	**sayl**kæsærkewæ

cold	nuha	noohah
cough	yskä	ewskæ
cramps	kouristuksia	koa°°ristooksiah
earache	korva|särky	koarvahsærkew
hay fever	heinä|nuha	hay'|nænoohah
headache	pään|särky	pænsærkew
indigestion	ruoan|sulatus|häiriö	r°°oahnsoolahtooshæiriur
nosebleed	veren|vuotoa nenästä	vayraynv°°oatoaah naynæstæ
palpitations	sydämen|tykytystä	sewdæmayntewkewtewstæ
rheumatism	reumatismi	ray°°mahtismi
sore throat	kurkku|kipu	koorkkookippoo
stiff neck	niska jäykkänä	niskah yæ°w'kkænæ
stomach ache	vatsa|kipuja	vahtsahkippooya
sunstroke	auringon|pisto	ah°°ringoanpistoa
I have difficulties breathing.	Minulla on hengitys|vaikeuksia.	minnoollah oan hayngittewsvah'kayooksiah
I have chest pains.	Minulla on rinta|kipuja.	minnoollah oan rintahkippooyah
I had a heart attack... years ago.	Minulla oli sydän|kohtaus... vuotta sitten.	minnoollah oali sewdænkoahtah°°ss... v°°attah sittayn
My blood pressure is too high/too low.	Veren|paineeni on liian korkea/matala.	vayraynpah'nǣyni oan leeahn koarkayah/mahtahlah
I'm allergic to...	Olen allerginen... -lle.	oalayn ahllayrgginnayn... -llay
I'm diabetic.	Minulla on sokeri-tauti	minnoollah oan soakayritah°°ti

Women's section *Naisten osasto*

I have period pains.	Minulla on kuukautis|kipuja.	minnoollah oan kookah°°tiskippooyah
I have a vaginal infection.	Minulla on emätin|tulehdus	minnoollah oan aymætintoolayhdooss
I'm on the pill.	Käytän ehkäisy|pillereitä.	kæ°w'tæn ayhkæisewpillayray'tæ
I haven't had a period for 2 months.	Minulla ei ole ollut kuukautisia 2:een kuukauteen.	minnoollah ay' oalay oalloot kookah°°tissiah kahtäyn kookah°°täyn
I'm (3 months) pregnant.	Olen (3:tta kuukautta) raskaana.	oalayn (koalmahttah kookah°°ttah) rahskaanah

Lääkäri

Kuinka kauan teillä on ollut näitä oireita?	How long have you been feeling like this?
Onko tämä teillä ensimmäistä kertaa?	Is this the first time you've had this?
Mittaan lämpönne/ veren|paineen.	I'll take your temperature/ blood pressure.
Käärikää hihanne, olkaa hyvä.	Roll up your sleeve, please.
Riisuuntukaa. (Riisukaa ylä|ruumis paljaaksi.)	Please undress (down to the waist).
Käykää makuulle tänne.	Please lie down over here.
Suu auki.	Open your mouth.
Hengittäkää syvään.	Breathe deeply.
Yskikää.	Cough, please.
Mihin koskee?	Where does it hurt?
Teillä on ...	You've got (a/an) ...
umpi|lisäkkeen tulehdus	appendicitis
rakko|tulehdus	cystitis
maha|katarri	gastritis
flunssa	flu
tulehtunut ...	inflammation of ...
ruoka|myrkytys	food poisoning
kelta|tauti	jaundice
keuhko|kuume	pneumonia
tuhka|rokko	measles
suku|puoli|tauti	venereal disease
Se ei ole tarttuvaa.	It's (not) contagious.
Se on allergiaa.	It's an allergy.
Annan teille ruiskeen.	I'll give you an injection.
Tarvitsen teiltä veri|/uloste|/ virtsa|näytteen.	I want a specimen of your blood/stools/urine.
Teidän täytyy pysyä vuoteessa ... **päivää.**	You must stay in bed for ... days.
Annan teille lähetteen erikois|lääkärille.	I want you to see a specialist.
Lähetän teidät sairaalaan yleis|tarkastukseen.	I want you to go to the hospital for a general check-up.

Prescription—Treatment *Lääke|määräys—Hoito*

This is my usual medicine.	Tavallisesti käytän tätä lääkettä.	tahvahllissaysti kæytæn tætæ lǣkayttæ
Can you give me a prescription for this?	Voitteko antaa minulle reseptin tätä varten?	voaˈttaykoa ahntaa minnoollay raysayptin tætæ vahrtayn
Can you prescribe a/an/some...?	Voitteko kirjoittaa reseptin... varten?	voaˈttaykoa keeryoaˈttaa raysayptin... vahrtayn
antidepressant sleeping pills tranquillizer	jotain piristävää uni|tabletteja jotain rauhoittavaa	yoataˈhn pirristævǣ oonitahblayttayyah yoataˈhn rahᵒᵒhoaˈttahvaa
I'm allergic to penicillin/certain antibiotics.	Olen allerginen penisilliinille/tiety-ille anti|biooteille.	oalayn ahllayrgginnayn paynissilleenillay/ tˈaytewˈllay ahnttibiōataillay
I don't want anything too strong.	En halua mitään vahvaa.	ayn hahlooah mittǣn vahvaa
How many times a day should I take it?	Montako kertaa päivässä minun pitää ottaa sitä?	moantahkoa kayrtaa pæivæssæ minnoon pittǣ oattaa sittæ
Must I swallow them whole?	Täytyykö ne niellä kokonaisina?	tæᵉʷtēwkur nay nˈayllæ koakoanahˈsinnah

---

🔊	🔊
Mitä hoitoa saatte?	What treatment are you having?
Mitä lääkkeitä otatte?	What medicine are you taking?
Ruiskeena vai suun kautta?	By injection or orally?
Ottakaa... tee|lusikallista tätä lääkettä...	Take... teaspoons of this medicine...
Ottakaa yksi pilleri vesi|lasillisen kanssa...	Take one pill with a glass of water...
joka...-s tunti	every... hours
... kertaa päivässä	... times a day
ennen ateriaa/aterian jälkeen	before/after each meal
aamulla/illalla	in the morning/at night
jos on kipuja	if there is any pain
... päivää	for... days

CHEMIST'S, see page 107

Fee *Maksu*

How much do I owe you?	**Paljonko olen vel-kaa?**	pah¹yoankoa oalayn tay¹llay vay¹kaa
May I have a receipt for my health insurance?	**Voinko saada kuitin sairaus|vakuutustani varten?**	voa¹nkoa saadah koo¹tin sah¹rah°°svahkōōtoostahni vahrtayn
Can I have a medical certificate?	**Voinko saada lääkärin|todistuksen?**	voa¹nkoa saadah lǣkǣrintoadistooksayn
Would you fill in this health insurance form, please?	**Täyttäisittekö tämän sairaus|vakuutus|lomakkeen.**	tæ°ʷttæissittaykur tæmæn sah¹rah°°svahkōōtoosloa mahkkāēn

Hospital *Sairaala*

Please notify my family.	**Ilmoittaisitteko perheelleni.**	ilmoa¹ttah¹sittaykoa payrhäʸllayni
What are the visiting hours?	**Mitkä ovat vierailu|ajat?**	mitkæ oavaht v¹ayrah¹looahyaht
When can I get up?	**Milloin voin nousta ylös?**	milloa¹n voa¹n noa°°stah ewlurs
When will the doctor come?	**Milloin lääkäri tulee?**	milloa¹n lǣkǣri toolāʸ
I'm in pain.	**Minulla on tuskia.**	minnoollah oan tooskiah
I can't eat/sleep.	**En voi syödä./En saa unta.**	ayn voa¹ s°ʷurdæ/ayn saa oontah
Where is the bell?	**Missä on soitto|kello?**	missæ oan soa¹ttoakaylloa

nurse	**hoitaja**	hoa¹tahyah
patient	**potilas**	poatillahs
anaesthetic	**puudutus|aine**	pōōdootoosah¹nay
blood transfusion	**veren|siirto**	vayraynseertoa
injection	**ruiske**	roo¹skay
operation	**leikkaus**	lay¹kkah°°s
bed	**vuode**	v°°oaday
bedpan	**alus|astia**	ahloosahstiah
thermometer	**lämpö|mittari**	læmpurmittahri

Dentist *Hammaslääkäri*

Can you recommend a good dentist?	**Voitteko suositella hyvää hammas|lääkäriä?**	voa'sittaykoa s°°asittayllah hewvǣ hahmmahslǣkæriæ
Can I make an appointment to see Dr... as soon as possible?	**Voinko päästä tohtori...-n vastaan|otolle?**	voa'nkoa pǣstæ toahtoari vahstaanoatoallay
Couldn't you make it earlier?	**Eikö löytyisi aikaisempaa aikaa?**	ay'kur lurᵉʷtew'si
I have a broken tooth.	**Minulta on murtunut hammas.**	minnooltah oan moortoonoot hahmmahs
I have toothache.	**Hammastani särkee.**	hahmmahstahni særkāy
I have an abscess.	**Minulla on märkä|pesäke.**	minnoollah oan mærkæpaysækay
This tooth hurts.	**Tätä hammasta särkee.**	tætæ hahmmahstah særkāy
at the top	**ylhäällä**	ewlhǣllæ
at the bottom	**alhaalla**	ahlhaallah
at the front	**edessä**	aydayssæ
at the back	**takana**	tahkahnah
Can you fix it temporarily?	**Voitteko paikata sen väli|aikaisesti?**	voa'ttaykoa pah'kahtah sayn væliah'kah'saysti
I don't want it pulled out.	**En halua, että se vedetään pois.**	ayn hahlooah ayttæ say vaydaytǣn poa'ss
Could you give me an anaesthetic?	**Voitteko antaa puudutuksen?**	voa'ttaykoa ahntaa pōōdootooksayn
I've lost a filling.	**Minulta on pudonnut paikka.**	minnooltah oan poodoannoot pah'kkah
My gums...	**Ikeneni...**	ikkaynayni
are very sore	**ovat hyvin arat**	oavaht hewvin ahraht
are bleeding	**vuotavat verta**	v°°oatahvaht vayrtah
I've broken my dentures.	**Hammas|proteesini on rikki.**	hahmmahsproatāysinni oan rikki
Can you repair my dentures?	**Voitteko korjata hammas|proteesini?**	voa'ttaykoa koaryahtah hahmmahsproatāysinni
When will they be ready?	**Milloin ne ovat valmiit?**	milloa'n nay oavaht vahlmeet

Reference section

Where do you come from? *Mistä olette kotoisin?*

Africa	**Afrikka**	ahfrikkah
Asia	**Aasia**	aassiah
Australia	**Australia**	ah°°straaliah
Europe	**Eurooppa**	ay°°rōappah
North America	**Pohjois-Amerikka**	poahyoaˈs-ahmayrikkah
South America	**Etelä-Amerikka**	aytaylæ-ahmayrikkah
Austria	**Itävalta**	itævahltah
Belgium	**Belgia**	baylgiah
Belorus	**Valkovenäjä**	vahlkoavaynæyæ
Canada	**Kanada**	kahnahdah
China	**Kiina**	keenah
Commonwealth of Independent States (CIS)	**Itsenäisten valtioiden yhteisö (IVY)**	itsaynæistayn vahltioaˈdayn ewhtayˈsur (IVY)
Denmark	**Tanska**	tahnskah
England	**Englanti**	aynglahnti
Estonia	**Viro**	virroa
Finland	**Suomi**	s°°oami
France	**Ranska**	rahnskah
Germany	**Saksa**	sahksah
Great Britain	**Iso-Britannia**	isoa-britahnniah
Greece	**Kreikka**	krayˈkkah
Ireland	**Irlanti**	eerlahnti
Italy	**Italia**	itahliah
Latvia	**Latvia**	lahtviah
Lithuania	**Liettua**	lᵃytttooah
Netherlands	**Hollanti**	hoallahnti
New Zealand	**Uusi-Seelanti**	ōosi-sāylahnti
Norway	**Norja**	noaryah
Portugal	**Portugali**	poartoogahli
Russia	**Venäjä**	vaynæyæ
Scotland	**Skotlanti**	skoatlahnti
Slovakia	**Slovakia**	sloavahkiah
South Africa	**Etelä-Afrikka**	eataylæ-ahfrikkah
Spain	**Espanja**	ayspahnyah
Sweden	**Ruotsi**	r°°oatsi
Switzerland	**Sveitsi**	svayˈtsi
Ukraine	**Ukraina**	ookrahˈnah
United States	**USA (Yhdys|vallat)**	ōōæssaa (ewhdewsvahllaht)
Wales	**Wales**	vayˈls

Numbers *Luvut*

0	nolla	noallah
1	yksi	ewksi
2	kaksi	kahksi
3	kolme	koalmay
4	neljä	naylyæ
5	viisi	veessi
6	kuusi	kōōssi
7	seitsemän	say'tsaymæn
8	kahdeksan	kahhdayksahn
9	yhdeksän	ewhdayksæn
10	kymmenen	kewmmaynayn
11	yksi|toista	ewksitoa'stah
12	kaksi|toista	kahksitoa'stah
13	kolme|toista	koalmaytoa'stah
14	neljä|toista	naylyætoa'stah
15	viisi|toista	veessitoa'stah
16	kuusi|toista	kōōssitoa'stah
17	seitsemän|toista	say'tsaymæntoa'stah
18	kahdeksan|toista	kahhdayksahntoa'stah
19	yhdeksän|toista	ewhdayksæntoa'stah
20	kaksi|kymmentä	kahksikewmmayntæ
21	kaksi|kymmentä|yksi	kahksikewmmayntæewksi
22	kaksi|kymmentä|kaksi	kahksikewmmayntækahksi
23	kaksi|kymmentä|kolme	kahksikewmmayntækoalmay
24	kaksi|kymmentä|neljä	kahksikewmmayntænaylyæ
25	kaksi|kymmentä|viisi	kahksikewmmayntæveessi
26	kaksi|kymmentä|kuusi	kahksikewmmayntækōōssi
27	kaksi|kymmentä|seitsemän	kahksikewmmayntæsay'tsaymæn
28	kaksi|kymmentä|kahdeksan	kahksikewmmayntækahhdayksahn
29	kaksi|kymmentä|yhdeksän	kahksikewmmayntæewhdayksæn
30	kolme|kymmentä	koalmaykewmmayntæ
31	kolme|kymmentä|yksi	koalmaykewmmayntæewksi
32	kolme|kymmentä|kaksi	koalmaykewmmayntækahksi
33	kolme|kymmentä|kolme	koalmaykewmmayntækoalmay
40	neljä|kymmentä	naylyækewmmayntæ
41	neljä|kymmentä|yksi	naylyækewmmayntæewksi
42	neljä|kymmentä|kaksi	naylyækewmmayntækahksi
43	neljä|kymmentä|kolme	naylyækewmmayntækoalmay
50	viisi|kymmentä	veessikewmmayntæ
51	viisi|kymmentä|yksi	veessikewmmayntæewksi
52	viisi|kymmentä|kaksi	veessikewmmayntækahksi
53	viisi|kymmentä|kolme	veessikewmmayntækoalmay
60	kuusi|kymmentä	kōōssikewmmayntæ
61	kuusi|kymmentä|yksi	kōōssikewmmayntæewksi
62	kuusi|kymmentä|kaksi	kōōssikewmmayntækahksi

63	kuusi|kymmentä|kolme	kōōssikewmmayntækoalmay
70	seitsemän|kymmentä	sayᵗtsaymænkewmmayntæ
71	seitsemän|kymmentä|yksi	sayᵗtsaymænkewmmayntæewksi
72	seitsemän|kymmentä|kaksi	sayᵗtsaymænkewmmayntækahksi
73	seitsemän|kymmentä|kolme	sayᵗtsaymænkewmmayntækoalmay
80	kahdeksan|kymmentä	kahdayksahnkewmmayntæ
81	kahdeksan|kymmentä|yksi	kahdayksahnkewmmayntæewksi
82	kahdeksan|kymmentä|kaksi	kahdayksahnkewmmayntækahksi
83	kahdeksan|kymmentä|kolme	kahdayksahnkewmmayntækoalmay
90	yhdeksän|kymmentä	ewhdayksænkewmmayntæ
91	yhdeksän|kymmentä|yksi	ewhdayksænkewmmayntæewksi
92	yhdeksän|kymmentä|kaksi	ewhdayksænkewmmayntækahksi
93	yhdeksän|kymmentä|kolme	ewhdayksænkewmmayntækoalmay

100	sata	sahtah
101	sata|yksi	sahtahewksi
102	sata|kaksi	sahtahkahksi
110	sata|kymmenen	sahtahkewmmaynayn
120	sata|kaksi|kymmentä	sahtahkahksikewmmayntæ
130	sata|kolme|kymmentä	sahtahkolmaykewmmayntæ
140	sata|neljä|kymmentä	sahtahnaylyækewmmayntæ
150	sata|viisi|kymmentä	sahtahveessikewmmayntæ
160	sata|kuusi|kymmentä	sahtahkōōssikewmmayntæ
170	sata|seitsemän|kymmentä	sahtahsayᵗtsaymænkewmmayntæ
180	sata|kahdeksan|kymmentä	sahtahkahhdayksahnkewmmayntæ
190	sata|yhdeksän|kymmentä	sahtahewhdayksænkewmmayntæ
200	kaksi|sataa	kahksisahtaa
300	kolme|sataa	koalmaysahtaa
400	neljä|sataa	naylyæsahtaa
500	viisi|sataa	veessisahtaa
600	kuusi|sataa	kōōssisahtaa
700	seitsemän|sataa	sayᵗtsaymænsahtaa
800	kahdeksan|sataa	kahhdayksahnsahtaa
900	yhdeksän|sataa	ewhdayksænsahtaa

1000	tuhat	toohaht
1100	tuhat sata	toohaht sahtah
1200	tuhat kaksi|sataa	toohaht kahksisahtaa
2000	kaksi|tuhatta	kahksitoohahttah
5000	viisi|tuhatta	veessitoohahttah

10,000	kymmenen|tuhatta	kewmmaynayntoohahttah
50,000	viisi|kymmentä|tuhatta	veessikewmmayntætoohahttah
100,000	sata|tuhatta	sahtahtoohahttah
1,000,000	miljoona	milyōānah
1,000,000,000	miljardi	milyahrdi

first	ensimmäinen	aynsimmæinayn
second	toinen	toa'nayn
third	kolmas	koalmahss
fourth	neljäs	naylyæss
fifth	viides	veedayss
sixth	kuudes	koodayss
seventh	seitsemäs	say'tsaymæss
eighth	kahdeksas	kahhdayksahs
ninth	yhdeksäs	ewhhdayksæs
tenth	kymmenes	kewmmaynayss
once/twice	kerran/kahdesti	kayrrahn/kahhdaysti
three times	kolme kertaa	koalmayah kayrtaa
a half	puolikas	p°°oalikkahs
half ...	puoli...-a	p°°oali...-ah
half of...	puolet...-sta	p°°oalayt...-stah
half (adj.)	puoli	p°°oali
a quarter/one third	neljännes (neljäs |osa)/kolmannes (kolmas|osa)	naylyænnays(naylyæsoa ssah)/koalmahnnays (koalmahsoassah)
a pair of	pari...-a	pahri
a dozen	tusina	toossinnah
one per cent	yksi prosentia	ewksi proasaynttiah
3.49%	3,49%	koalmay pilkkoo naylyæ kewmmayntæewh- dayksæn proasaynttiah
1981	tuhat yhdeksän- |sataa |kahdeksan- |kymmentä|yksi	toohaht ewhhdayksænsah- taakahhdayksahnkewm- mayntæewksi
1995	tuhat yhdeksän- |sataa|yhdeksän- |kymmentä|viisi	toohaht ewhhdayksænsah- taaewhdayksænkewm- mayntæveessi
2009	kaksi tuhatta- |yhdeksän	kahksi toohahttah ewhdayksæn

Year and age *Vuosi ja ikä*

year	vuosi	v°°oassi
leap year	karkaus|vuosi	kahrkah°°sv°°oassi
decade	vuosi|kymmen	v°°oassikewmmayn
century	vuosi|sata	v°°oassisahtah
this year	tämä vuosi	tæmæ v°°oassi
last year	viime vuosi	veemay v°°ooassi
next year	ensi vuosi	aynssi v°°oassi
each year	joka vuosi	yoakah v°°oassi
2 years ago	kaksi vuotta sitten	kahksi v°°oattah sittayn

in one year	**yhden vuoden kuluttua**	ewhdayn v°°oadayn kooloottooah
in the eighties	**kahdeksan-|kymmentä-|luvulla**	kahhdayksahnkewm-mayntæloovoollah
the 16th century	**1500-luku**	toohatveessisahtaalookoo
in the 20th century	**tuhat|yhdeksän-|sataa|luvulla**	toohahtewhdayksænsah-taaloovoollah
How old are you?	**Kuinka vanha olet(te)?**	koo'nkah vahnhah oalayt(tay)
I'm 30 years old.	**Ole 30 vuotias.**	oalayn koalmaykewm-mayntæ v°°oatiahss
He/She was born in 1960.	**Hän on syntynyt vuonna 1960.**	hæn oan sewntewnewt v°°oanah toohahtewh-dayksænsahtaakōōssi kewmmayntæ
What is his/her age?	**Minkä ikäinen hän on?**	minkæ ikæinayn hæn oan
Children under 16 are not admitted.	**Kielletty lapsilta alle 16.**	k'ayllayttew lahpsiltah ahl-lay kōōssitoa'stah

Seasons *Vuoden\|ajat*

spring/summer	**kevät/kesä**	kayvæt/kayssæ
autumn/winter	**syksy/talvi**	sewksew/tahlvi
in spring	**keväällä**	kayvællæ/kayssællæ
during the summer	**kesä|aikana**	kayssæah'kahanah
in autumn	**syksyllä**	sewksewllæ
during the winter	**talvi|aikana**	tahlviah'kaan
high season	**sesonki|aika**	saysoankiah'kah
low season	**hiljainen aika**	hillyah'nayn ah'kah

Months *Kuukaudet*

January	**tammi|kuu**	tahmmikkōō
February	**helmi|kuu**	haylmikōō
March	**maalis|kuu**	maalisskōō
April	**huhti|kuu**	hoohtikkōō
May	**touko|kuu**	toa°°koakōō
June	**kesä|kuu**	kayssækōō
July	**heinä|kuu**	hay'nækōō
August	**elo|kuu**	ayloakōō
September	**syys|kuu**	sēwskōō
October	**loka|kuu**	loakahkōō
November	**marras|kuu**	mahrrahskōō
December	**joulu|kuu**	yoa°°lookōō

in September	syys|kuussa	sēwskōossah
since October	loka|kuusta asti	loakahkōostah ahsti
the beginning of January	tammi|kuun alku	tahmmikkōōn ahlkoo
the middle of February	helmi|kuun puoli|väli	haylmikkōōn p°°oalivæli
the end of March	maalis|kuun loppu	maaliskōōn loappoo

Days and Date *Päivät ja päivämäärät*

What day is it today?	Mikä päivä tänään on?	mikkæ pæivæ tænǣn oan
Sunday	sunnuntai	soonnoontah[i]
Monday	maanantai	maanahntah[i]
Tuesday	tiistai	teestah[i]
Wednesday	keski|viikko	kayskiveekkoa
Thursday	torstai	toarstah[i]
Friday	perjantai	payryahntah[i]
Saturday	lauantai	lah°°ahntah[i]
It's...	Nyt on...	newt oan
July 1	ensimmäinen heinä|kuuta	aynsimmæ[i]nayn hay[i]næk°°tah
March 10	maalis|kuun kymmenes	maaliskōōn kewm maynayss
in the morning	aamulla	aamoollah
during the day	päivällä	pæ[i]vællæ
in the afternoon	ilta|päivällä	iltahpæ[i]vællæ
in the evening	illalla	illahllah
at night	yöllä	ew[w]llæ
the day before yesterday	toissa|päivänä	toa[i]ssahpæ[i]vænæ
yesterday	eilen	ay[i]layn
today	tänään	yænǣn
tomorrow	huomenna	h°°oamaynnah
the day after tomorrow	yli|huomenna	ewlih°°oamaynnah
the day before	edellisenä päivänä	aydayllisaynæ pæ[i]vænæ
the next day	seuraavana päivänä	say°°raavahnah pæ[i]vænæ
two days ago	kaksi päivää sitten	kahksi pæ[i]vǣ sittayn
in three days' time	kolmessa päivässä	koalmayssæ pæ[i]væssæ
last week	viime viikolla	veemay veekoallah
next week	ensi viikolla	aynsi veekoallah
for a fortnight (two weeks)	kahden viikon ajan	kahhdayn veekoan ahyahn
birthday	syntymä|päivä	sewntewmæpæ[i]væ
day off	vapaa|päivä	vahpaapæ[i]væ

holiday	loma|päivä	loamahpæʲvæ
holidays/vacation	loma	loamah
week	viikko	veekkoa
weekend	viikon|loppu	veekoanloappoo
working day	työ|päivä	tewᵘʳpæⁱvæ
on weekdays	arkisin	ahrkissin

Public holidays *Yleiset vapaa\|päivät*

January 1	uuden|vuoden |päivä	New Year's Day
May 1	vappu	Labour Day
December 6	itsenäisyys|päivä	National Day
December 24	joulu|aatto	Christmas Eve
December 25	joulu|päivä	Christmas Day
December 26	tapanin|päivä	St Stephen's Day

Greetings and wishes *Tervehdykset ja toivotukset*

Merry Christmas!	Hyvää Joulua!	hewvæ yoa°°looah
Happy New Year!	Onnellista Uutta Vuotta!	oannayllistah ōōttah v°°oattah
Happy Easter!	Iloista Pääsiäistä!	illoaⁱstah pǣsiæⁱstæ
Happy birthday!	Hyvää syntymä-|päivää!	hewvæ sewntewmæpæⁱ-vǣ
Best wishes	Parhain terveisin	pahrhahⁱn tayrvayⁱssin
Congratulations!	Onneksi olkoon!	oannayksi oalkōān
Good luck/All the best!	Onnea!	oannaea
Have a good trip!	Hauskaa matkaa!	hah°°skaa mahtkaa
Have a good holiday!	Hauskaa lomaa!	hah°°skaa loamaa
Best regards from ...	Terveisiä ...-lta.	tayrvayⁱsⁱæ ...-ltah
My regards to ...	Terveiset ...-lle.	tayrvayⁱsayt ...-llay

What time is it? *Mitä kello on?*

In Finland, for everyday speech people often prefer the 12-hour clock but in all official or even semi-official contexts the 24-hour clock is used.

| Excuse me. Can you tell me the time? | Anteeksi. Voitteko sanoa, mitä kello on? | ahntāȳksi voaⁱttaykoa sah-noah mittæ kaylloa oan |

It's...	Se on...	say oan
(exactly) one	(tasan) yksi	(tahsahn) ewksi
five past one	viittä yli yksi	veettæ ewli ewksi
ten past two	kymmentä yli kaksi	kewmmayntæ ewli kahksi
a quarter past three	neljännestä/vartin yli kolme	naylyænnaystæ/vahrtin ewli koalmay
twenty past four	kahta|kymmentä yli neljä	kahhtahkewmmayntæ ewli naylyæ
twenty-five past five	viittä vaille puoli kuusi	veettæ vah'llay pºoali kōōssi
half past six	puoli seitsemän	pºoali say'tsaymæn
twenty-five to seven	kahta|kymmentä-|viittä vaille seitsemän	kahhtahkewmmayntæveet-tæ vah'llay say'tsaymæn
twenty to eight	kahta|kymmentä vaille kahdeksan	kahhtahkewmmayntæ vah'llay kahhdayksahn
a quarter to nine	viisitoista minuuttia vaille yhdeksän	veesitoa'stah minoottiah vah'llay ewhhdayksæn
ten to ten	kymmentä vaille kymmenen	kewmmayntæ va'llay kewmmaynayn
five to eleven	viittä vaille yksi-|toista	veettæ vah'llay ewksitoa's-tah
twelve o'clock (noon/ midnight)	kaksitoista (keski-|päivällä/keski-|yöllä)	kahksitoa'stah (kayski-pæ'vællæ/kayskiew"llæ)
in the morning	aamulla	aamoollah
in the afternoon	päivällä	pæ'vællæ
in the evening	illalla	illahllah
The train leaves at ...	Juna lähtee kello...	yoonah læhtāȳ kaylloa
13.04 (1.04 p.m.)	kolme|toista nolla neljä	koalmaytoa'stah noallah naylyæ
0.40 (0.40 a.m.)	nolla neljä-|kymmentä	noallah naylyækewm-mayntæ
in five minutes	viiden minuutin päästä	veedayn minnōōtin pāēstæ
in a quarter of an hour	viidentoista minuutin kuluttua	veedayntoa'stah minōōtin koolōottooah
half an hour ago	puoli tuntia sitten	pºoali toontiah sittayn
about two hours	noin kaksi tuntia	noa'n kahksi toontiah
more than 10 minutes	yli 10 minuuttia	ewli kewmmaynayn minnōōttiah
less than 30 seconds	alle 30 sekunttia	ahllay koalmaykewm-mayntæ saykoonttiah
The clock is fast/ slow.	Kello edistää/jätät-tää	kaylloa aydistāē/yætættāē

Common abbreviations *Yleisiä lyhenteitä*

ap.	aamu|päivällä	a.m.
as.	asema	railway station
esim.	esi|merkiksi	for instance
fil. tri	filosofian tohtori	Ph.D.
Hki	Helsinki	Helsinki
HKL	Helsingin Kaupungin Liikenne |laitos	Helsinki Municipal Transport Company
hra	herra	Mr.
huom.	huomaa, huomautus	note
hv	hevos|voima(a)	horsepower
ip.	ilta|päivällä	p.m
J.K, P.S.	jälki|kirjoitus	postscript
jne.	ja niin edelleen	etc.
joht.	johtaja	director
klo	kello	o'clock
kpl	kappaletta	pieces
ks.	katso	see
lääket. tri	lääke|tieteen tohtori	MD/GP
mk	markka(a)	Finnish mark(s)
n.	noin	approximately
nro	numero	number
nti	neiti	Miss
os.	osoite	address
OY	osake|yhtiö	Ltd., Inc.
p	penni(ä)	penni (100 = 1 mark)
puh.	puhelin	telephone
pvm.	päivä|määrä	date
rva	rouva	Mrs.
s, ss.	sivu, sivut	page(s)
t, h	tunti(a)	hour(s)
v.	vuosi, vuonna	year
VP	vastausta pyydetään	RSVP
VR	Valtion Rauta|tiet	Finnish State Railways
YK	Yhdistyneet Kansa|kunnat	United Nations
ym.	ynnä muuta	etc.

Signs and notices *Kylttejä ja varoituksia*

Alas	Down
Alennus|myynti/Ale	Sale
Avoinna	Open
Älkää tukkiko sisään|käyntiä	Do not block entrance
Ei saa häiritä	Do not disturb
Ei saa koskea	Do not touch
Epä|kunnossa	Out of order
(Hengen|)vaara	Danger (of death)
Hissi	Lift
Hätä|/Vara|ulos|käytävä	Emergency exit
Kassa	Cash desk
... kielletty	... forbidden
Koputtamatta sisään	Enter without knocking
Kuuma	Hot
Kylmä	Cold
Loppuun|myyty	Sold out
Läpi|kulku (sakon uhalla) kielletty	Tresspassers will be prosecuted
Miehille	Gentlemen
Myydään	For sale
Naisille	Ladies
Neuvonta	Information
Odottakaa	Please wait
Pääsy kielletty	No admittance
Roskaaminen kielletty	No littering
Sisään(|käynti)	Entrance
Soitto|kello/Soittakaa	Please ring
Tupakointi kielletty	No smoking
Työnnä	Push
Täynnä	No vacancies
Ulos(|käynti)	Exit
Vapaa	Vacant
Vapaa pääsy	Free admittance
Varattu	Occupied/Reserved
Varo(kaa)	Caution
Varokaa koiraa	Beware of the dog
Vasta maalattu	Wet paint
Vedä	Pull
Vuokralle tarjotaan	To let
Vuokrataan	For hire
Yksityis|tie	Private road
Ylös	Up

Emergency *Hätä|tilanne*

Call the police.	Kutsukaa poliisi.	kootsookaa poaleesi
Consulate	Konsulaatti	koansoolaatti
DANGER!	VAARA!	vaarah
Embassy	Lähetystö	læhaytewstur
FIRE!	TULI|PALO!	toolipahloa
Gas	Kaasua	kaassooah
Get a doctor.	Hakekaa lääkäri.	hahkaykaa lǣkæri
Go away!	Menkää tiehenne!	maynkǣ t'aynaynnay
HELP!	APUA!	ahpooah
Get help quickly!	Hakekaa apua– nopeasti!	hahkaykaa ahpooah noapayahsti
I'm ill.	Olen sairas.	oalayn sah'rahs
I'm lost.	Olen eksynyt.	oalayn ayksewnewt
Leave me alone!	Jättäkää minut rauhaan!	yættækǣ minnoot rah°°haan
LOOK OUT!	VAROKAA!	vahroakaa
Poison	Myrkkyä	mewrkkewæ
POLICE!	POLIISI!	poaleesi
Stop that man/ woman!	Pysäyttäkää tuo mies/nainen!	pewsæ°wttækǣ t°°oa m'ays/nah'nayn
STOP THIEF!	OTTAKAA VARAS KIINNI!	oattahkaa vahrahs keenni

Emergency telephone numbers *Hätä|puhelin|numerot*

In Helsinki dial 000 to report police, fire and medical emergencies. In other towns, hotels and tourist offices keep lists of local emergency numbers.

Lost property—Theft *Kadonnut omaisuus—Varkaus*

Where's the ...?	Missä on ...?	missæ oan
lost property (lost and found) office	löytö|tavara- |toimisto	lur°wturtahvahrahtoa'- mistoa
police station	poliisi|asema	poaleesiahsaymah
I want to report a theft.	Tekisin ilmoituksen varkaudesta	taykissin ilmoa'tooksayn vahrkah°°daystah
My... has been stolen.	...-ni on varastettu	-ni oan vahrahstayttoo
I've lost my ...	Olen kadotta- nut...-ni.	oalayn kahdoattahnoot...-ni
handbag	käsi|laukku	kæssilah°°kkooni
passport	passi	pahssi
wallet	lompakko	loampahkkoa

CAR ACCIDENTS, see page 78

Conversion tables

Centimetres and inches

To change centimetres into inches, multiply by .39.

To change inches into centimetres, multiply by 2.54.

	in.	feet	yards
1 mm	0.039	0.003	0.001
1 cm	0.39	0.03	0.01
1 dm	3.94	0.32	0.10
1 m	39.40	3.28	1.09

	mm	cm	m
1 in.	25.4	2.54	0.025
1 ft.	304.8	30.48	0.304
1 yd.	914.4	91.44	0.914

(32 metres = 35 yards)

Temperature

To convert Centigrade into degrees Fahrenheit, multiply Centigrade by 1.8 and add 32.

To convert degrees Fahrenheit into Centigrade, subtract 32 from Fahrenheit and divide by 1.8.

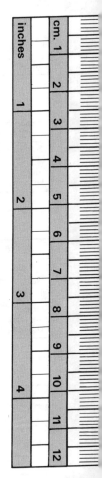

Kilometres into miles

1 kilometre (km.) = 0.62 miles

km.	10	20	30	40	50	60	70	80	90	100	110	120	130
miles	6	12	19	25	31	37	44	50	56	62	68	75	81

Miles into kilometres

1 mile = 1.609 kilometres (km.)

miles	10	20	30	40	50	60	70	80	90	100
km.	16	32	48	64	80	97	113	129	145	161

Fluid measures

1 litre (l.) = 0.88 imp. quart or 1.06 U.S. quart
1 imp. quart = 1.14 l.　　1 U.S. quart = 0.95 l.
1 imp. gallon = 4.55 l.　　1 U.S. gallon = 3.8 l.

litres	5	10	15	20	25	30	35	40	45	50
imp. gal.	1.1	2.2	3.3	4.4	5.5	6.6	7.7	8.8	9.9	11.0
U.S. gal.	1.3	2.6	3.9	5.2	6.5	7.8	9.1	10.4	11.7	13.0

Weights and measures

1 kilogram or kilo (kg.) = 1000 grams (g.)

100 g. = 3.5 oz.	½ kg. = 1.1 lb.
200 g. = 7.0 oz.	1 kg. = 2.2 lb.
1 oz. = 28.35 g.	
1 lb. = 453.60 g.	

CLOTHING SIZES, see page 114/YARDS AND INCHES, see page 111

Basic Grammar

Finnish, which belongs to the small Finno-Ugrian group of languages, is very different from English, Swedish or Russian, which all belong to the big Indo-European group of languages.*

Finnish uses many more suffixes (word endings) than is usual in European languages. Because of a certain melodic logic, the suffixes are not attached mechanically to words. Vowel harmony and some sound changes associated with inflexional suffixes, although quite regular, complicate the grammar.

Nouns

Finnish has no grammatical gender and no definite or indefinite article.

Finnish nouns can have four kinds of suffixes. They always follow the same order: number + case + possessive + particle.

To simplify presentation here, the sign = indicates a vowel which is the same as the nearest preceding vowel.

1. **Number:** If plural, then -**t** in the nominative case and -**i**- in other cases (between two vowels this plural -**i**- changes to -**j**-).

2. **Case:**

The cases used mainly as subject or object:

case	suffix	basic meaning	example	meaning
nominative	–, (pl. -**t**)	(basic form)	auto	a/the car
genitive	-**n**, (pl. -**en**, -**den**, -**ten**)	possession	auton	of the car
partitive	-**a**, -**ta**, -**tta**	indefinite quantity	autoa	(some) car

* Finnish is similar to some of the languages around the Gulf of Finland, Estonian being the most widely-spoken. The difference between Finnish and Hungarian, the most widely-spoken of Finno-Ugrian languages, is greater than that between Swedish and Italian.

The local cases:

inessive	-ssa	inside	autossa	in the car
elative	-sta	out of	autosta	out of the car
illative	-=n, -h=n, -seen, -siin	into	autoon	into the car
adessive	-lla	on	autolla	at the car
ablative	-lta	off	autolta	from the car
allative	-lle	onto	autolle	to the car

The cases expressing a state:

essive	-na	in a state	autona	as a car
translative	-ksi	into a state	autoksi	to (become) a car

There are another *three* cases in Finnish but these are rarely used.

Cases are used in many other ways in Finnish and this is just the briefest outline of their use with nouns.

3. **Possessive:** Instead of possessive determiners ('my', 'your' etc.) Finnish uses the genitive forms of the personal pronouns (see table). These are not always necessary, because possessive suffixes indicate the owner.

	singular			plural		
1st person	-ni	autoni	my car	-mme	automme	our car
2nd person	-si	autosi	your car	-nne	autonne	your car
3rd person	-nsa	autonsa	his/her car	-nsa	autonsa	their car

4. **Particle:** Some particles are added to words as suffixes. The most important of these is -**ko** which is used to form direct questions. The question word (usually a verb) appears first in the sentence e.g:

Tuletko?   Are you coming?
Autollako tulet?   Are you coming by car?

Other common suffix particles are **-kin** ('also/too') and **-kaan** ('also' in negative sentences), e.g. Minä**kin**! 'Me too!'

Suffixes are also added to pronouns, adjectives, numbers and some forms of verbs. As attributes these almost always agree with the headword in number and case.

Personal pronouns

You will notice that Finnish has only one word for 'he' and 'she' - **hän**.

subject			object		possessive	
nominative			accusative	partitive	genitive	
I	**minä**	me	**minut**	**minua**	mine	**minum**
you	**sinä**	you	**sinut**	**sinua**	yours	**sinum**
he/she	**hän**	him/her	**hänet**	**häntä**	his/hers	**hänen**
we	**me**	us	**meidät**	**meitä**	ours	**meidän**
you	**te**	you	**teidät**	**teitä**	yours	**teidän**
they	**he**	them	**heidät**	**heitä**	theirs	**heidän**

The 2nd person plural (**te**) is also used as a polite singular 'you' form. When using this form, verbs and suffixes must of course be in the plural form that corresponds to **te**.

Verbs

Subject pronouns in the 1st and 2nd person are often omitted (sometimes also in the 3rd person), because the ending of the verb is enough to indicate the subject. The verb endings are:

I	**-n**	we	**-mme**
you	**-t**	you	**-tte**
he/she	two vowels*	they	**-vat**

* the last vowel of the stem is doubled, if it is not the second vowel of a long vowel or a diphthong.

To form the negative in Finnish a special *verb* is used. This negative verb inflects according to the subject of the sentence just like any other verb. The 'action' verb does not change. This construction is similar to the way 'do not, does not' are used as a negative auxiliary in English.

I	**en**	we	**emme**
you	**et**	you	**ette**
he/she	**ei**	they	**eivät**

Verbs in Finnish can be divided into four groups for inflection:

Present tense:

	ostaa (to buy)	tuoda (to bring)	tulla (to come)	pelata (to play)
I	ostan	tuon	tulen	pelaan
you	ostat	tuot	tulet	pelaat
he/she/it	ostaa	tuo	tulee	pelaa
we	ostamme	tuomme	tulemme	pelaamme
you	ostatte	tuotte	tulette	pelaatte
they	ostavat	tuovat	tulevat	pelaavat

Present tense negative:

I	en osta	en tuo	en tule	en pelaa
you	et osta	et tuo	et tule	et pelaa
he/she/it	ei osta	ei tuo	ei tule	ei pelaa
we	emme osta	emme tuo	emme tule	emme pelaa
you	ette osta	ette tuo	ette tule	ette pelaa
they	eivät osta	eivät tuo	eivät tule	eivät pelaa

Past tense:

The ending for the past tense is **-i-**. It causes many vowel and consonant changes.

I	ostin	toin	tulin	pelasin
you	ostit	toit	tulit	pelasit
he/she/it	osti	toi	tuli	pelasi
we	ostimme	toimme	tulimme	pelasimme
you	ostitte	toitte	tulitte	pelasitte
they	ostivat	toivat	tulivat	pelasivat

Irregular verbs

olla (to be)			
Present tense		Present tense negative	Past tense
I am	(minä) olen	en ole	I was	olin
you are	(sinä) olet	et ole	you were	olit
he/she is	hän on	hän ei ole	he/she was	hän oli
it is	se on	se ei ole	it was	se oli
we are	(me) olemme	emme ole	we were	olimme
you are	(te) olette	ette ole	you were	olitte
they are	he ovat	he eivät ole	they were	he olivat

The personal pronouns in brackets are used for emphasis only. Normally they are required only with the 3rd person singular and plural forms.

To have

There is no corresponding verb for 'to have' in Finnish. Instead the possessor appears in the adessive case combined with the 3rd person singular of the verb **olla** (to be) in the appropriate tense:

I have a card.	**Minu*lla* on kortti.**
Do you have money?	**On*ko* sinu*lla*/teil*lä* rahaa?**
He does not have time.	**Hänel*lä* ei ole aikaa.**
We had fun.	**Meil*lä* oli hauskaa.**
They have had fun.	**Heil*lä* on ollut hauskaa.**

Some adverbs of place

Missä?	Where?	Mistä?	From where?	Minne?	Where to?
siellä	there (place mentioned before)	sieltä	from there	sinne	(in) there
täällä	here	täältä	from there	tänne	(in) here
tuoola	there (place pointed to)	tuolta	from there	tuonne	(in) there

Dictionary
and alphabetical index

English-Finnish

itr intransitive   *tr* transitive

A

abbey luostari 80
abbreviation lyhennys 154
about *(approximately)* noin 153
above yllä, yli 15; yläpuolella 63
abscess märkäpesäke 145
absorbent cotton vanu 108
accept, to ottaa 61; hyväksyä 102
accessories asusteet 115; lisälaitteet 125
accident onnettomuus 78, 139
account tili 130
ache särky 141
adaptor adapteri, sovitin 118
address osoite 21, 31, 76, 79, 102
address book osoitekirja 104
adhesive liima 104, 105
adhesive tape teippi 104
admission (sisään)pääsy 82, 90, 155
admitted päästää sisään 150
Africa Afrikka 146
after jälkeen 15, 77
after-shave lotion partavesi 109
afternoon, in the iltapäivällä 151, 153
again uudelleen 96, 136
against vastaan 140
age ikä 149, 150
ago sitten 149, 151
air bed ilmapatja 106
air conditioning ilmastointi 23, 28
air mattress ilmapatja 106
airmail lentoposti 132
airplane lentokone 65
airport lentokenttä 16, 21; lentoasema 65
aisle seat käytävä-paikka 65
alarm clock herätyskello 121
alcohol alkoholi 37, 58
alcoholic alkoholi 58
all kaikki 103
allergic allerginen 141, 143

almond manteli 53
alphabet aakkoset 9
also myös 15
alter, to *(garment)* korjata 114
altitude sickness lentopahoinvointi 107
amazing hämmästyttävä 83
amber meripihka 122
ambulance ambulanssi 79
American amerikkalainen 93, 105, 126
American plan täysihoito 24
amethyst ametisti 122
amount summa 61, 131
amplifier vahvistin 118
anaesthetic puudutusaine 144; puudutus 145
analgesic kipua lievittävä 108
anchovy anjovis 44
and ja 15
animal eläin 85
aniseed anis 51
ankle nilkka 139
anorak anorakki 115
another toinen 56, 123
answer vastaus 136
antibiotic antibiootti 143
antidepressant piristävä lääke 143
antique shop antiikkikauppa 98
antiques antiikki 83
antiseptic cream antiseptinen voide 108
any yhtään 14
anyone kukaan 12, 16
anything mitään 17, 25, 101, 112
anywhere jossain, missään 89
apartment huoneisto 23
aperitif aperitiivi 58
appendicitis umpilisäkkeen tulehdus 142
appendix umpilisäke 138
appetizer alkuruoka 41

apple omena 53, 63, 119
apple juice omenamehu 59
appliance koje 118
appointment sovittu tapaaminen 131; aika 137; vastaanotto 145
apricot aprikoosi 52
April huhtikuu 150
archaeology arkeologia 83
architect arkkitehti 83
area code suuntanumero 134
arm käsivarsi 138, 139
around (approximately) suunnilleen 31
arrangement (set price) sopimus 20
arrival saapuvat 65
arrive, to olla perillä 65; saapua 68, 70; tulla 130
art taide 83
art gallery taidegalleria 80, 98
artichoke artisokka 49
article tavara 101
artificial keino 124
artificial light keinovalo 124
artist taiteilija 81, 83
ashtray tuhkakuppi 36
Asia Aasia 146
ask for, to pyytää 25, 60
asparagus parsa 49
aspirin aspiriini 108
asthma astma 140
astringent kasvovesi 109
at kohdalla 15
at least vähintään 24
at once heti 31
aubergine munakoiso 49
August elokuu 150
aunt täti 93
Australia Australia 146
Austria Itävalta 146
automatic automaatti 20, 122, 124
autumn syksy 150
average keskinkertainen 91
awful kaamea 84, 94

B
baby pikkulapsi 25; vauva 110
baby food vauvan ruoka 110
babysitter lapsenvahti 27
back selkä 138
back, to be/to get tulla takaisin 21, 80; palata 136
backache selkäsärky 140
bacon pekoni 40

bacon and eggs pekonia ja munia 40
bad huono 14; kehno 95
bag laukku 18; kassi 103
baggage matkatavara 18, 26, 31, 71
baggage cart (työntö)kärry 18, 70
baggage check matkatavarasäilytys 67, 71
baggage locker säilytyslokero 18, 67, 70
baked uunissa paistettu 45, 47
baker's leipomo 98
balance (finance) saldo 131
balcony parveke 24
ball (inflated) pallo 128
ball-point pen kuulakärkikynä 104
ballet baletti 87
banana banaani 52, 63
Band-Aid ® laastari 108
bandage side 108
bangle rannerengas 121
bangs otsatukka 30
bank (finance) pankki 98, 129, 130
banknote seteli 130
bar (room) baari 33
barber's parturi 30, 98
basil basilika 51
basketball koripallo 89
bath kylpyhuone 24, 25, 27
bath salts kylpysuola 109
bath towel kylpypyyhe 27
bathing cap uimalakki 115
bathing hut uimakoppi 90
bathing suit uimapuku 115
bathrobe kylpytakki 115
bathroom kylpyhuone 27
battery akku 75, 78; paristo 118, 121, 125
be, to olla 163
beach ranta 90
beach ball rantapallo 128
bean papu 49
beard parta 31
beautiful kaunis 14, 83
beauty salon kauneushoitola 30, 98
bed sänky 24; vuode 28, 142, 144
bed and breakfast (yösija) aamiaisen kanssa 25
bedpan alusastia 144
beef naudanliha 46
beer olut 55, 63
beet(root) punajuuri 49
before (time) ennen 15
begin, to alkaa 80, 86
beginner aloittelija 91
beginning alku 150

behind takana, taakse 15, 77
beige beige 112
Belgium Belgia 146
bell (electric) soittokello 144
below alla, alle 15
belt vyö 116
berth makuupaikka 69; vuodepaikka 70
better parempi 14, 25, 101
between välissä, välillä 15
bicycle (polku)pyörä 74
big suuri 14; iso 101, 117
bilberry mustikka 53
bill lasku 28, 31, 61, 102
bill (banknote) seteli 130
billion (Am.) miljardi 148
binoculars kiikari 123
bird lintu 85
birth syntymä 26
birthday syntymäpäivä 151, 152
biscuit (Br.) keksi 63
bitter kitkerä 61
black musta 112
black and white (film) mustavalkoinen 124, 125
black coffee kahvi mustana 40, 60
blackcurrant musta viinimarja 53
bladder virtsarakko 138
blade terä 109
blanket peitto 27
bleed, to vuotaa verta 139, 145
blind (window shade) kaihdin 29
blister rakko 139
blocked tukossa 29
blood veri 142
blood pressure verenpaine 141, 142
blood transfusion verensiirto 144
blouse pusero 115
blow-dry föönaus 30
blue sininen 112
blueberry mustikka 53
blusher poskipuna 109
boat vene, lautta, alus 73, 74
bobby pin hiusneula 110
body ruumis 138
boil paise 139
boiled keitetty 47
boiled egg keitetty muna 40
bone luu 138
book kirja 12, 104
booking office lippumyymälä 19; lipunmyynti 67
bookshop kirjakauppa 98, 104
boot saapas 117
boring ikävystyttävä 83

born syntynyt 150
botanical gardens kasvitieteellinen puutarha 80
botany kasvitiede 83
bottle pullo 17, 57
bottle-opener pullonavaaja 120
bottom alaosa 145
bow tie rusetti 115
bowel suoli 138
boxing nyrkkeily 89
boy poika 111, 128
boyfriend poikaystävä 93
bra rintaliivit 115
bracelet rannekoru 121
braces (suspenders) henkselit 115
braised haudutettu 47
brake jarru 78
brake fluid jarruneste 75
brandy konjakki 58
bread leipä 36, 40, 63
break down, to mennä epäkuntoon 78
break, to mennä rikki 29, 118, 123; murtua 139, 145
breakdown konerikko 78
breakdown van hinausauto 78
breakfast aamiainen 24, 27, 40
bream lahna 44
breast rinta 138
breathe, to hengittää 141, 142
bridge silta 85
bring down, to tuoda alas 31
bring, to tuoda 13, 57
British britti 93
broiled (Am.) grillattu 47
broken rikki 118, 123; murtunut 139, 140
brooch rintakoru 121
brother veli 93
brown ruskea 112
bruise mustelma 139
brush harja 110
Brussels sprouts ruusukaali 49
bubble bath kylpyvaahto 109
bucket ämpäri 120, 128
buckle solki 116
build, to rakentaa 83
building rakennus 81, 83
building blocks/bricks rakennuspalikat 128
bulb (light) lamppu 29, 75, 118
burn palohaava 139
burn out, to (bulb) palaa (loppuun) 29
bus bussi 18, 19, 65, 72, 80
bus stop bussipysäkki 72, 73
business liikeasia 16; liike- 130

business class business-luokka 65
business district liikekeskus 81
business trip liikematka 94
busy (muussa) puuhassa 96
but mutta 15
butane gas butaani, nestekaasu 32, 106
butcher's lihakauppa 98
butter voi 36, 40, 64
button nappi 29, 116
buy, to ostaa 82, 100, 104, 123

C

cabana uimakoppi 91
cabbage kaali 49
cabin (ship) hytti 74
cable sähke 133
cable release lankalaukaisin 125
café kahvio, kahvila 33
cake kakku 37, 54, 63
calculator laskin 104
calendar kalenteri 104
call (phone) puhelu 134, 136
call back, to soittaa takaisin 136
call, to (give name) nimittää 11
call, to (phone) soittaa 134, 136
call, to (summon) kutsua 78, 156
calm tyyni 90
cambric hieno palttina 113
camel-hair kamelinkarva 113
camera kamera 124, 125
camera case kameralaukku 125
camera shop valokuvausliike 98
camp site leirintäalue 32
camp, to leiriytyä 32
campbed telttasänky 106
camping leirintä 32
camping equipment leirintävarusteet 106
can (be able to) voida 12
can (container) purkki, tölkki 119
can opener purkinavaaja 120
Canada Kanada 146
Canadian kanadalainen 93
cancel, to peruuttaa 65
candle kynttilä 120
candy makeinen 126
candy store makeiskauppa 98
cap lakki 115
capers kapris 51
capital (finance) pääoma 131
car auto 19, 20, 32, 75, 78
car hire auton vuokraus 20

car mechanic (auton)korjaaja 78
car park pysäköintialue 77
car racing kilpa-ajot 89
car radio autoradio 118
car rental auton vuokraus 20
carat karaatti 121
caravan asuntovaunu 32
caraway kumina 51
carbon paper hiilipaperi 104
carbonated (fizzy) hiilihapollinen 59
carburettor kaasutin 78
card kortti 131
card game korttipeli 128
cardigan neuletakki, villatakki 115
carrot porkkana 49
carry, to kantaa 21
cart (työntö)kärry 18
carton (of cigarettes) kartonki 17, 126
cartridge (camera) kasetti 124
case kotelo 123; laukku 125
cash desk kassa 103, 155
cash, to vaihtaa rahaksi 130; lunastaa 133
cassette kasetti 118, 127
cassette recorder kasettinauhuri 118
castle linna 81
catacombs katakombit 81
catalogue luettelo 82
cathedral tuomiokirkko 81
Catholic katolinen 84
cauliflower kukkakaali 49
caution varo 155
cave luola 81
celery selleri 49
cemetery hautausmaa 81
centimetre senttimetri 111
centre keskusta 19, 21, 76, 81
century vuosisata 149
ceramics keramiikka 83
cereal hiutaleita 40
certificate todistus 144
chain (jewellery) ketju 121
chain bracelet rannekoru 121
chair tuoli 106
chamber music kamarimusiikki 128
change (money) vaihtoraha 62, 130; kolikoita 77
change, to vaihtaa 60, 68, 73, 75, 123; muuttaa 25
change, to (money) vaihtaa 18, 130
chapel kappeli 81
charcoal grillihiili 106
charge maksu 20, 32, 77, 89, 136
charge, to veloittaa 25, 130
charm (trinket) amuletti 121

charm bracelet ranneketju 121
cheap halpa 14, 101
cheaper halvempi 24, 25, 101
check *(money)* shekki 130, 131
check *(restaurant)* lasku 61
check in, to *(airport)* ilmoittautua (lähtöön) 65
check out, to lähteä (ilmoittautua lähteväksi) 31
check, to tarkistaa 75, 123
check, to *(luggage)* lähettää matkatavara 71
check-up *(medical)* tarkastus 142
cheers! kippis 56
cheese juusto 51, 64
chemist's apteekki 98, 107
cheque shekki 130, 131
cherry kirsikka 52
chervil kirveli 51
chess set shakkipeli 128
chest rintakehä 138, 141
chestnut kastanja 52
chewing gum purukumi 126
chewing tobacco purutupakka 126
chicken kana 48, 62
chicken breast kanan rinta 48
chicory endive 49
chiffon shifonki 113
child lapsi 24, 60, 82, 93, 139, 150
children's doctor lastenlääkäri 137
China Kiina 146
chips ranskalaiset perunat 62; perunalastut 63
chives ruoholaukka 51
chocolate suklaa 64, 119, 126
chocolate *(hot)* kaakao 40, 60
chocolate bar suklaapatukka 64
choice valinta 39
chop *(meat)* kyljys 46
Christmas joulu 152
chromium kromi 122
church kirkko 81, 84
cigar sikaari 126
cigarette savuke 17, 95, 126; tupakka 121
cigarette case savukekotelo 121, 126
cigarette holder imuke 126
cigarette lighter (tupakan) sytytin 121, 126
cinema elokuva 86, 96
cinnamon kaneli 51
circle *(theatre)* parveke 87
city kaupunki 81
city centre kaupungin keskusta 81
classical klassinen 128

clean puhdas 61
clean, to puhdistaa 29, 76
cleansing cream puhdistusvoide 109
cliff jyrkänne 85
cloakroom vaatesäilö 89
clock kello 121; aika 153
clock-radio kelloradio 118
close, to sulkea *tr* 11, 82, 107, 132
closed suljettu 155
clothes vaatteet 29, 115
clothes peg/pin pyykkipoika 120
clothing vaatetus 111
cloud pilvi 94
clove mausteneilikka 51
coach *(bus)* linja-auto 71
coast rannikko 85
coat takki 115
coconut kookospähkinä 52
cod turska 44
coffee kahvi 40, 60, 64
coin (metalli)raha 83
cold kylmä 14, 25, 40, 61, 94, 155
cold *(illness)* vilustuminen 107, 141
cold cuts leikkeleet 64
collar kaulus 116
collect call vastaanottaja maksaa-puhelu 134
colour väri 103, 111, 124, 125
colour chart värikartta 30
colour rinse värihuuhtelu 30
colour shampoo värishampoo 110
colour slide väridia 124
colourfast väriäpäästämätön 113
comb kampa 110
come, to tulla 36, 92, 95, 137, 144, 146
comedy komedia 86
commission *(fee)* välityspalkkio 130
common *(frequent)* yleinen 154
compact disc CD-levy 127
compartment *(train)* vaunuosasto 70
compass kompassi 106
complaint valitus 60
concert konsertti 87
concert hall konserttisali, talo 81, 88
condom kondomi 108
conductor *(orchestra)* kapellimestari 88
confectioner's makeiskauppa 98
conference room kokoushuone 24
confirm, to vahvistaa 65
confirmation vahvistus 23
congratulation onnittelu 152
connection *(transport)* yhteys 65, 67
constipation ummetus 140
consulate konsulaatti 156

contact lens kontaktilinssi 123
contagious tarttuva 142
contain, to sisältää 37
contraceptive ehkäisyväline 108
contract sopimus 131
control tarkastus 16
convent nunnaluostari 81
cookie keksi 64
cool box kylmäkassi 106
copper kupari 122
coral koralli 122
corduroy vakosametti 113
corn *(Am.)* maissi 49
corn *(foot)* liikavarsi 108
corn plaster liikavarvaslaastari 108
corner kulma 21, 77; nurkka 36
cosmetics kosmetiikka 109
cost kustannukset 131, 136
cost, to maksaa 11, 80, 133
cot lapsen sänky 24
cotton puuvilla 113
cotton wool vanu 108
cough yskä 107, 141
cough drops yskänlääke 108
cough syrup yskänlääke 108
cough, to yskiä 142
counter luukku 133
country maa 93, 146
countryside maaseutu 85
courgette munakoiso 49
court house oikeustalo 81
cousin serkku 93
cracker voileipäkeksi 64
cramp kouristus 141
crayfish *(river)* rapu 44
crayon värikynä 104
cream kerma 60
cream *(toiletry)* voide 109
crease resistant rypistymätön 113
credit luotto 130
credit card luottokortti 20, 31, 62, 102, 130
crepe kreppi 113
crockery astiat 120
cross risti 121
cross-country skiing murtomaahiihto 91
crossing *(maritime)* ylitys 74
crossroads tienhaara 77
cruise risteily 73
crystal kristalli 122
cucumber kurkku 49
cuff link kalvosinnappi 121
cuisine keittiö 34
cup kuppi 36, 60, 120

curler papiljotti 110
currency valuutta 129
currency exchange office valuutanvaihto(toimisto) 18, 67, 129
current virtaus 90
curtain verho 29
customs tulli 16, 102
cut *(wound)* (viilto)haava 139
cut glass hiottu lasi 122
cut off, to *(interrupt)* mennä poikki 135
cut, to *(with scissors)* leikata 30
cuticle remover kynsinauhavesi 109
cutlery ruokailuvälineet 120, 121
cutlet kotletti 46
cycling pyöräily 89
cystitis rakkotulehdus 142

D
dairy maitokauppa 98
dance tanssi 88, 96
dance, to tanssia 88, 96
danger vaara 155, 156
dangerous vaarallinen 90
dark pimeä 25; tumma 101, 111, 112
date *(appointment)* treffit 95
date *(day)* päivä 26; päivämäärä 151
date *(fruit)* taateli 53
daughter tytär 93
day päivä 20, 25, 80, 94, 150, 151
day off vapaapäivä 151
daylight päivänvalo 124
decade vuosikymmen 149
decaffeinated kafeiinitonta 40, 60
December joulukuu 150
decision päätös 25, 102
deck *(ship)* kansi 74
deck chair kansituoli 90
declare, to *(customs)* ilmoittaa tullattavaksi 17
deep syvä 142
degree *(temperature)* aste 140
delay myöhässä 68
delicatessen herkkumyymälä 98
delicious herkullinen 62
deliver, to toimittaa 102
delivery toimitus 102
denim farkkukangas 113
Denmark Tanska 146
dentist hammaslääkäri 98, 145
denture hammasproteesi 145
deodorant deodorantti 109
department *(museum)* osasto 83
department *(shop)* osasto 100

department store tavaratalo 98
departure lähtö 65
deposit *(down payment)* ennakkomaksu 20; *(bank)* pano 130
dessert jälkiruoka 37, 54
diabetic diabeetikko 37; sokeritautinen 141
dialling code suuntanumero 134
diamond timantti 122
diaper vaippa 110
diarrhoea ripuli 140
dictionary sanakirja 104
diesel dieselöljy 75
diet dieetti 37
difficult vaikea 14
difficulty vaikeus 28, 102, 141
digital digitaali 122
dill tilli 51
dining car ravintolavaunu 66, 68, 71
dining room ruokasali 28
dinner päivällinen 34, 95
direct suora 65
direct, to opastaa 13
direction suunta 76
director *(theatre)* ohjaaja 86
directory *(phone)* puhelinluettelo 134
disabled vammainen 82
disc kiekko 77; levy 127
discotheque disko 88, 96
discount alennus 131
disease tauti 142
dish ruokalaji 36
disinfectant desinfiointiaine 108
dislocated pois sijoiltaan 140
display case esittelyteline 100
dissatisfied tyytymätön 103
district *(of town)* alue 81
disturb, to häiritä 155
dizzy huimaus 140
doctor lääkäri 79, 137, 144, 145
doctor's office lääkärin vastaanotto 137
dog koira 155
doll nukke 128
dollar dollari 18, 102, 130
door ovi 155
double bed kaksoisvuode 23
double room kahden hengen huone 19, 23
down alhaalla, alas 15
downhill skiing laskettelu 91
downtown keskusta 81
dozen tusina 149
drawing paper piirustuspaperi 104

drawing pins piirustusneuloja 104
dress leninki 115
dressing gown aamutakki 115
drink juoma 55, 59, 60, 61, 95
drink, to juoda 35, 36, 37
drinking water juomavesi 32
drip, to tippua 28
drive, to ajaa 21, 76
driving licence ajokortti 20, 79
drop *(liquid)* tippa 108
drugstore apteekki 98, 107
dry kuiva 30, 57, 110
dry cleaner's pesula 29, 98
dry shampoo kuivashampoo 110
duck ankka 48
dummy *(baby's)* tutti 110
during aikana 15, 150
duty *(customs)* tulli 17
duty-free shop verovapaa myymälä 19
dye värjäys 30; hiusväri 110

E
each joka 149
ear korva 138
ear drops korvatipat 108
earache korvasärky 141
early *(a)* aikainen 14; aikaisin 31
earring korvakoru 121
east itä 77
Easter pääsiäinen 152
easy helppo 14
eat, to syödä 36, 37, 144
eel ankerias 44
egg muna 40, 64
eggplant munakoiso 49
eight kahdeksan 147
eighteen kahdeksantoista 147
eighth kahdeksas 149
eighty kahdeksankymmentä 148
elastic elastinen, kimmo 108
elastic bandage kimmoside, ideaaliside 108
electric(al) sähkö 118
electrical appliance sähkökoje 118
electrical goods shop sähköliike 98
electricity sähkö 32
electronic elektroninen 128
elevator hissi 28, 100
eleven yksitoista 147
embarkation point laivaan nousukohta 73
embassy lähetystö 156
emerald smaragdi 122

DICTIONARY

emergency hätä 156
emergency exit hätäuloskäynti 28, 99
emery board hiekkapaperiviila 109
empty tyhjä 14
enamel emali 122
end loppu 150
engaged (phone) varattu 136
engagement ring kihlasormus 122
engine (car) moottori 78
England Englanti 134, 146
English englantilainen 93, 126
English (language) englanti 11, 16, 80, 82, 84, 104, 105
enjoy oneself, to pitää hauskaa 96
enjoyable viihtyisä 31
enlarge, to suurentaa 125
enough tarpeeksi 14, 68
entrance sisään(käynti) 67, 99, 155
entrance fee pääsymaksu 82
envelope kirjekuori 104
equipment varusteet 90, 91, 106
eraser pyyhekumi 104
estimate (cost) (kustannus)arvio 78, 131
Estonia Viro 146
Eurocheque euroshekki 130
Europe Eurooppa 146
evening ilta 95, 96
evening dress iltapuku 88
evening dress (woman's) iltapuku 115
evening, in the illalla 151, 153
every joka 143
everything kaikki 31, 61
examine, to tutkia 137
exchange rate vaihtokurssi 18, 130
exchange, to vaihtaa 103
excursion retki 80
excuse me anteeksi 11, 152
excuse, to antaa anteeksi 11
exercise book kirjoitusvihko 104
exhaust pipe pakoputki 78
exhibition näyttely 81
exit ulos(käynti) 67, 99, 155
expect, to odottaa 130
expenses kulut 131
expensive kallis 14, 19, 25, 101
exposure (photography) kuva 124, 125
exposure counter kuvalaskuri 125
express pika 132
expression ilmaisu 10, 100
expressway moottoritie 76
extension (phone) alanumero 135
extension cord/lead jatkojohto 118
extra lisä 27
eye silmä 138, 139

eye drops silmätipat 108
eye shadow luomiväri 109
eye specialist silmälääkäri 137
eyebrow pencil kulmakynä 109
eyesight näkö 123

F
fabric (cloth) kangas 112
face kasvot 138
face pack kasvonaamio 30
face powder kasvopuuteri 109
factory tehdas 81
fair messut, markkinat 81
fall (autumn) syksy 150
fall, to kaatua 139
family perhe 93, 144
fan belt tuulettimen hihna 75
far kaukana 14, 100
fare (ticket) maksu 67, 73
farm maatalo 85
fast herkkä (nopea) 124
fat (meat) rasva 37
father isä 93
faucet vesihana 28
fax faksi 133
February helmikuu 150
fee (doctor's) maksu 144
feeding bottle tuttipullo 110
feel, to (physical state) tuntea 140, 142
felt huopa 113
felt-tip pen huopakärkikynä 104
ferry lautta 74
fever kuume 140
few harva 14
few (a few) muutama 14
field pelto 85
fifteen viisitoista 147
fifth viides 149
fifty viisikymmentä 147
file (tool) viila 109
fill in, to täyttää 26, 144
filling (tooth) paikka 145
filling station bensiiniasema 75
film filmi 86, 124, 125
film winder filminkelaaja 125
filter suodatin 125
filter-tipped suodattimella 126
find, to löytää tr 11, 12, 76; löytyä itr 84, 100
fine (OK) hyvin 11, 92; hyvä 25, 92
fine arts taide-esineet 83
finger sormi 138
Finland Suomi 146

Sanakirja

Finnish suomalainen 34, 113, 135
fire tulipalo 156
first ensimmäinen 69, 72, 77, 149
first class ensimmäinen luokka 68
first name etunimi 26
first-aid kit ensiapupakkaus 108
fish kala 43
fishing kalastus 90
fishing permit kalastuslupa 90
fishing tackle kalastusvälineet 106
fishmonger's kalakauppa 98
fit, to sopia 114
fitting room sovituskoppi 114
five viisi 147
fix, to korjata 75; paikata 145
fizzy *(mineral water)* hiilihapollinen 59
flannel flanelli 113
flash *(photography)* salamavalo 125
flash attachment salamalaite 125
flashlight taskulamppu 106
flat *(apartment)* huoneisto 23
flat *(shoe)* matalakorkoinen 117
flat tyre rengas tyhjänä 78
flea market kirpputori 81
flight lento 65
floor kerros 27
floor show ohjelma 88
florist's kukkakauppa 98
flounder kampela 44
flour jauho 37
flower kukka 85
flu flunssa 142
fluid neste 75, 123
foam rubber mattress
vaahtomuovipatja 106
fog sumu 94
folding chair kokoonpantava tuoli 106
folding table kokoontaitettava pöytä
106
folk music kansanmusiikki 128
follow, to seurata 77
food ruoka 37, 61
food poisoning ruokamyrkytys 142
foot jalka 138
foot cream jalkavoide 109
football jalkapallo 89
footpath polku 85
for *(direction, position)* suuntaan,
sijaan 15
forbidden kielletty 155
forecast ennuste 94
forest metsä 85
forget, to unohtaa 61
fork haarukka 36, 60, 120
form *(document)* kortti 26; kaavake
133; lomake 144
fortnight kaksi viikkoa 151
fortress linnoitus 81
forty neljäkymmentä 147
foundation cream alusvoide 109
fountain lähde 81
fountain pen täytekynä 104
four neljä 147
fourteen neljätoista 147
fourth neljäs 149
frame *(glasses)* sangat 123
France Ranska 146
free vapaa 14, 70, 80, 82, 96, 155
French fries ranskalaiset perunat 62
fresh tuore 52, 61
Friday perjantai 151
fried paistettu 45, 47
fried egg paistettu muna 40
friend ystävä 95
fringe otsatukka 30
from suunnasta 15
front edessä 75
frost pakkanen 94
fruit hedelmä 52
fruit cocktail hedelmäcocktail 52
fruit juice hedelmämehu 40, 59
frying pan paistinpannu 120
full täysi 14
full board täysihoito 24
full insurance täysvakuutus 20
furniture huonekalut 83
furrier's turkisliike 98

G

gabardine gabardiini 113
gallery galleria 80, 98
game peli 128
game *(food)* riista 48
garage autotalli 26; korjaamo 78
garden puutarha 85
gardens puutarha 81
garlic valkosipuli 51
gas kaasu 156
gasoline bensiini, bensa 75, 78
gastritis mahakatarri 142
gate *(airport)* portti 65
gauze sideharso 108
gem jalokivi 121
general yleinen 27, 100, 137
general delivery poste restante 133
general practitioner yleislääkäri 137
genitals sukuelimet 138
gentleman mies 155

genuine aito 117
geology geologia 83
Germany Saksa 146
get off, to nousta pois 73
get past, to päästä ohi 69
get to, to päästä 19, 76
get up, to nousta ylös 144
get, to *(find)* saada 11, 19, 21, 32; hankkia 21
gherkin suolakurkku 64
gift lahja 17
gin gini 58
gin and tonic gintonic 58
ginger inkivääri 51
girdle (naisten) liivit 115
girl tyttö 111, 128
girlfriend tyttöystävä 93
give, to antaa 13, 123, 135; saada 63, 75, 126, 130
gland rauhanen 138
glass lasi 36, 57, 60
glasses silmälasit 123
gloomy synkkä 83
glove hansikas 115
glue liima 104
go away! menkää tiehenne! 156
go back, to palata 77
go out, to lähteä ulos 96
go, to mennä 72; ajaa 21, 77; lähteä 96
gold kulta 121, 122
gold plated kullattu 122
golden kullanvärinen 112
golf golf 89
golf course golf-rata 89
good hyvä 14, 86, 101
good afternoon (hyvää) päivää 10
good evening (hyvää) iltaa 10
good morning (hyvää) huomenta 10
good night hyvää yötä 10
goodbye näkemiin 10
goose hanhi 48
gooseberry karviaismarja 52
gram gramma 119
grammar kielioppi 159
grammar book kielioppi 105
grandfather isoisä 93
grandmother isoäiti 93
grape viinirypäle 53, 64
grapefruit greippi 52
grapefruit juice greippimehu 40, 59
gray harmaa 112
graze raapaisu, verinaarmu 139
greasy rasvainen 30, 110
great *(excellent)* hieno, oikein mukava 95

Great Britain Iso-Britannia 146
Greece Kreikka 146
green vihreä 112
greengrocer's vihannesmyymälä 98
greeting tervehdys 10, 152
grey harmaa 112
grilled grillattu 45, 47
grocer's sekatavarakauppa 98, 119
groundsheet telttapatja 106
group ryhmä 82
guesthouse matkustajakoti 19, 23
guide opas 80
guidebook opaskirja 82, 104, 105
gum *(teeth)* ikenet 145
gynaecologist gynekologi 137, 141

H
habit tapa 34
hair hiukset 30, 110
hair dryer hiustenkuivaaja 118
hair gel hiusgeeli 30, 110
hair lotion hiusvesi 110
hair slide hiussolki 110
hair spray hiuslakka 30, 110
hairbrush hiusharja 110
haircut tukanleikkuu 30
hairdresser kampaaja 30, 98
hairgrip hiussolki 110
hairpin hiusneula 110
half *(a)* puoli 149
half an hour puoli tuntia 153
half board puolihoito 24
half, a puolikas 149
hall *(large room)* sali, halli 81, 88
hall porter portieeri 27
ham kinkku 40, 64
ham and eggs kinkkua ja munia 40
hammer vasara 120
hammock riippumatto 106
hand käsi 138
hand cream käsivoide 109
hand washable käsinpestävä 113
handbag käsilaukku 115, 156
handicrafts käsityö(tuotteet) 83, 127
handkerchief nenäliina 115
handmade käsitehty 112
hanger vaateripustin 27
happy onnellinen 152
harbour satama 73, 81
hard kova 123
hard-boiled *(egg)* kovaksi keitetty 40
hardware store kodinkonemyymälä 98

hare jänis 48
hat hattu 115
have to, to *(must)* on -ttava 17, 68;
  täytyy 68, 77, 95, 140
have, to -lla on 163
hay fever heinänuha 107, 141
hazelnut hasselpähkinä 52
he hän 161
head pää 138, 139
head waiter hovimestari 61
headache päänsärky 141
headphones kuulokkeet 118
health food shop
  luontaistuotemyymälä 98
health insurance *(company)*
  sairausvakuutus 144
health insurance form
  sairausvakuutuslomake 144
heart sydän 138
heart attack sydänkohtaus 141
heat, to lämmittää 90
heavy raskas 14; painava 101
heel korko 117
helicopter helikopteri 74
hello hei, terve 10, 135
help apu 156
help! apua! 156
help, to auttaa 13, 21, 70, 100, 134
help, to *(oneself)* ottaa (itse) 119
her hän 161
herb tea yrttitee 59
herbs yrtit 51
here täällä 14
herring silli 44
hi hei, terve 10
high korkea 85, 90, 141
high season sesonkiaika 150
highlights raidat 30
hill mäki 85
hire vuokraus 20, 74
hire, to vuokrata 19, 20, 74, 90, 91, 119,
  155; palkata 80
his hänen 161
history historia 83
hitchhike, to liftata 74
hold on! *(phone)* hetkinen 136
hole reikä 30
holiday lomapäivä, loma 152
holidays loma 16; lomapäivä 152
home koti 96
home address kotiosoite 31
home town kotikaupunki 26
home-made kotitekoinen 39
honey hunaja 40
hope, to toivoa 96

horseback riding ratsastus 89
hospital sairaala 98, 142, 144
hot *(warm)* kuuma 14, 24, 25, 40, 94,
  155
hot water kuuma vesi 24, 28
hot-water bottle kuumavesipullo 28
hotel hotelli 19, 21, 22, 26, 80, 96, 102
hotel directory/guide hotelliopas 19
hotel reservation hotellin varaus 19
hour tunti 80, 143, 153
house talo 83, 85
household article taloustarvike 119
how kuinka 11
how far kuinka kaukana 11, 76, 84
how long *(time)* kuinka kauan 11, 25
how many kuinka monta 11
how much kuinka paljon 11; paljonko
  24, 80
hundred sata 148
hungry nälkäinen 13, 35
hunting metsästys 90
hurry, to be in a on kiire 21
hurt *(to be)* loukata 139
hurt, to koskee 139, 140, 142; särkee
  145
husband aviomies 93
hydrofoil kantosiipialus 74

I
I minä 161
ice jää 95
ice cream jäätelö 54
ice cube jääkuutio 28
ice pack jääpussi 106
iced tea jäätee 60
if jos 143
ill sairas 140
illness tauti 140
important tärkeä 13
imported maahantuotu 112
impressive vaikuttava 83
in sisässä, sisällä 15
include, to sisällyttää 24, 31, 32, 80
included sisältyy 20, 61; 31, 32, 80
indigestion ruoansulatushäiriö 141
indoor sisä 90
inexpensive edullinen 35; huokea 124
infected tulehtunut 140
infection tulehdus 141
inflammation tulehdus 142
inflation inflaatio 131
inflation rate inflaatiotaso 131
influenza influenssa 142

information neuvonta 67, 155
injection ruiske 142, 143, 144
injure, to loukata 139
injured loukkaantunut 79, 139
injury vamma 139
ink muste 105
inquiry tiedustelu 67
insect bite hyönteisen pistos 108, 139
insect repellent hyttysöljy 108
insect spray hyönteissuihke 106
inside sisässä, sisälle 15
instead of asemasta 37
insurance vakuutus 20, 144
insurance company vakuutusyhtiö 79
interest *(finance)* korko 131
interested, to be olla kiinnostunut 83, 96
interesting mielenkiintoinen 83
international kansainvälinen 133, 134
interpreter tulkki 131
intersection risteys 77
introduce, to esitellä 92
introduction *(social)* esittely 92
investment investointi 131
invitation kutsu 95
invite, to kutsua 94
invoice lasku 131
iodine jodi 108
Ireland Irlanti 146
Irish irlantilainen 93
iron *(for laundry)* silitysrauta 118
iron, to silittää 29
ironmonger's rautakauppa 98
Italy Italia 146
ivory norsunluu 122

J
jacket (lyhyt) takki, pusakka 115
jade jade 122
jam *(preserves)* hillo 40
jam, to juuttua kiinni 29, 125
January tammikuu 150
jar *(container)* purkki 119
jaundice keltatauti 142
jaw leuka 138
jazz jatsi 128
jeans farmarihousut 115
jersey villatakki 115
jewel box korulipas 121
jeweller's kultaseppä 98, 121
joint nivel 138
journey matka 71
juice mehu 37, 40, 59

July heinäkuu 150
jumper villapusero 115
June kesäkuu 150
just *(only)* vain 16, 37, 100

K
keep, to pitää 62
kerosene valopetroli 106
key avain 27
kidney munuainen 138
kilo(gram) kilo 119
kilometre kilometri 20, 78
kind ystävällinen 95
kind of, what *(type)* minkä lajin 85; millainen 140
knee polvi 138
kneesocks polvisukat 115
knife veitsi 36, 60, 120
knock, to koputtaa 155
know, to tietää 16, 25, 96; tuntea 113

L
label nimilappu 105
lace pitsi 113
lady nainen 155
lake järvi 81, 85, 90
lamb *(meat)* lammas 46
lamp lamppu 29, 106, 118
lamprey nahkiainen 45
lane *(traffic)* kaista 79
language kieli 104
lantern lyhty 106
large suuri 20, 130; suurta kokoa 101
last viimeinen 14, 68, 73; viime 149, 151
last name sukunimi 26
late myöhäinen 14
late, to be olla myöhässä 153
later myöhemmin 135
Latvia Latvia 146
laugh, to nauraa 95
launderette itsepalvelupesula 98
laundry *(clothes)* pesula 29
laundry *(place)* pesula 29, 98
laundry service pyykkipalvelu 24
laxative ulostuslääke 108
lead *(theatre)* pääosa 86
leap year karkausvuosi 149
leather nahka 113, 117
leave, to lähteä 31; 68, 95
leave, to *(deposit)* jättää (talteen) 26

leave, to *(leave behind)* jättää 20, 70
leeks purjo(sipuli) 49
left vasen 21, 68, 77
left-luggage office matkatavaran säilytys 67, 70
leg sääri 138
lemon sitruuna 37, 40, 53, 59
lemonade limonaadi 59
lens *(camera)* objektiivi 125
lens *(glasses)* linssi 123
lentils linssit 49
less vähemmän 14
lesson (oppi)tunti 90
let, to *(hire out)* antaa vuokralle 155
letter kirje 132
letter box postilaatikko 132
letter of credit remburssi 130
lettuce lehtisalaatti 49
library kirjasto 81, 99
licence *(driving)* ajokortti 20, 79
lie down, to käydä makuulle 142
life belt pelastusliivi 74
life boat pelastusvene 74
life guard *(beach)* hengenpelastaja 90
lift *(elevator)* hissi 28, 100
light valo 28, 124
light *(weight)* kevyt 14, 55, 101
light *(colour)* vaalea 101, 112
light *(for cigarette)* tuli 95
light meter valotusmittari 125
lighter sytytin 126
lighter fluid/gas sytytinbensiini, sytytinkaasu 126
lightning salama 94
like kuten 111
like, to haluta 13, 20, 23, 112; pitää 61
like, to *(please)* pitää 25, 102; on mukavaa 92
linen *(cloth)* pellava 113
lip huuli 138
lipsalve huulirasva 109
lipstick huulipuna 109
liqueur likööri 58
listen, to kuunnella 128
Lithuania Liettua 146
litre litra 75, 119
little *(a little)* vähän 14
live, to elää 83
liver maksa 138
lobster hummeri 42
local paikallinen 36
long pitkä 115
long-sighted kaukonäköinen 123
look for, to hakea 13
look out! varokaa! 156

look, to katsella 100; katsoa 123, 139
loose *(clothes)* väljä 114
lose, to hukata 123; kadottaa 156
loss tappio 131
lost eksynyt 13
lost and found office/lost property office löytötavaratoimisto 67, 156
lot *(a lot)* paljon 14
lotion neste, vesi 109
loud *(voice)* kova 135
love to, to mielellään 95
lovely ihana 94
low matala 141
low season hiljainen kausi 150
lower ala(vuode) 69, 70
luck onni 135, 152
luggage matkatavarat 17, 18, 21, 26, 31, 71
luggage locker säilytyslokero 18, 67, 70
luggage trolley (työntö)kärry 18, 70
lump *(bump)* kyhmy 139
lunch lounas 34, 80, 95
lung keuhko 138

M

machine *(washable)* konepestävä 113
mackerel makrilli 44
magazine aikakauslehti 105
magnificent komea 84
maid siivooja 27
mail posti 28, 133
mail, to postittaa 28
mailbox postilaatikko 132
main tärkein 100
make up, to *(prepare)* sijata 29; laittaa kuntoon 70
make, to ottaa 131; tehdä 162
make-up meikki 109
make-up remover pad meikinpoistovanu 109
mallet nuija 106
man mies 156
manager johtaja 27
manicure käsien hoito 30
many monta 15
map kartta 76, 105
March maaliskuu 150
marinated marinoitu 45
marjoram meirami 51
mark *(currency)* markka 18
market *(kauppa)*tori 81, 99
marmalade marmelaadi 40

DICTIONARY

married naimisissa 93
mass *(church)* messu 84
match *(matchstick)* tulitikku 106, 120, 126
match *(sport)* ottelu 89
match, to *(colour)* sopia yhteen 111
matinée varhaisnäytäntö 87
matt *(finish)* mattapintainen 125
mattress patja 106
May toukokuu 150
may *(can)* saada 12
meadow niitty 85
meal ateria 24, 34, 143
mean, to tarkoittaa 11, 26
means väline 74
measles tuhkarokko 142
measure, to mitata 113
meat liha 37, 46, 47, 60
meatball lihapyörykkä 46
mechanic korjaaja 78
mechanical pencil lyijytäytekynä 105, 121
medical certificate lääkärintodistus 144
medicine lääketiede 83
medicine *(drug)* lääke 143
medium *(meat)* keski-kypsä 47
medium-sized keskikokoinen 20
meet, to tavata 96
melon melooni 52
memorial muistomerkki 81
mend, to korjata 75
mend, to *(clothes)* korjata 29
menthol *(cigarettes)* mentholi 126
menu ruokalista 36, 38, 39
merry iloinen 152
message viesti 28, 136
metre metri 111
mezzanine *(theatre)* parveke 87
middle keski(vuode) 69; puoliväli 150
midnight keskiyö 153
mild *(light)* mieto 126
mileage kilometrimäärä 20
milk maito 40, 60, 64
milkshake pirtelö 59
million miljoona 148
mineral water mineraalivesi 59
minister *(religion)* pappi 84
mint minttu 51
minute minuutti 21, 68, 153
mirror peili 114, 123
miscellaneous sekalaista 127
Miss neiti 10
miss, to puuttua 18, 29; uupua 60
mistake virhe 31, 61, 102; erehdys 60

moccasin mokkasiini 117
modified American plan puolihoito 24
moisturizing cream kosteusvoide 109
monastery munkkiluostari 81
Monday maanantai 151
money raha 18, 130, 156
money order maksumääräys 133
month kuukausi 16, 150
monument monumentti 81
moon kuu 94
moped mopo 74
more enemmän 12, 14; lisää 15, 37
morning, in the aamulla 143, 151, 153
mortgage kiinnitys 131
mosque moskeija 84
mosquito net hyttysverkko 106
motel motelli 22
mother äiti 93
motorbike moottoripyörä 74
motorboat moottorivene 91
motorway moottoritie 76
mountain vuori 85
mountaineering vuoristokiipeily 89
moustache viikset 31
mouth suu 138, 142
mouthwash suuvesi 108
move, to liikuttaa 139
movie elokuva 86
movies elokuva 86, 96
Mr. herra 10
Mrs. rouva 10
much paljon 11, 14
mug muki 120
muscle lihas 138
museum museo 81
mushroom sieni 49
music musiikki 83, 128
musical musikaali 86
mussel sinisimpukka 44
must *(have to)* täytyä 31, 60, 95, 142
my minun 161
myself *(minä)* itse 119

N
nail *(human)* kynsi 109
nail brush kynsiharja 109
nail clippers kynsileikkuri 109
nail file kynsiviila 109
nail polish kynsilakka 109
nail polish remover kynsilakanpoistoaine 109
nail scissors kynsisakset 109
name nimi 23, 26, 79, 92, 131, 136

Sanakirja

napkin lautasliina 36, 120
nappy vaippa 110
narrow kapea 117
nationality kansallisuus 26, 93
natural luonnon 83
natural history luonnonhistoria 83
nauseous pahoinvointi, kuvotus 140
near lähellä, lähelle 14, 15
nearby lähellä 32, 77
nearest lähin 75, 78, 98
neat *(drink)* sekoittamaton 58
neck niska 30; kaula (ja niska) 138
necklace kaulakoru 121
need, to tarvita 29, 90, 137
needle neula 28
negative negatiivi 124, 125
nephew veljen/sisaren poika 93
nerve hermo 138
Netherlands Hollanti 146
never ei koskaan 15
new uusi 14
New Year uusi vuosi 152
New Zealand Uusi-Seelanti 146
newsagent's lehtimyymälä 99
newspaper sanomalehti 104, 105
newsstand lehtimyymälä 19, 67;
lehtikioski 99, 104
next seuraava 14, 65, 68, 73, 76, 151;
ensi 149, 151
next time ensi kerralla 95
next to vieressä 15, 77
nice *(beautiful)* kaunis 94
niece veljen/sisaren tytär 93
night yö 10, 25, 151
night cream yövoide 109
night, at yöllä 151
nightclub yökerho 88
nightdress/-gown yöpaita 115
nine yhdeksän 147
nineteen yhdeksäntoista 147
ninety yhdeksänkymmentä 148
ninth yhdeksäs 149
no ei 10
noisy meluisa 26
nonalcoholic alkoholiton 59
none ei yhtään 15
nonsmoker ei-tupakoijille 36;
tupakointi kielletty 69
noon puolipäivä 31; keskipäivä 153
normal normaali 30
north pohjoinen 77
North America Pohjois-Amerikka 146
Norway Norja 146
nose nenä 138
nose drops nenätipat 108

nosebleed verenvuoto nenästä 141
not ei 15
note *(banknote)* seteli 130
note paper kirjoituspaperi 105
notebook muistikirja 105
nothing ei mitään 15, 17
notice *(sign)* varoitus 155
notify, to ilmoittaa 144
November marraskuu 150
now nyt 15
number numero 26, 65, 135, 136, 147
nurse hoitaja 144
nutmeg muskotti 51

O
occupation *(profession)* ammatti 26
occupied varattu 14, 155
October lokakuu 150
office myymälä 19; myynti 67;
toimisto 80, 99, 132, 156
oil öljy 37, 75, 110
oily *(greasy)* rasvainen 30, 110
old vanha 14
old town vanha kaupunki 81
on päällä, päälle 15
on foot jalan 76
on time aikataulussa 68
once kerran 149
one yksi 147
one-way *(traffic)* yksisuuntainen 77
one-way ticket menolippu 65, 69
onion sipuli 49
only vain 15, 25, 80, 87, 108
onyx onyks 122
open avoin 14; auki 82, 142; avoinna
155
open, to aueta *itr* 11, 107, 132; avata *tr*
17, 130
open-air ulko 90
opera ooppera 88
opera house oopperatalo 81, 88
operation leikkaus 144
operator keskus 134
operetta operetti 88
opposite vastapäätä 77
optician optikko 99, 123
or tai 15
orange appelsiini 52, 64
orange *(colour)* oranssi 112
orange juice appelsiinimehu 40, 59
orangeade appelsiinilimonaadi 59
orchestra orkesteri 88
orchestra *(seats)* etupermanto 87

order *(goods, meal)* tilaus 102
order, to *(goods, meal)* tilata 60, 102, 103
oregano oregano 51
ornithology lintutiede 83
other muu 74, 101
our meidän 161
out of order epäkunnossa 136, 155
out of stock ei varastossa 103
outlet *(electric)* (sähkö)pistorasia 27
outside ulkona, ulos 15; ulkoa 36
oval soikea 101
overalls haalarit 115
overdone *(meat)* ylikypsä 60
overheat, to *(engine)* ylikuumeta 78
owe, to olla velkaa 144
oyster osteri 44

P
pacifier *(baby's)* tutti 110
packet rasia 126
pail ämpäri 128
pain kipu 140, 141; tuska 144
painkiller särkylääke 140, 144
paint maali 155
paint, to maalata 83
paintbox vesivärirasia 105
painter taidemaalari 83
painting maalaus 83
pair pari 115, 117, 149
pajamas pyjama 115
palace palatsi 81
palpitations sydämen tykytys 141
panties pikkuhousut 115
pants *(trousers)* housut 115
panty girdle housuliivit 115
panty hose sukkahousut 115
paper paperi 105
paper napkin paperilautasliina 105, 120
paperback taskukirja 105
paperclip liitin 105
paraffin *(fuel)* valopetroli 106
parcel paketti 132, 133
pardon, I beg your *(pyydän)* anteeksi 11
parents vanhemmat 93
park puisto 81
park, to pysäköidä 26, 77
parka sadepusakka 115
parking pysäköinti 77, 79
parking disc pysäköintikiekko 77
parking meter pysäköintimittari 77
parliament building eduskuntatalo 81

parsley persilja 51
part osa 138
partridge peltopyy 48
party *(social gathering)* kutsut 95
pass *(mountain)* sola 85
pass through, to kulkea läpi 16
passport passi 16, 17, 25, 26, 156
passport photo passikuva 124
paste *(glue)* liima 105
pastry shop konditoria 99
patch, to *(clothes)* paikata 29
path polku 85
patient potilas 144
pattern kuvioitus 112
pay, to maksaa 17, 31, 62, 100, 102, 136
payment maksu 102, 131
pea herne 49
peach persikka 53
peak huippu 85
peanut maapähkinä 52
pear päärynä 53
pearl helmi 122
pedestrian jalankulkija 155
peg *(tent)* telttapuikko 106
pen kynä 105
pencil lyijykynä 105
pencil sharpener kynänteroitin 105
pendant riipus 121
penicillin penisilliini 143
penknife kynäveitsi 120
pensioner eläkeläinen 82
people ihmiset 92
pepper pippuri 37, 40, 51, 64
per cent prosentti 149
per day päivältä 20, 32, 89
per hour tunnilta 77, 89
per night yöltä 24
per person hengeltä 32
per week viikolta 20, 24
percentage prosentti 131
perch ahven 44
perform, to *(theatre)* esittää 86
perfume hajuvesi 109
perhaps ehkä 15
period *(monthly)* kuukautiset 141
period pains kuukautiskivut 141
perm(anent) permanentti 30
permit lupa 90
person henki(lö) 32
personal henkilökohtainen 17, 130
personal call/person-to-person call henkilöpuhelu 134
personal cheque henkilökohtainen shekki 130

DICTIONARY

petrol bensiini, bensa 75, 78
pewter tina 122
pharmacy apteekki 107
pheasant fasaani 48
photo valokuvata 82, 124, 125
photocopy valokopio 131
photograph, to valokuvata 82
photographer valokuvaamo 99
photography valokuvaus 124
phrase sanonta 12
pick up, to *(person)* hakea 80, 96
picnic piknik 62
picnic basket eväskori 106
picture *(painting)* taulu 83
picture *(photo)* (valo)kuva 82
piece kappale 18; pala 63, 119
pike hauki 44
pill pilleri 141; tabletti 143
pillow tyyny 28
pin neula 109, 110, 121
pineapple ananas 52
pink vaaleanpunainen 112
pipe piippu 126
pipe cleaner piipun puhdistin 126
pipe tobacco piipputupakka 126
pipe tool piippukalu 126
place paikka 26, 76
place of birth syntymäpaikka 26
place, to *(call)* tilata 134
plaice punakampela 44
plain *(colour)* yksivärinen 112
plane lento(kone) 65
planetarium planetaario 81
plaster kipsi 140
plastic muovi 120
plastic bag muovikassi 120
plate lautanen 36, 60 120
platform *(station)* laituri 67, 68, 69
platinum platina 122
play *(theatre)* näytelmä 86
play, to esittää 86; soittaa 88; pelata 89, 93
playground leikkikenttä 32
playing card pelikortti 105
please olkaa hyvä 10
plimsolls kumitossu 117
plug *(electric)* pistoke 29, 118
plum luumu 52
pneumonia keuhkokuume 142
poached keitetty 45
pocket tasku 116
pocket calculator taskulaskin 105
pocket watch taskukello 121
point of interest *(sight)* nähtävyys 80
point, to osoittaa 12

poison myrkky 108, 156
poisoning myrkytys 142
pole *(ski)* sauva 91
pole *(tent)* telttaseiväs 106
police poliisi 78, 79, 156
police station poliisiasema 99, 156
pond lampi 85
poplin popliini 113
pork porsaanliha 46
port *(harbour)* satama 73
portable kannettava 118
porter kantaja 18, 26, 70
portion annos 37, 54, 60
Portugal Portugali 146
possible, (as soon as) mahdollista, (niin pian kuin) 137
post *(mail)* posti 28, 133
post office posti(toimisto) 19, 99, 132
post, to postittaa 28
postage kirjemaksu 132
postage stamp postimerkki 28, 126, 132, 133
postcard postikortti 105, 126; 132
poste restante poste restante 133
pottery savenvalanta 83
poultry lintu 48
pound punta 18, 102, 130
powder puuteri 109
powder compact puuterirasia 122
powder puff puuterihuisku 109
prawn katkarapu 44
pregnant raskaana 141
premium *(gasoline)* korkeaoktaaninen 75
prescribe, to kirjoittaa resepti 143
prescription resepti 107; lääkemääräys 143
press stud painonappi 116
press, to *(iron)* prässätä 29
pressure paine 75, 141
pretty sievä 84
price hinta 24
priest (katolinen) pappi 84
print *(photo)* kuva 125
private oma 24; yksityinen 80, 155
processing *(photo)* kehitys 125
profession ammatti 26
profit voitto 131
programme ohjelma 87
pronounce, to ääntää 12
pronunciation ääntäminen 6
propelling pencil lyijytäytekynä 105, 121
Protestant protestanttinen 84
provide, to järjestää, hankkia 131

Sanakirja

prune kuivattu luumu 52
public holiday yleinen vapaapäivä 152
pull, to vetää 155
pull, to *(tooth)* vetää pois 145
pullover villapaita 115
pump pumppu 106
purchase osto 131
pure täyttä (puhdasta) 113
purple sinipunainen 112
push, to työntää 155
put, to tuoda 24
pyjamas pyjama 116

Q

quality laatu 103, 112
quantity määrä 14
quarter of an hour neljännestunti 153
quartz kvartsi 122
question kysymys 11
quick(ly) nopea(sti) 14, 79, 137, 156
quiet hiljainen 24; rauhallinen 25

R

rabbi rabbi 84
race kilpailu 89
race course (track) kilparata 89
racket *(sport)* maila 90
radiator *(car)* jäähdyttäjä 78
radio radio 23, 28, 118
radish retiisi 49
railway station rautatieasema 19, 21, 66, 69
rain sade 94
rain, to sataa 94
raincoat sadetakki 117
raisin rusina 53
rangefinder etäisyysmittari 125
rare *(meat)* raaka 47, 61
rash ihottuma 139
raspberry vadelma 52
rate *(inflation)* taso 131
rate *(of exchange)* vaihtokurssi 18, 130
rate *(price)* hinta 20
razor partakone 109
razor blades partakoneen terä 109
read, to lukea 39
reading lamp lukulamppu 28
ready valmis 30, 117, 123, 125, 145
real *(genuine)* aito 117, 121
rear takana 69; 75

receipt kuitti 103, 144
reception vastaanotto 23
receptionist vastaanotto 27
recommend, to suositella 35, 36, 80, 86, 88, 137, 145
record *(disc)* levy 127, 128
record player levysoitin 118
recorder nauhuri 118
rectangular suorakulmainen 101
red punainen 105, 112
red *(wine)* puna 57
reduction alennus 24, 82
refill *(pen)* säiliö 105
refund *(to get a)* maksun palautus 103
regards terveiset 152
region alue 92
register, to *(luggage)* lähettää matkatavara 71
registered mail kirjattu lähetys 132
registration kirjoittautuminen 26
registration form matkustajakortti 26
regular *(petrol)* matalaoktaaninen 75
religion uskonto 83
religious service jumalanpalvelus 84
rent, to vuokrata 19, 20, 74, 90, 91, 119, 155
rental vuokraus 20, 74
repair korjata 125
repair, to korjata 29, 117, 118, 121, 123, 125, 145
repeat, to toistaa 12
report, to *(a theft)* tehdä ilmoitus 156
required vaaditaan 88
requirement tarve 27
reservation varaus 19, 23, 65, 69
reservations office paikanvaraus 67
reserve, to varata 19, 23, 35, 69, 87
reserved varattu 155
rest loput 130
restaurant ravintola 19, 32, 33, 35, 67
return ticket menopaluu 65, 69
return, to *(come back)* palata 21, 80
return, to *(give back)* palauttaa 103
rheumatism reumatismi 141
rib kylkiluu 138
ribbon värinauha 105
right *(correct)* oikea 14
right *(direction)* oikea 21, 68, 77
ring *(jewellery)* sormus 122
ring, to *(doorbell)* soittaa 155
river joki 85, 90
river cruise jokiristeily 74
road tie 76, 77, 85
road assistance tiepalvelu 78
road map tiekartta 105

Sanakirja

road sign liikennemerkki 79
roasted paahdettu 47
roll sämpylä 40, 64
roll film filmirulla 124
roller skate rullaluistin 128
room huone 19, 23, 24, 25, 27, 28, 155
room *(space)* tila 32
room number huonenumero 26
room service huonepalvelu 24
rope köysi 106
rosary rukousnauha 122
rosemary rosmariini 51
rouge poskipuna 109
round pyöreä 101
round *(golf)* kierros 89
round up, to pyöristää 62
round-neck pyöreä kaula-aukko 115
round-trip ticket menopaluu 65, 69
route reitti 85
rowing boat soutuvene 90
royal kuninkaan 81
rubber *(eraser)* pyyhekumi 105
rubber *(material)* kumi 117
ruby rubiini 122
rucksack reppu 106
ruin raunio 81
ruler *(for measuring)* viivotin 105
rum rommi 58
running water juokseva vesi 24
Russia Venäjä 146

S

safe tallelokero 26
safe *(free from danger)* turvallinen 90
safety pin hakaneula 109
saffron sahrami 51
sage salvia 51
sailing purjehdus 89
sailing boat purjehdusvene 90
salad salaatti 42
sale myynti 131
sale *(bargains)* alennusmyynti, ale 100
salmon lohi 44
salt suola 37, 40, 64
salty suolainen 61
same sama(nlainen) 117
sand hiekka 90
sandal sandaali 117
sandwich voileipä 63
sanitary napkin/towel terveysside 108
sapphire safiiri 122
sardine sardiini 44
satin satiini 113

Saturday lauantai 151
sauce kastike 51
saucepan kattila 120
saucer teevati, kahvilautanen 120
sausage makkara 46, 64
scarf huivi 116
scarlet helakanpunainen 112
scenery maisema 92
scenic route kaunis reitti 85
school koulu 79
scissors sakset 120
scooter skooteri 74
Scotland Skotlanti 146
scrambled eggs munakokkeli 40
screwdriver ruuvimeisseli 120
sculptor kuvanveistäjä 83
sculpture kuvanveisto(taide) 83
sea meri 85, 90
seafood äyriäiset 44
season vuodenaika 150
seasoning mauste 37
seat paikka 65, 69; 70, 87
seat belt turvavyö 75
second toinen 149
second *(time)* sekuntti 153
second class toinen luokka 69
second hand sekunttiviisari 122
second-hand shop osto- ja myyntiliike 99
secretary sihteeri 27, 131
section osasto 104
see, to katsoa 12, 121; nähdä 25, 26, 87, 89, 96
self-service shop itsepalvelumyymälä 32
sell, to myydä 100
send, to lähettää 78, 102, 103, 132, 133
sentence lause 12
separately kukin erikseen 61
September syyskuu 150
seriously vakavasti 139
service palvelupalkkio 24; tarjoilupalkkio 62; palvelu 98, 100
service *(church)* jumalanpalvelus 84
serviette lautasliina 36
set *(hair)* kampaus 30
set menu vakiolista 36
setting lotion kampausneste 30, 110
seven seitsemän 147
seventeen seitsemäntoista 147
seventh seitsemäs 149
seventy seitsemänkymmentä 148
sew, to ommella 29
shade *(colour)* sävy 111
shampoo shampoo 30, 110

shampoo and set pesu ja kampaus 30
shape muoto 103
share *(finance)* osake 131
sharp *(pain)* pistävä 140
shave parranajo 31
shaver parranajokone 27, 118
shaving brush partasuti 109
shaving cream partavaahdoke 109
she hän 161
shelf hylly 119
ship laiva 74
shirt paita 116
shiver puistatus 140
shoe kenkä 117
shoe polish kengänkiilloke 117
shoe shop kenkäkauppa 99
shoelace kengännauha 117
shoemaker's suutari 99
shop myymälä, kauppa, liike 98
shop window näyteikkuna 100
shopping ostos 97
shopping area ostosalue 81, 100
shopping centre ostoskeskus 99
short lyhyt 30, 114
short-sighted likinäköinen 123
shorts shortsit 116
shoulder olkapää, hartiat 138
shovel lapio 128
show näytös 87; ohjelma 88
show, to näyttää 12, 13, 76, 100, 101, 103, 118, 124
shower suihku 23, 32
shrimp katkarapu 44
shrink, to kutistua 113
shut suljettu 14
shutter *(camera)* suljin 125
shutter *(window)* ikkunaluukku 29
sick *(ill)* sairas 140
sickness *(illness)* sairaus 140
side sivu 31
sideboards/-burns pulisongit 31
sight nähtävyys 80
sightseeing kiertoajelu 80
sightseeing tour nähtävyyskierros 80
sign *(notice)* viitta 77; merkki 77, 79; kyltti 155
sign, to allekirjoittaa 26, 131
signature allekirjoitus 26
signet ring sinettisormus 122
silk silkki 113
silver hopea 121, 122
silver *(colour)* hopeanvärinen 112
silver plated hopeoitu 122
silverware hopeaesineitä 122
simple yksinkertainen 124

since alkaen 15; -sta asti 151
sing, to laulaa 88
single *(ticket)* menolippu 65, 69
single *(unmarried)* naimaton 93
single cabin yhden hengen hytti 74
single room yhden hengen huone 19, 23
sister sisko 93
sit down, to istuutua 95
six kuusi 147
sixteen kuusitoista 147
sixth kuudes 149
sixty kuusikymmentä 147
size koko 113, 117, 124
skate luistin 91
skating rink luistinrata 91
ski suksi 91
ski boot hiihtokengät 91
ski lift hiihtohissi 91
ski run latu 91
ski, to hiihtää 91
skiing hiihto 89, 91
skiing equipment hiihtovarusteet 91, 106
skiing lessons hiihtotunti 91
skin iho 138
skin-diving sukellus 91
skin-diving equipment sukellusvarusteet 90, 106
skirt hame 116
sky taivas 94
sleep, to nukkua 144
sleeping bag makuupussi 106
sleeping car makuuvaunu 68, 69, 70
sleeping pill unitabletti 108, 143
sleeve hiha 116, 142
sleeveless hihaton 116
slice siivu 119
slide *(photo)* dia 124
slip *(underwear)* alushame 116
slipper tohveli 117
slow hidas 14
slowly, more hitaammin 21, 135
small pieni 14, 20, 25, 101, 117, 130
smoke, to polttaa 95
smoked savustettu 45
smoker tupakoitsija 69
snack välipala 62
snack bar pikabaari 62
snap fastener painonappi 116
sneaker kumitossu 117
snorkel snorkkeli 128
snow lumi 94
snow, to sataa lunta 94
snuff nuuska 126

DICTIONARY

Sanakirja

soap saippua 28, 110
soccer jalkapallo 89
sock (nilkka)sukka 116
socket *(electric)* (sähkö)pistorasia 27
soft pehmeä 123
soft drink (alkoholiton) juoma 64
soft-boiled *(egg)* pehmeäksi keitetty 40
sold out loppuunmyyty 87
sole *(fish)* meriantura 44
sole *(shoe)* pohja 117
soloist solisti 88
some hieman 14
someone joku 96
something jotain 30, 36, 107, 111, 112, 139
somewhere jossain 87
son poika 93
song laulu 128
soon pian 15
sore *(painful)* arka 145
sore throat kurkkukipu 141
sorry anteeksi 11, 16; valitettavasti 87, 103
sort *(kind)* laatu 119
soup keitto 42
south etelä 77
South Africa Etelä-Afrikka 146
South America Etelä-Amerikka 146
souvenir muistoesine 127
souvenir shop matkamuistomyymälä 99
spade lapio 128
Spain Espanja 146
spare tyre vararengas 75
spark(ing) plug sytytystulppa 76
sparkling *(wine)* kuohu 57
speak, to puhua 11, 12, 16, 84; tavata (puhutella) 135
speaker *(loudspeaker)* kaiutin 118
special erikois 20; 37
special delivery pikajakelu 132
specialist erikoislääkäri 142
speciality erikoisuus 39
specimen *(medical)* näyte 142
spectacle case simälasikotelo 123
speed nopeus 79
spell, to tavata 12
spend, to kuluttaa 101
spice mauste 51
spinach pinaatti 49
spine selkäranka 138
sponge pesusieni 110
spoon lusikka 36, 60, 120
sport urheilu 89

sporting goods shop urheiluvälinekauppa 99
sports jacket urheilupusero 116
sprained nyrjähtänyt 140
spring *(season)* kevät 150
spring *(water)* lähde 85
square neliskulmainen 101
square *(town)* tori 81
stadium stadion 81
staff *(personnel)* henkilökunta 27
stain tahra 29
stainless steel ruostumaton teräs 120
stalls *(theatre)* etupermanto 87
stamp *(postage)* postimerkki 28, 126, 132, 133
staple niitti 105
star tähti 94
start, to alkaa 80, 86; *(car)* käynnistyä 78
starter *(meal)* alkuruoka 41
station *(railway)* (rautatie)asema 19, 21, 66, 69
station *(underground/subway)* asema 71
stationer's paperikauppa 99, 104
statue patsas 81
stay oleskelu 31, 92
stay, to viipyä 16, 25, 26; pysyä 142
stay, to *(reside)* asua 94
steak pihvi 46
steal, to varastaa 156
steamed höyryssä keitetty 45
stewed muhennettu 47
stiff neck niska jäykkänä 141
still *(mineral water)* hiilihapoton 59
sting pistos 139
sting, to pistää 139
stitch, to ommella 29; 117
stock exchange pörssi 81
stocking (naisten) sukka 116
stomach maha, vatsa 138
stomach ache vatsakipu 141
stools uloste 142
stop *(bus)* pysäkki 72, 73
stop thief! varas kiinni! 156
stop! seis! 156
stop, to pysähtyä *itr* 21, 68; seisoa 70; pysäyttää *tr* 156
store *(shop)* myymälä, kauppa, liike 98
straight *(drink)* sekoittamaton 58
straight ahead suoraan eteenpäin 21, 77
strange outo 84
strawberry mansikka 52
street katu 26, 77

street map kaupungin kartta 19, 105
streetcar raitiovaunu 72
string naru 105
strong väkevä 126; vahva 143
student opiskelija 82, 93
study, to opiskella 93
sturdy tanakka 111
sturgeon sampi 44
subway (railway) metro 71
suede mokka 113, 117
sugar sokeri 37, 64
suit (man's) puku 116
suit (woman's) kävelypuku, jakkupuku
116
suitcase matkalaukku 18
summer kesä 150
sun aurinko 94
sun-tan cream aurinkovoide 110
sun-tan oil aurinköljy 110
sunburn auringon polttama iho 107
Sunday sunnuntai 151
sunglasses aurinkolasit 123
sunshade (beach) aurinkovarjo 90
sunstroke auringonpisto 141
super (petrol) korkeaoktaaninen 75
superb loistava 84
supermarket valintamyymälä 99
suppository peräpuikko 108
surgery (consulting room) vastaanotto
(huone) 137
surname sukunimi 26
suspenders (Am.) henkselit 116
swallow, to niellä 143
sweater neulepusero, villapaita 116
sweatshirt college-paita 116
Sweden Ruotsi 146
sweet makea 57, 61
sweet (confectionery) makeinen 126
sweet corn maissi 49
sweet shop makeiskauppa 99
sweetener makeutusaine 37
swell, to turvota 139
swelling turvotus 139
swim, to uida 90
swimming uinti 89, 91
swimming pool uimaallas 32, 90
swimming trunks uimahousut 116
swimsuit uimapuku 116
switch (electric) katkaisija 29
switchboard operator keskus 27
Switzerland Sveitsi 146
swollen turvoksissa 139
synagogue synagooga 84
synthetic tekokuitu 113

T
T-shirt T-paita 116
table pöytä 36, 106
tablet (medical) tabletti 108
tailor's räätäli 99
take away, to ottaa mukaan 62, 102
take to, to viedä 21, 66
take, to ottaa 18, 25, 102, 143; päästä
72, 73
taken (occupied) varattu 69
talcum powder talkki 110
tampon tamponi 108
tangerine mandariini 53
tap (water) vesihana 28
tape recorder magnetofoni, nauhuri 118
tarragon rakuna 51
tax vero 32, 102
taxi taksi 19, 21, 31, 67
taxi rank/stand taksiasema 21
tea tee 40, 60, 64
team joukkue 89
tear, to revähdyttää 140
teaspoon teelusikka 120, 143
telegram sähke 133
telegraph office lennätin 99
telephone puhelin 28, 78, 79, 134
telephone booth puhelinkioski 134
telephone call puhelu 134, 136
telephone directory puhelinluettelo 134
telephone number puhelinnumero 134,
136, 156
telephone, to (call) soittaa 134
telephoto lens teleobjektiivi 125
television televisio 24, 28, 118
telex teleksi 133
telex, to lähettää teleksi 130
tell, to sanoa 12, 73, 152; neuvoa 76;
kertoa 136
temperature lämpötila 90; kuume 140;
lämpö 142
temporary väliaikainen 145
ten kymmenen 147
tendon jänne 138
tennis tennis 89
tennis court tennis-kenttä 89
tennis racket tennis-maila 89
tent teltta 32, 106
tent peg telttapuikko 106
tent pole telttaseiväs 106
tenth kymmenes 149
term (word) termi 131
terrace terassi 36
terrifying pelottava 84
tetanus jäykkäkouristus 140

than kuin 14
thank you kiitos 10
thank, to kiittää 10, 96
that tuo 11, 100
theatre teatteri 81, 86
theft varkaus 156
their heidän 161
then sitten 15
there tuolla 14
thermometer lämpömittari 108, 144
they he 161
thief varas 156
thigh reisi 138
thin ohut 113
think, to (believe) taitaa olla 31, 61, 102; luulla 94
third kolmas 149
third, one kolmannes 149
thirsty, to be janoinen 13, 35
thirteen kolmetoista 147
thirty kolmekymmentä 147
this tämä 11, 100
thousand tuhat 148
thread lanka 28
three kolme 147
throat kurkku 138, 141
throat lozenge kurkkutabletti 108
through läpi 15
through train suora (juna)yhteys 67
thumb peukalo 138
thumbtack piirustusnasta 105
thunder ukkonen 94
thunderstorm ukkosmyrsky 94
Thursday torstai 151
thyme tinjami 51
ticket lippu 65, 69, 72, 87, 89
ticket office lipputoimisto 67
tie solmio, kravatti 116
tie clip solmion pidike 122
tie pin solmioneula 122
tight (close-fitting) tiukka 114
tights sukkahousut 116
time aika 68, 80; kello 152
time (occasion) kerta 95, 142, 143
timetable (trains) aikataulu 68
tin (container) tölkki 119
tint hiusväri 110
tinted värjätyt 123
tire rengas 75, 76
tired väsynyt 13
tissue (handkerchief) paperipyyhe 110
tissue paper silkkipaperi 105
to luokse 15
to get (fetch) hankkia 31; hakea 137
to get (go) päästä 100

to get (obtain) saada 90, 107; päästä 134
toast paahtoleipä 40
tobacco tupakka 126
tobacconist's tupakkakauppa 99, 126
today tänään 29, 151
toe varvas 138
toilet paper vessapaperi 110
toilet water eau de toilette 110
toiletry kosmetiikka 109
toilets WC:t 24, 28, 37, 67; vessat 32
tomato tomaatti 49
tomato juice tomaattimehu 59
tomb hauta 81
tomorrow huomenna 29, 96, 151
tongue kieli 138
tonic water tonic-vesi 59
tonight tänä iltana 29, 86, 87, 96
tonsils kitarisat 138
too liiaksi 14
too (also) myös 15
too much liiaksi 14
tools työkalut 120
tooth hammas 145
toothache hammassärky 145
toothbrush hammasharja 110, 118
toothpaste hammastahna 110
top, at the päällä 30; ylhäällä 145
torch (flashlight) taskulamppu 106
torn revähtänyt 140
touch, to koskea 155
tough (meat) sitkeä 60
tour kierros 73, 80
tourist office matkailutoimisto 19, 23, 80
tourist tax matkailijavero 32
tow truck hinausauto 78
towards kohti 15
towel pyyhe 27, 110
towelling (terrycloth) pyyhekangas 113
tower torni 81
town kaupunki 19, 76, 88
town centre kaupungin keskusta 21, 72, 76
town hall kaupungintalo, raatihuone 82
toy leikkikalu 128
toy shop lelukauppa 99
tracksuit verryttelypuku 116
traffic liikenne 79
traffic light liikennevalo 77
trailer asuntovaunu 32
train juna 66, 68, 69, 70, 153
tram raitiovaunu 72

tranquillizer rauhoittava lääke 108, 143
transfer *(finance)* siirto 131
transformer muuntaja 118
translate, to kääntää 12
transport, means of kulkuväline 74
travel agency matkatoimisto 99
travel guide matkaopas 105
travel sickness matkapahoinvointi 107
travel, to matkustaa 93
traveller's cheque matkashekki 18, 60, 102, 130
travelling bag (matka)laukku 18
treatment hoito 143
tree puu 85
tremendous valtava 84
trim, to *(a beard)* siistiä 31
trip matka 71, 94, 152
trolley (työntö)kärry 18, 70
trousers (pitkät) housut 116
trout taimen 44
try on, to sovittaa 114
try, to yrittää 135
tube putkilo 119
Tuesday tiistai 151
tumbler juomalasi 120
tuna tonnikala 44
tunny tonnikala 44
turbot kampela 45
turkey kalkkuna 48
turn, to *(change direction)* kääntyä 21, 77
turnip nauris 49
turquoise *(colour)* turkoosi 112
turquoise *(gem)* turkoosi 122
turtleneck poolo-kaulus 115
tweezers pinsetit 110
twelve kaksitoista 147
twenty kaksikymmentä 147
twice kahdesti 149
twin beds kaksi vuodetta 23
two kaksi 147
typewriter konekirjoittaja 27
typing paper konekirjoituspaperi 105
tyre rengas 75, 76

U

ugly ruma 14, 84
umbrella sateenvarjo 116
umbrella *(beach)* aurinkovarjo 90
uncle setä 93
unconscious tajuton 139
under alla, alle 15

underdone *(meat)* puolikypsä 47, 61
underground *(railway)* metro 71
underpants (miesten) alushousut 116
undershirt aluspaita 116
understand, to ymmärtää 12, 16
undress, to riisua 142
United States USA (Yhdysvallat) 146
university yliopisto 82
unleaded lyijytön 75
until asti 15
up ylhäällä, ylös 15
upper ylä(vuode) 69
upset stomach vatsavaiva 107
upstairs yläkerrassa 15
urgent kiire 13
urine virtsa 142
use käyttö 17, 108
use, to käyttää 78, 134
useful hyödyllinen 15
usually tavallisesti 94, 143

V

V-neck V-aukko 116
vacancy vapaa huone 23
vacant vapaa 14, 155
vacation loma 152
vaccinate, to rokottaa 140
vacuum flask termospullo 120
vaginal infection emätintulehdus 141
valley laakso 85
value arvo 131
value-added tax liikevaihtovero 24, 102
vanilla vanilja 54
VAT *(sales tax)* liikevaihtovero 24, 102
veal vasikanliha 46
vegetable vihannes 49
vegetable store vihanneskauppa 99
vegetarian kasvissyöjä 37
vein suoni 138
velvet sametti 113
velveteen puuvillasametti 113
venereal disease sukupuolitauti 142
venison hirvenliha 48
vermouth vermutti 59
very tosi 15
vest aluspaita 116
vest *(Am.)* (miesten) liivit 116
veterinarian eläinlääkäri 99
video camera videokamera 124
video cassette videokasetti 118, 124, 127
video recorder videonauhuri 118

view *(panorama)* näköala 23, 25
village kylä 76, 85
vinegar viinietikka 37
vineyard viinitarha 85
visit käynti 92
visit, to tulla käymään 95
visiting hours vierailuajat 144
vitamin pill vitamiinipilleri 108
vodka vodka 59
volleyball lentopallo 89
voltage jännite 27, 118
vomit, to oksentaa 140

W

waist vyötärö 142
waistcoat liivi, hihaton (villa)takki 116
wait, to odottaa 21, 96, 107
waiter tarjoilija 26, 36
waiting room odotushuone 67
waitress tarjoilija 27, 36
wake, to herättää 27, 70
Wales Wales 146
walk, to kävellä 74, 85
wall muuri 85
wallet lompakko 156
walnut saksanpähkinä 53
want, to haluta 13, 101, 102
warm lämmin 94
wash, to pestä 29, 113
washable pestävä 113
washbasin pesuallas 29
washing powder pesupulveri 120
washing-up liquid nestemäinen pesuaine 120
watch kello 121, 122
watchmaker's kelloseppä 99, 121
watchstrap kellon hihna 122
water vesi 24, 28, 32, 40, 90; neste 75
water flask kenttäpullo 106
water melon vesimelooni 53
water-skis vesisukset 91
waterfall vesiputous 85
waterproof vedenpitävä 122
wave aalto 90
way tie 76
we me 161
weather sää 94
weather forecast sääennuste 94
wedding ring vihkisormus 122
Wednesday keskiviikko 151
week viikko 16, 20, 25, 80, 92, 151
weekday arkipäivä 152

weekend viikonloppu 20
well hyvin 10, 140
well-done *(meat)* hyvin/kypsäksi paistettu 47
west länsi 77
what mitä 11
wheel pyörä 78
when milloin 11
where missä 11
where from mistä 92, 146
which mikä, kumpi 11
whipped cream kermavaahto 54
whisky viski 17, 58
white valko 57; valkoinen 112
who kuka 11
whole kokonainen 143
why miksi 11
wick sytyttimen sydän 126
wide leveä 117
wide-angle lens laajakulmaobjektiivi 125
wife vaimo 93
wig peruukki 110
wild boar villisika 48
wind tuuli 94
window ikkuna 29, 36, 65, 69, 100, 111
windscreen/shield tuulilasi 76
windsurfer purjelauta 91
wine viini 56, 57, 61
wine list viinilista 56
wine merchant's viinimyymälä, alkoholiliike 99
winter talvi 150
winter sports talviurheilu 91
wiper *(car)* pyyhkijän sulka 76
wish toivotus 152
with kanssa 15
withdraw, to *(from account)* nostaa 130
withdrawal otto 130
without ilman 15
woman nainen 156
wonderful ihana 96
wood metsä 85
wool villa 113
word sana 12, 15, 133
work, to toimia 28, 118
working day työpäivä 152
worse huonompi 14
worsted kampalankaa 113
wound haava 139
wrap up, to panna pakettiin 103
wrapping paper käärepaperi 105
wrinkle-free rypistymätöntä 113
wristwatch rannekello 122

Suomi hakemisto

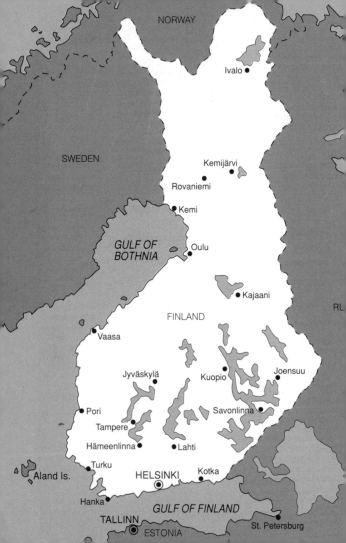